Intrepid Lover *of* Perfect Grace

ALEXANDER Y. HWANG

Intrepid Lover *of* Perfect Grace

The Life and Thought of Prosper of Aquitaine

THE CATHOLIC UNIVERSITY OF AMERICA PRESS
Washington, D. C.

The paper used in this publication meets the minimum requirements of American National Standards for Information Science—Permanence of Paper for Printed Library Materials, ANSI Z39.48–1984.

∞

Library of Congress Cataloging-in-Publication Data
Hwang, Alexander Y.
Intrepid lover of perfect grace : the life and thought of Prosper of Aquitaine / Alexander Y. Hwang.
p. cm.
Includes bibliographical references and index.
ISBN 978-0-8132-1670-6 (pbk. : alk. paper) 1. Prosper, of Aquitaine, Saint, ca. 390–ca. 463. I. Title.
BR1720.P8H83 2009
230′.14092—dc22 2008047244

For my wife, Lydia T. Kim

Contents

Abbreviations

ACW	Ancient Christian Writers
AS	*Augustinian Studies*
ATA	*Augustine through the Ages*
CCL	Corpus Christianorum, series Latina
CH	*Church History*
CSEL	Corpus Scriptorum Ecclesiasticorum Latinorum
CSQ	*Cistercian Studies Quarterly*
DTC	Dictionnaire de théologie catholique
FC	Fathers of the Church
JEH	*Journal of Ecclesiastical History*
JTS	*Journal of Theological Studies*
MGH, AA	Monumenta Germaniae Historica, Auctores Antiquissimi
PG	Patrologia Graeca
PL	Patrologia Latina
PLS	Patrologia Latina, Supplementum
PS	*Patristic Studies*

RB	*Revue bénédictine*
RE	Realenzyklopädie für protestantische Theologie und Kirche
RechScRel	*Recherches de science religieuse*
RTAM	*Recherches de théologie ancienne et médiévale*
SC	Sources chrétiennes
SP	Studia Patristica
TS	*Theological Studies*
TU	Text und Untersuchungen zur Geschichte der altchristlichen Literatur
VC	*Vigiliae Christianae*
WSA	Works of Saint Augustine: A Translation for the 21st Century

Chronology of Prosper

ca. 388	Prosper born in Aquitaine
406–416	Captive of the barbarians for some or all of these years
416	Relocated to Marseilles and wrote *De providentia Dei*
416–426	First period of reflection
425–428	Cassian's *Conlationes*
426/427	Hadrumetum affair
426	Prosper's first pro-Augustine work: *Epistula ad Rufinum*
427	*Epistula ad Augustinum*
428/429	Augustine's *De praedestinatione sanctorum*
430	Death of Augustine
431	Prosper and Hilary appeal to Celestine in Rome
435–440	Second period of reflection
440	Meets Leo and joins papal staff as advisor
440s	Editing of Augustine's teaching on grace: *Epigrammata* and *Liber Sententiarum*
450	Prosper's theological maturity: *De vocatione omnium gentium*
early 450s	Prosper's ecclesiological maturity: *Auctoritates*
455	Final edition of *Chronicon*
	Death of Prosper

Preface

The following study on the life and works of Prosper of Aquitaine is the first biography of the much-neglected theologian. My interest in Prosper stemmed from my study of Augustine's later doctrine of grace and the Church's initial reactions to it following his death in 430. Although it was clear that Prosper played a pivotal role in the controversy that ensued in Provence over Augustine's doctrine of grace, there was less scholarly work on Prosper than one might expect. In addition, as his importance in other areas of fifth-century ecclesiastical history became apparent after further study, I was even more puzzled by the lack of scholarly attention.

Prosper was not as astute a theologian as Augustine, as ascetically accomplished as Cassian, or as charismatic as Leo. However, I found Prosper's life just as interesting, if not more so. It is precisely because of his many failings and flaws that he drew and repulsed me at the same time. The Church recognizes Prosper as a saint for his service to the Church, but it is the story of how Prosper served the Church, which was not exactly saintly, that is fascinating.

This work could not have been possible without the encouragement and help of some extraordinary people. Professors Paul Rorem and Kathleen McVey at Princeton Theological Seminary; Professors Thomas Shelley, Elizabeth Johnson, Mary Callaway, Joseph Pearson, George Demacapoulos, Maryanne Kowaleski, and Richard Gyug of Fordham University; the library staffs at Fordham University and Westmont College; my friends at Fordham, especially Christophe Chalamet and Ed Siecienceski; Peter Brown of Princeton University whose kindness and generosity continues to inspire me to be a better scholar and person; and my three amigos: Mark Rothweiler, John Ballard, and Marco Almeida—lifelong friends and excellent fishing companions.

My thanks to James C. Kruggel at the Catholic University of America Press for his encouragement and guidance throughout the process, and the readers of this manuscript, Fr. Roland Teske, S. J., and Dr. Augustine Casiday, who made valuable corrections and suggestions. I also wish to thank Wayne Hellmann at Saint Louis University for allowing me the time and space to finish the manuscript, and my graduate students Eric Wickman and Joseph Rajpaul Sundararaj.

I am deeply indebted to my *Doktorvater,* Fr. Joseph Lienhard, S. J. Fr. Lienhard has carefully guided me through this ordeal, and has read and corrected the rough drafts of this work with meticulous care and attention to every detail. What scholarly accomplishment there may be in this work belongs to Fr. Lienhard most of all.

Lastly, I wish to thank my family, especially my wife, Lydia, for her unfailing love and patience throughout this long and difficult journey, and my daughter, Zoe, who is responsible for the delay of this book, but who has more than compensated me with the daily joy and beauty she brings to my life.

A little over than a century ago, Valentin justified his thousand-page dissertation on Prosper by stating, "Une étude sur saint Prosper n'est donc pas inutile."[1] It is my hope that this is true.

1. L. Valentin, *Saint Prosper d'Aquitaine: Étude sur la littérature latine ecclésiastique au cinquième siècle en Gaule* (Paris: Picard, 1900), 4.

Intrepid Lover *of* Perfect Grace

Introduction

THE IMPORTANCE of Prosper of Aquitaine for the history of dogma—his defense and interpretation of Augustine's doctrine of grace—and for early medieval historiography—his continuation of Jerome's chronicle to 455—have long been acknowledged by both historians and theologians; however, the limited scholarship exclusively devoted to Prosper has not reflected his importance. Only three books on Prosper have appeared since the beginning of the twentieth century. These books, along with articles and brief introductions to translations of Prosper's works, have only treated certain aspects of Prosper's life and writings: individual writings, his writings in the context of fifth-century ecclesiastical literature, his chronicle, the question of his Augustinianism, and his relationship with Pope Leo. However, none has adequately explored Prosper's life and writings as a whole to present a biography of the person. The purpose of this study is to provide a historical biography of Prosper that presents his life and theological development within his historical context. This study is the first English language book-length study on Prosper.

The main thesis is that Prosper's theological development is marked by his evolving understanding of the Church. There are four stages in this development. Prosper initially had a very limited and general understanding of the Church. Then came a period of study and encounter with south Gallic monasticism, Augustine, and the Church. Based on these initial encounters, Prosper naively assumed Augustine represented the catholic Church's view and defended him accordingly. Prosper's understanding of the catholic Church then became increasingly connected with the Roman Church and Prosper attempted to synthesize Augustine's doctrine to conform to his emerging appreciation of the Roman Church. The final stage in his development was Prosper's full conviction that the Roman Church was the center of the catholic Church. Thus, on the question of grace, it was the Roman Church—the pronouncements of its popes and its liturgical practices—that determined the catholic view on grace. It was Prosper's evolving ecclesiology that informed and determined his evolving doctrine of grace.

Before proceeding any further it is necessary to clarify the terms used to describe the theological conflict that is inextricably linked with Prosper's life. The conflict over Augustine's doctrine of grace that took place among the monks of Hadrumetum and Provence is traditionally termed the semi-Pelagian controversy, which encompasses the period from its beginnings in Hadrumetum—the late 420s—to its resolution at the Second Council of Orange in 529. This term is historically and theologically incorrect. Instead, the conflict should apply only to the opposition in Provence and is more accurately described as the Augustinian controversy. The opponents of Augustine in Provence, insofar as they reacted to Augustine's doctrine of grace, are appropriately termed *doctores Gallicani.*[1]

The term "semi-Pelagian" made its first appearance during the late-sixteenth- and early-seventeenth-century controversy known as the *de auxiliis.* Prosper's designation for the opponents of Augustine's doctrine of grace in Marseilles—*Pelagianorum reliquiae*—was translated as semi-Pelagian.[2] By the seventeenth century, semi-Pelagianism became the established term used for the conflict over Augustine's doctrine of grace, which included the brief confusion over his doctrine of

1. The designation *doctores Gallicani* was first employed by Gennadius of Marseilles, *De virus inlustribus* 60 (ed. E. C. Richardson, TU 14/1 [Leipzig: Hindrichs, 1896], 81). Mark Vessey ("Peregrinus against the Heretics: Classicism, Provinciality, and the Place of the Alien Writer in Late Roman Gaul," *Studia Ephemerides Augustinianum* 46 [Rome, 1994], 533ff.) elaborates this term. See also D. Ogliari, *Gratia et Certamen: The Relationship between Grace and Free Will in the Discussion of Augustine with the So-Called Semipelagians* (Leuven: Leuven University Press, 2003), 5–7; and Conrad Leyser, "Semi-Pelagianism," *Augustine through the Ages,* 761–62 (hereafter *ATA*).

2. Prosper, [among the letters of Augustine] *Ep.* 225.7 (CSEL 57: 465); see Ogliari, *Gratia et Certamen,* 6–7.

grace among the monks of Hadrumetum and the subsequent opposition in Provence.[3]

The bases for the terms are flawed, as is the scope of the designations. The use of these well-established terms is based on Prosper's partisan label, which he himself only used once. The inclusion of the monks of Hadrumetum in this group implies a similarity to the opposition in Provence, which, as will be shown, is false. The monks of Hadrumetum had no connection to the opponents of Augustine in Provence, and what happened there was dramatically different in tone, scope, and quality compared to the opposition in Provence. The semi-Pelagian controversy, whose term will be shortly addressed, should be limited to the reaction in Provence.

The terms themselves are theologically inaccurate. Semi-Pelagian denotes a connection to Pelagianism, which is wholly incorrect. The opponents of Augustine in Provence were not "part" Pelagian, but in fact anti-Pelagian. In addition, the term is deeply misleading since the conflict was over Augustine's doctrine of grace, not the Provencals' understanding of grace.

A more positive term is "Massilians."[4] This designation also came about during the *de auxiliis* controversy and is based loosely on Prosper's description.[5] However, Massilians is both too broad and too narrow a term. Massilians is too broad in that it implies a consensus among the inhabitants of Marseilles—Prosper and the other supporters of Augustine were also Massilians, and there were residents in Marseilles who showed varying degrees of affinity to both sides. It is too narrow because the opposition to Augustine's doctrine of grace was not limited to Marseilles, which Hilary pointed out in his letter to Augustine.[6] Thus, these terms are in need of revision.

3. M. Jacquin, "A quelle date apparaît le terme 'semipélagien'?" *Revue des sciences philosophiques et theologiques* 1 (1907): 508; Ogliari, *Gratia et Certamen*, 7.

4. The most recent advocate of the term is Ogliari (*Gratia et Certamen*, 9), who qualifies the terms "Massilian" and "Massilianism" to apply only to the "particular theological discussion concerning the relationship between grace, free will and predestination, and to no other issues."

5. Prosper (*Ep.* 225.1 [CSEL 57: 455]): "Multi ergo seruorum Christi, qui in Massiliensi urbe consistunt."

6. Hilary ([among the letters of Augustine] *Ep.* 226.2 [CSEL 57: 469]): "Haec sunt itaquae Massiliae vel etiam aliquibus locis in Gallia ventilantur."

Although a near consensus is apparent among current scholars on the incorrectness of these terms, they are still in use to this day.[7] The tenacity of the terms is helped by the fact that they are well established in historical and theological literature, and by the absence of any agreed-upon alternative terms. Thus, scholarship, when dealing with this subject, has had to employ the terms in order to refer to the subject and then refute these very terms. This approach is evident in the titles of three of the most recent works dealing with the subject: Ogliari's book, *Gratia et Certamen: The Relationship between Grace and Free Will in the Discussion of Augustine with the So-Called Semipelagians;* Casiday's article, "Rehabilitating John Cassian: An Evaluation of Prosper of Aquitaine's Polemic against the 'Semipelagians'"; and Conrad Leyser's entry, "Semi-Pelagianism," in *Augustine through the Ages.*[8] The pattern of referring to and then refuting the terms, ironically, serves to continue the tradition it seeks to correct.

The best alternative to the term "semi-Pelagian controversy" is the "Augustinian controversy." This term is theologically and historically more accurate. The conflict was over Augustine's doctrine of grace; it was his doctrine that was controversial. The problem with this term is that the name attached to a controversy is traditionally associated with those who opposed catholic teaching, and was in turn vigorously persecuted by the Church, for example, the Origenist and Pelagian controversies. However, because Augustine's orthodoxy is so well established, such a designation would hardly suggest any connection with heresy. In fact, Augustine's orthodoxy may be too well established in some circles. That is, Augustine's later orthodoxy is assumed to have been readily acknowledged in his

7. Among the most influential and vocal opponents of the terms is Owen Chadwick (*John Cassian: A Study in Primitive Monasticism,* 2nd ed. [Cambridge: Cambridge University Press, 1968], 127): "The name [Semi-pelagian] is wrong. The leaders of the school [opponents of Augustine in Provence] were not half-way to being disciples of Pelagius." However, Chadwick goes on to employ the term. Rebecca Harden Weaver (*Divine Grace and Human Agency: A Study of the Semi-Pelagian Controversy,* Patristic Monograph Series, 15 [Macon, Ga.: Mercer University Press, 1996]) is one of the very few contemporary scholars to continue to employ the term without reservation.

8. Augustine Casiday, "Rehabilitating John Cassian: An Evaluation of Prosper of Aquitaine's Polemic against the 'Semipelagians,'" *Scottish Journal of Theology* 58, no. 3 (2005): 270–84; Leyser, "Semi-Pelagianism," *ATA,* 761–66.

time. This assumption is anachronistic. At issue in the controversy in Provence was the question of Augustine's orthodoxy. Designating the controversy the Augustinian controversy helps illuminate the historical reality of the Church's initial struggle to appropriate Augustine's doctrine of grace.

A number of alternatives have been proposed to denote the opponents of Augustine's doctrine of grace in Provence. Among the terms are "semi-Augustinians," "anti-Augustinians," "anti-Augustinian/anti-predestinarian," "masters of Provence," and "monks of Provence."

Semi-Augustinians is wholly unacceptable considering Augustine's opponents objected to what was fundamentally Augustinian: predestination.[9] Moreover, the label seems more appropriately to denote a stage in Prosper's theological development. Anti-Augustinian/anti-predestinarian is technically correct, but seems redundant.[10] Predestination cannot be properly detached from the sole originator of the doctrine, Augustine. To be anti-Augustinian is to be antipredestinarian and vice versa. Masters of Provence or Provençal Masters is elegant, but not all the "masters"—ecclesial and ascetical—of Provence were opposed to him.[11] In addition, the term is popularly used to denote painters. Monks of Provence point to the important connection between asceticism and the opponents of Augustine, but the term "monk" is rather ambiguous in the context of the fifth century, as it suggests both a uniformity of all monks and that the opposition was limited to monks.[12]

Nora Chadwick, in 1955, remarked that anti-Augustinianism was becoming the preferred term of choice and cited Harnack as an ex-

9. For the term, see F. Grützmacher, "Cassianus, Johannes," RE 3 (1897): 747; quotation in Ogliari, *Gratia et Certamen*, 8 n. 36.

10. Ralph W. Mathisen, *Ecclesiastical Factionalism and Religious Controversy in Fifth-Century Gaul* (Washington: The Catholic University of America Press, 1989), 131.

11. C. Tibeletti, "Valeriano di Cimiez e la teologia dei Maestri Provenzali," *Augustinianum* 22 (1982): 513–32; Augustine Casiday, *Tradition and Theology in the Writings of St. John Cassian*, Oxford Early Christian Studies (Oxford: Oxford University Press, 2006), 22.

12. C. Tibeletti, "Introduction," in *Pagine monastiche provenzali: Il monachesimo nella Gallia del quinto secolo* (Rome: Borla, 1990), 8–59; see also Roland Teske, "General Introduction," in *Answers to the Pelagians*, vol. 4, trans. Roland Teske, WSA I/26 (Hyde Park, N.Y.: New City Press, 1999), 22–34.

ample.[13] Though far from gaining complete acceptance, the term has been advocated by notable scholars including Amann, Daniélou, Marrou, Owen Chadwick, and, most recently, Augustine Casiday.[14] However, this term too is flawed. The opponents of Augustine in Gaul were not completely opposed to Augustine. Moreover, anti-Augustinianism only describes what they were opposed to and does not reflect their own theological views. They certainly were anti-Augustinian, in terms of their opposition to Augustine's doctrine of grace, but they did so because it conflicted with their own understanding of grace. Thus, *doctores Gallicani* best describes this group, reflecting their own theological tradition.

These then are the terms of the conflict: the controversy will be referred to as the Augustinian controversy or conflict, the opponents of Augustine in Provence as *doctores Gallicani,* and the supporters of Augustine as Augustinians. The two groups made up what can be best described as factions, united by social and theological ties and loyalties.[15] These terms may be too simple, but in the course of this study the complexity and diversity of the participants in the controversy will be drawn out.

It is not without good reason that a comprehensive biography of Prosper has not been attempted in the past. There is simply very little that is known about Prosper's life apart from his writings. Valentin concluded at the end of his chapter on the details of Prosper's life, "Mais saint Prosper est bien plus célèbre par ce qu'il a écrit que par ce qu'il a fait, et sa vraie biographie consiste surtout dans l'étude historique de ses ouvrages."[16] A little more than a century of scholar-

13. Nora Chadwick, *Poetry and Letters in Early Christian Gaul* (London: Bowes & Bowes, 1955), 180; quoting Adolf Harnack, *History of Dogma,* vol. 5, trans. Neil Buchanan (New York: Russell & Russell, 1958), 245 n. 3.

14. E. Amann, "Semi-Pélagiens," DTC 14 (1939): 1796; Jean Daniélou and Henri Marrou, *The Christian Centuries,* vol. 1, trans. Victor Cronin (New York: McGraw-Hill, 1964), 407; O. Chadwick, *John Cassian,* 113; quotation in Ogliari, *Gratia et Certamen,* 9 n. 37. Augustine Casiday, "Rehabilitating John Cassian." Oddly, Chadwick, after employing the terms "Massilian" and "anti-Augustinian" (*John Cassian,* 119), rejects the term "semi-Pelagian" (*John Cassian,* 127), but then employs semi-Pelagian in his discussion (*John Cassian,* 127–36).

15. The two groups, the Augustinians and the *doctores Gallicani,* belonged to the larger context of factionalism in southern Gaul; see Mathisen, *Ecclesiastical Factionalism.*

16. Valentin, *Saint Prosper,* 155.

ship has passed since Valentin's work, and a better understanding of Prosper, his works, and his historical context has emerged. Though much of his life remains a mystery, there is enough information to warrant an attempt at a biography of Prosper.

The biography of Prosper will be chronological in nature, with special attention devoted to his theological development, namely, his changing views on grace in light of his developing ecclesiology. Once the discussion on the history of scholarship on Prosper and the list of authentic writings of Prosper have been established, Prosper's life and work will be traced from his origins in Aquitaine to his last years in Rome. The chapters will be divided roughly into chronological periods of Prosper's life. Each period will discuss the relevant writings—both his and those he reacted against—and will seek to situate Prosper in his historical context.

The portrait of Prosper that emerges is that of an intensely private and somber individual, impressionable but able to abandon those influences, and whose life revolved around the insatiable and fanatical desire to know the deepest mysteries of grace. At each stage of his understanding on grace, Prosper fervently believed his views perfectly catholic. Prosper left behind a body of writings that attest to these theological convictions, but nothing of his personal life. Prosper's writings were wholly concerned with the explication of his theological views. That insatiable curiosity was satisfied, in the end, when he submitted to the authority of the Roman Church and accepted the Roman Church's limited pronouncements on grace.

Prosper's life can be seen as a series of refinements to his conviction that he represents the catholic view on grace. Yet, at each stage of his development, Prosper never acknowledges any changes and corrections he has made, and proceeds to defend his views at each turn with the same tenacity and polemical aggression. He belittles, demonizes, mischaracterizes, and even attempts to rewrite history, all for the sake of proving whatever convictions he held about the catholic view of grace at the time. Though Augustine represents a profound influence upon his life, once he becomes aware that Augustine did not represent the catholic view on grace, he first attempts to synthesis Augustine's theology to conform it along acceptable catholic limits, and then abandons him, along with the supporters of Augustine. Prosper was quick to abandon positions and loyalties, but he did not forget his Provencal opponents and took every opportunity to attack them. In this regard, Prosper was successful—the Church made Prosper a saint and tainted his opponents with the label of semi-Pelagians.

Prosper can be viewed with even a certain admiration for his struggle and tenacity in attempting to understand the catholic view on grace and for helping to define it. However misguided and misinformed, Prosper attempted to explain and defend the catholic view on grace. Still, it is the manner in which he struggled that casts Prosper in a negative light. J. N. D. Kelly described Orosius as "[t]alented, opinionated, narrowly orthodox, impetuous," and Bonner added that in Orosius, "a burning zeal for the Faith was united with a narrow and ungenerous nature, and the whole allied to an impetuous temperament, and a remarkable naïvety."[17] These judgments seem to apply to Prosper all too well. In the end, Prosper concluded that the Roman Church determined the catholic view on grace he had long labored to defend. However, Prosper left behind a body of work whose tone and intent were anything but gracious.

In Gelasius's list of saints, Prosper's name follows Jerome's name, not Augustine's.[18] This makes little chronological and relational sense, but it seems, after studying his life, appropriate. In terms of Prosper's personality, he was closer to the spirit of Jerome than Augustine, unfortunately.

Prosper's theological development has traditionally been viewed in terms of his Augustinianism. This view begins with Prosper as an enthusiastic follower of Augustine who over time moved away from the more controversial elements of Augustine's later views on grace. This tells only part of the story. Instead, when viewing Prosper's whole life, it is not Augustinianism, but his dedication to the

17. J. N. D. Kelly, *Jerome: His Life, Writings, and Controversies* (London: Duckworth, 1975), 317; Gerald Bonner, *St Augustine of Hippo: Life and Controversies,* 2nd ed. (Norwich, U.K.: Canterbury Press, 1986), 332.

18. Gelasius (pope 492–496), "Concilium Romanum I," *Appendix tertia: Concilia quaedam a Gelasio celebrata* (PL 59: 160).

Church that is at the center of his life and works. Prosper's theological development must be seen primarily through his evolving ecclesiology.

Prosper's first known work, *De providentia Dei* in 416, reflects the views of a Christian unaware of the Church, in general, and its role in determining the life and theology of its members. After a decade of reflection and literary silence, Prosper emerged as a lifelong dedicated disciple of the Church, broadly defined at this stage. This came about around the same time that Prosper encountered Augustine. Prosper became enamored of Augustine, and the relatively young man assumed Augustine represented the Church's view on grace. Prosper did not misunderstand Augustine—far from it, he was the most able exponent of Augustine's teaching on grace—rather, he misunderstood the Church.

Toward the end of his participation in the defense of Augustine in Marseilles, Prosper began to move away from strict adherence to Augustine's doctrine of predestination as Prosper's appreciation of the Roman Church began to emerge. This understanding of the Roman Church underwent further and significant changes shortly before joining Leo's papal staff in 440. During this second period of reflection and literary inactivity, Prosper concluded that Augustine's doctrine of grace was not the doctrine of the catholic Church, which he now understood was the Roman Church. In the last stage of his development, Prosper no longer defended Augustine's doctrine of grace, but devoted himself solely to defending the catholic Church, which Prosper equated with the Roman Church. Prosper came to the conclusion that the Roman Church—through what it teaches through the popes and by its liturgy—determined the catholic doctrine on grace.

Thus, the question of Prosper's Augustinianism has been overemphasized and obscures the essential feature in Prosper's life and theology: his fidelity to the catholic Church, which Prosper eventually concluded was centered in Rome. Prosper's theological development is the story of the evolution of his understanding of the catholic Church.

This appreciation of Prosper's life and works was expressed

shortly after his death. In 494, Gelasius listed Prosper's name after Jerome's, which followed Augustine's, and before Leo's.[19] In addition, neither Gelasius nor Gennadius (490s) explicitly mentioned Prosper's relationship to Augustine.[20] These two accounts viewed Prosper apart from Augustine. Prosper's theological erudition is emphasized by Gennadius, and his faith emphasized by Gelasius. Both attach him to the papacy.[21] What is apparent in the two early estimations of Prosper is that they viewed him as a worthy catholic Christian—who was saintly and theologically sophisticated—without regard to his relationship to Augustine. That is, Prosper was exclusively recognized as a theologian and saint who served the Church, the Roman Church. This view of Prosper has not been appreciated in the Middle Ages down to the present, until this study.

Augustine's doctrine of grace was at the center of the controversy, but Prosper was primarily responsible for its inception and continuation. There may not have been a controversy, at least not as intense and drawn out, without Prosper. Prosper was the key figure in the controversy, and a better appreciation of him adds to a better understanding of the controversy. While attention is focused primarily on Prosper, his relationships to his associates and his opponents are detailed. This controversy was a battle of ideas, but the ideas and the battle itself reflect the personal and social elements. The conflict was as much about personal backgrounds, experiences, and social connections as it was about the conflict of ideas over the way grace operated.

19. Gelasius, "Concilium Romanum I," (PL 59: 160).

20. Gelasius ("Concilium Romanum I" [PL 59: 160]): "Prosperi viri religiossimi." Gennadius (*De viris inlustribus* 85 [TU 14/1: 90]: "Prosper, homo Aquitanicae regionis, sermone scholasticus et adsertionibus nervosus. . . . Epistulae quoque Papae Leonis . . . ad diversos datae ab isto dictatae creduntur."

21. Leo is listed immediately after Prosper, and the fact that Prosper was a theological advisor to Leo would have been well known in Rome, and thus the relationship between the two is implied in this ordering.

~1

The Works of Prosper and Literature

THIS CHAPTER is divided into two sections. The first addresses the question of authorship and establishes a list of authentic works by Prosper. The second details the important literature on Prosper from the early twentieth century to the present.

The lack of certainty surrounding the details of Prosper's life has led scholars to focus primarily on his theology, particularly in relationship to Augustine's doctrine of grace. In all, from the twentieth century to the present, scholarship on Prosper is rather sparse—only three books and about a dozen articles, besides a number of translations that contain brief introductions.

The question of the authorship of certain works attributed to Prosper has been much debated. The last century has witnessed a number of new editions and translations of Prosper's individual works, as well as new arguments for and against Prosper's authorship. Twenty-six works have been attributed to Prosper at one time or another, but only seventeen are authentic.

Works of Prosper

Editions

The two most important editions of the works of Prosper are the 1539 edition by Sebastian Gryphius at Lyons *(Divi Prosperi Aqui-*

tanici, Episcopi Regiensis . . . Opera), and the 1711 edition by J. B. Le Brun des Marettes and Luc Urbain Mangeant at Paris *(Sancti Prosperi Aquitani . . . Opera).*[1] The Gryphius edition was the most comprehensive at the time and was succeeded by the 1711 edition, which came about during a time of renewed interest in Augustine's theology of grace as a result of the Jansenist controversy.[2]

The 1711 edition contains Prosper's vita—copied from the sixteenth volume of Tillemont's *Mémoires pour servir à l'histoire ecclésiastique des six premiers siècles*—, 952 columns of Prosper's works, and 416 columns of documents related to Prosper's work, including the canons of the Second Council of Orange (529) and Cassian's *Conlatio* 13.[3]

The 1846 Migne edition (PL 51) marks the end of the history of the attempt to establish the corpus of Prosper's works. The Migne edition is essentially a reprint of the 1711 edition, but includes Schoenneman's note on the history of the editions.[4]

The list of Prosper's works, contained in the Migne edition and the edition of 1711, includes the following eighteen works:

Pro Augustino responsiones ad capitula obiectionum Gallorum calumniantium
Pro Augustino responsiones ad capitula obiectionum Vincentiarum
Pro Augustino responsiones ad excerpta Genuensium
Carmen de ingratis
Confessio
Epigrammata ex sententiis sancti Augustini

1. For the history of the editions of Prosper's works, see K. Schoeneman, *Bibliotheca historico-literaria patrum latinorum,* 2 (Leipzig, 1794), 1012–49, and Couture, "Saint Prosper d'Aquitaine," *Bulletin de littérature ecclésiastique* 2 (1900): 269–82. Prosper, at one point, was mistaken for another Prosper, the bishop of Reggio; see G. Morin, "Saint Prosper de Reggio," *Revue bénédictine* 12 (1895): 241–57 (hereafter *RB*). The full title of the two editions are: *Divi Prosperi Aquitanici, Episcopi Regiensis Opera, accurata vestustorum exemplarium collatione per viros eruditos recognita* (1539) and *Sancti Prosperi Aquitani, sancti Augustini discipuli, sancti Leonis Papae Primi notarii, opera omnia, ad manuscriptos codices necnon primum secundum ordinem temporum disposita* (1711).

2. Couture, "Saint Prosper d'Aquitaine," 272–76.

3. Couture, "Saint Prosper d'Aquitaine," 277. Le Brun and Mangeant had access to Tillemont's vita of Prosper before Tillemont's sixteenth volume was published in 1712. Cf. Tillemont, *Mémoires pour servir à l'histoire ecclésiastique des six premiers siècles,* 16 (Paris: Chez Charles Robustel, 1712), 1–30, 730–36.

4. Schoenneman, *Patrum latinorum,* 1012–49; repr. in PL 51: 43–63.

Epigrammata in obtrectatorem Augustini
Epistula ad Augustinum
Epistula ad Rufinum
Epitaphium Nestorianae et Pelagianae haereseon
Epitoma Chronicon
Expositio psalmorum a centesimo usque ad centesimum quinquagesimum
De gratia Dei et libero arbitrio liber contra collatorem
Liber sententiarum ex operibus sancti Augustini delibatarum
Poema coniugis ad uxorem
Praeteritorum episcoporum sedis apostolicae auctoritates de gratia Dei et libero voluntatis arbitrio
De providentia Dei
De vocatione omnium gentium

Questions of Authorship

Beginning with Valentin, scholars have addressed the problem of authorship by dividing these works into three groups: authentic, probable, and doubtful or spurious. Of the scholars who have reviewed this question, Valentin, Elberti, and Dekkers provide the most comprehensive treatment of the content of Prosper's corpus. All three differed in the total number of texts considered and the exact makeup of the three groups—authentic, probable, and doubtful or spurious.[5] However, there is agreement by all three scholars on the authenticity of the following works. Furthermore, no scholars have raised serious concerns about the authenticity of these texts. The following is a list of the authentic works with a brief description for each. Unless otherwise noted, the dates will be discussed in the relevant chapters.

5. Surprisingly, Dekkers failed to include Prosper's letter to Augustine in his list (Eligius Dekkers, *Clavis Patrum Latinorum,* 3rd ed. [Turnhout: Brepols, 1995], 184–88); Valentin, *Saint Prosper,* 156–221; Arturo Elberti, *Prospero d'Aquitania: Teologo e Discepolo* (Rome: Edizioni Dehoniane, 1999), 28–32. Due to Pelland's focus on a specific doctrinal issue, the list and discussion of authentic and dubious works are uncritical and limited, thus Pelland's list will be excluded from the discussion. Cf. Pelland, *S. Prosperi Aquitani doctrina de predestinatione et voluntate Dei salvifica* (Montreal: Studia Collegii Maximi Immaculatae Conceptionis, 1936), 20–21.

The *Tome to Flavian* will not be included in the discussion below. That Prosper participated in the writing of the *Tome* is all that can be affirmed. The text will be addressed in chapter 6.

Authentic Works

Carmen de ingratis

While awaiting Augustine's response to his letter, Prosper wrote a 1,002-line poem excoriating the opponents of Augustine in Marseilles. The work was written at some point between late 429 and early 430. The text is in PL 51: 91–148. In 1962, Charles T. Huegelmeyer edited the work and provided the first English translation.[6]

Epitoma Chronicon

Prosper wrote four different editions of the *Chronicon* between 433 and 455. Prosper's *Chronicon* epitomizes Jerome's chronicle and continues it where Jerome ended, in 378, to 455. The *Chronicon* details the important religious and secular events of Prosper's day. The most recent critical edition of the text was made in 1894, and can be found in MGH, AA 9: 385–499. The only English translation of Prosper's continuation was made in 2000 by Alexander Courtney Murray.[7]

De gratia Dei et libero arbitrio liber contra collatorem

This work was directed against the views of grace expressed by John Cassian in *Conlatio* 13, which Prosper exaggerated and caricatured.[8] The text is in PL 51: 213–76 and was translated by Letter.[9]

6. *Carmen de ingratis.* [Critical edition of the text and facing translation in] *Carmen de ingratis: A Translation with an Introduction and a Commentary,* trans. Charles Huegelmeyer, *Patristic Studies* 95 (Washington, D.C.: The Catholic University of America Press, 1962) (hereafter *PS*).

7. *Epitoma Chronicon* (MGH, AA 9: 385–499; *Chronicle* [Prosper's chronicle from years 379 to 455], in *From Roman to Merovingian Gaul: A Reader,* trans. Alexander Callander Murray [Orchard Park, N.Y.: Broadview Press, 2000], 62–76). See Jerome, *Chronicon,* ed. Rudolf Helm, 2d ed. (Berlin: Akademie-Verlag, 1956); *A Translation of Jerome's Chronicon with Historical Commentary,* trans. M. C. Donalson (Lewiston, Pa.: Carnegie Mellon University Press, 1996).

8. John Cassian, *Conlationes* (CSEL 13; *The Conferences,* trans. Boniface Ramsey, ACW 57 [New York: Paulist Press, 1997]).

9. *De gratia Dei et libero arbitrio liber contra collatorem* (PL 51: 213–76; *On Grace and Free Will, Against Cassian the Lecturer,* in *Defense of St. Augustine,* 70–138).

Epigrammata ex sententiis sancti Augustini

The *Epigrammata* is the longer, verse version of the *Liber sententiarum* and is in PL 51: 498–532.

Epigrammata in obtrectatorem Augustini

The *Epigrammata* contains two very short epigrams: the *Epigramma in obtrectatorem Augustini* (PL 51: 149A–50A), consisting of fourteen lines, and the *Epigramma in eumdem aut alium quempiam Augustini obtrectatorem* (PL 51: 149C–152A), containing twelve lines. Their similar tone and view of Augustine's opponents in Marseilles suggests they were written around the same period as the *Carmen de ingratis*.

Epistula ad Augustinum [lost]

Prosper wrote two letters to Augustine. Only the second is extant, which refers to this first letter.[10]

Epistula ad Augustinum

This second letter informed Augustine about the reactions to his doctrine of grace in Marseilles. The letter is contained in PL 51: 67–74, reprinted among the works of Augustine in PL 44: 947–54, and also among the collection of Augustine's letters in CSEL 57: 454–68. The most recent translation was made by Roland Teske in 2005 for the new series *Works of Saint Augustine: A Translation for the 21st Century.*[11]

Epistula ad Rufinum

This is Prosper's first known work as a defender of Augustine. The letter was written around 426 and addressed to an otherwise unknown Rufinus to allay his concerns over Prosper's association with Augustine's doctrine of grace. The text is in PL 51: 77–90 under the title *Epistula ad Rufinum de gratia et libero arbitrio,* and was translated by Letter in 1963.[12]

10. Prosper, *Ep.* 225.1 [among the letters of Augustine] (CSEL 57: 454–55; *Letter* 225, in *Letters 211–270, 1*–29**, vol. 4, trans. Roland Teske, WSA II/4 [Hyde Park, N.Y.: New City Press, 2005], 87): "I [Prosper] am, if you recall, known to you by my thoughts and words. For I sent you a letter and received one back from you."

11. *Ep.* 225 (CSEL 57: 454–68; *Letter* 225, 87–102).

12. *Epistola ad Rufinum de gratia et libero arbitrio* (PL 51: 77–90; *Letter to Rufinus,* in

Epitaphium Nestorianae et Pelagianae haereseon

This allegory linking the Pelagian and Nestorian heresies was Prosper's thinly veiled attack on Prosper's Gallic opponents. The work, consisting of a little more than two dozen lines, was written between 431 and 433, and is contained in PL 51: 153–54.

Expositio psalmorum a centesimo usque ad centesimum quinquagesimum

The next three works are summaries of Augustine's thoughts and are textually related. They belong to the period of Prosper's residence in Rome from 440 to his death in 455. The *Expositio psalmorum* is a summary of the last third of the Psalter, Psalms 100 to 150, from Augustine's *Enarrationes in Psalmos.*[13] The *Expositio psalmorum* is in CCL 68A: 1–211.

Liber sententiarum ex operibus sancti Augustini delibatarum

The *Liber sententiarum* is composed of three hundred and ninety-two brief statements primarily drawn from Augustine's works. Almost the entire first seventy sentences are drawn from Prosper's *Expositio psalmorum,* while the rest are drawn directly from Augustine's works. This work was recently edited in 1972 in CCL 68A: 257–365.

Pro Augustino responsiones ad capitula obiectionum Gallorum calumniantium

This work was in response to a series of Gallic objections drawn from Augustine's doctrine of grace. These responses, along with Prosper's next set of responses, mark a change in Prosper's view on grace and his defense of Augustine. The text is in PL 51: 155–74 and was translated by Letter.[14]

Defense of St. Augustine, trans. P. de Letter, ACW 32 [Westminster, Md.: Newman Press, 1963], 21–37).

13. Aug., *Enarrationes in psalmos* (CCL 38–40; *Expositions of the Psalms,* trans. Maria Boulding, WSA III/15–20 [Hyde Park, N.Y.: New City Press, 2000–2004]).

14. *Pro Augustino responsiones ad capitula obiectionum Gallorum calumniantium* (PL 51: 155–74; *Answers to the Objections of the Gauls,* in *Defense of St. Augustine,* 139–62).

Pro Augustino responsiones ad capitula obiectionum Vincentiarum

This work was also a response to a series of objections drawn from Augustine's doctrine of grace, but the origin of the objections is associated with Vincent of Lérins. The text is in PL 51: 177–86 and was translated by Letter. Both responses were written around the same time, 433 to 435.[15]

Pro Augustino responsiones ad excerpta Genuensium

Shortly after the death of Augustine, but before the Council of Ephesus (431), Prosper replied to two priests, Camille and Theodore, who were seeking clarification on certain passages of Augustine's *De praedestinatione sanctorum* and *De dono perseverantiae.*[16] This work is in PL: 187–202 and was translated by Letter in 1963.[17]

Disputed, but Authentic Works

The following texts have been judged authentic or probable by at least one notable scholar, and will be treated as authentic for the reasons stated below.

De providentia Dei

The authorship of this poem set in the tumultuous years of the barbarian invasions in Gaul has been heavily contested. The long-held argument against Prosper's authorship has been the supposed Pelagian or anti-Augustinian elements contained in the poem.[18] Miroslav Marcovich, following Duckworth, L. Tillemont, Max Manitius,

15. *Pro Augustino responsiones ad capitula obiectionum Vincentiarum* (PL 51: 177–86; *Answers to the Vincentian Articles*, in *Defense of St. Augustine*, 70–138).

16. The *terminus post quem* and *ante quem* are established by Prosper's reference to the "blessed memory" of Augustine, and the absence of reference to the Council of Ephesus.

17. *Pro Augustino responsiones ad exerpta Genuensium* (PL 51: 187–202; *Answers to the Extracts of the Genoese*, in *Defense of St. Augustine*, 49–69).

18. For a judgment against Prosper's authorship, see the introduction by Michael McHugh, *The Carmen de providentia Dei Attributed to Prosper of Aquitaine: A Revised Text with an Introduction, Translation, and Notes, PS* 98 (Washington, D.C.: The Catholic University of America Press, 1964), 10–18.

Valentin, and R. Helm, attributed the work to Prosper.[19] Marcovich asserted that the Pelagian or anti-Augustinian elements, if there are any, can be explained by attributing this text to an early stage of Prosper's theological development.[20] As for the proofs of Prosper's authorship, Marcovich pointed to the textual tradition of the text, and the doctrinal and literary coincidences between the poem and *De ingratis* and *Epigrams*—works definitely written by Prosper. Hincmar of Rheims quoted passages from the poem and named Prosper as its author.[21] The only extant manuscript of the poem (cod. *Mazarinensis* 3896) and the Gryphius edition of 1539 names Prosper as the author of the poem.[22] The coincidence in doctrine, imagery, diction, and lexicon between *De providentia Dei* and *De ingratis* and *Epigrams* are of such magnitude that Marcovich concluded it is undoubtedly the work of Prosper.[23] In addition, Marcovich pointed to the conclusions of various scholars who see virtually identical metrics of *De providentia Dei* and *De ingratis*.[24] McHugh and Marcovich,

19. Tillemont, *Mémoires,* 731; G. E. Duckworth, "Five Centuries of Latin Hexameter Poetry: Silver Age and Late Empire," *Transactions and Proceedings of the American Philological Association,* 98 (1967): 77–150; Max Manitius, "Über das Gedicht *de Providentia divina,*" *Zeitschrift für die österreichischen Gymnasien* 39 (1888): 580–84; idem, "Beiträge zur Geschichte frühchristlicher Dichter im Mittelatter," *SB Akademie Wien* 117 (1889), Abh. 12, 20 f; 121 (1890), Abh. 7, 14; idem, *Geschichte der christlich-lateinischen Poesie bis zur Mitte des 8 Jahrhunderts* (Stuttgart: J. G. Cotta, 1891), 171–80; Valentin, *Saint Prosper,* 790–837; Rudolf Helm, "Prosper Tiro," *Realencyclopädie de classischen Altertumswissenschaft* 23 (1957): 884–87. Miroslav Marcovich briefly argued against McHugh's judgment and proceeded to correct a number of McHugh's translations in "The Text of St. Prosper's De providentia Dei," *Illinois Classical Studies* 8 (1983): 108–21. Marcovich, a few years later, provided his own text, translation, and commentary on the work and expanded the argument for Prosper's authorship in the preface (Marcovich, "Preface," *De providentia Dei: Text, Translation and Commentary,* Supplements to *Vigiliae Christianae* 10 [New York: E. J. Brill, 1989], ix–xii).

20. Marcovich, "Preface," *De providentia Dei,*" x.

21. Hincmar of Rheims, *De praedestinatione dissertatio posterior* (PL 125: 65–474).

22. Paris, Bibliothèque Mazarine 3896. Gryphius, *Divi Prosperi Aquitanici . . . Opera* (Lyons, 1539), 264–90.

23. Marcovich, "Preface," x.

24. Marcovich, "Preface," xi. Marcovich cites these authors: U. Moricca, *Storia della letteratura latina cristiana,* 3/1 (Turin: Società Editrice Internazionale, 1932), 41ff.; McHugh, *Carmen de Providentia Dei,* 182–255; Duckworth, "Latin Hexameter Poetry," 77–150; A. Longpré, "Le De Providentia divina de Prosper d'Aquitaine et la question de son authenticité," *Revue des études anciennes* 80 (1978): 108–13.

following the majority of scholarly opinion, assign the date of composition to 416.[25]

McHugh's revised text and translation, which was the first English translation, was published in 1964. James Walsh and P. G. Walsh translated the poem in a collection of patristic texts addressing divine providence and human suffering in 1985. This translation was intended for a wide audience and is not a critical translation.[26]

Marcovich felt McHugh's text was not critical enough and his translation faulty in places, and, in 1989, published a critical edition of the text along with a new translation on facing pages.[27] McHugh's translation is more of a literal translation, while Marcovich took a phrase-for-phrase approach.

De vocatione omnium gentium

This poem has been the subject of some controversy, but the weight of scholarly opinion has established its authenticity. Valentin, after a lengthy and careful discussion, was inclined to attribute the work to Prosper, as did Cappuyns in 1927.[28] In 1952, Joseph J. Young published a thorough and detailed study on the vocabulary and *clausulae* of the poem to determine Prosper's authorship.[29] Young concluded Prosper's authorship based on vocabulary inconclusive, but found strong evidence of his authorship based on *clausulae*.

Dekkers, following Cappuyns and J. J. Young, listed the work as authentic.[30] A. G. Hamman in 1993, following Cappuyns, in the introduction of his study of the text, affirmed Prosper's authorship, which he claimed was universally accepted.[31] The same conclusion

25. For the discussion of the scholarly opinion of the composition date, see McHugh, "Introduction," *Carmen de Providentia Dei*, 18–24, and Marcovich, "Preface," ix.

26. McHugh, *Carmen de providentia Dei; De providentia Dei,* in *Divine Providence and Human Suffering,* trans. James Walsh and P. G. Walsh, Message of the Fathers of the Church, 17 (Wilmington, Del.: Michael Glazier, 1985), 64–91.

27. Marcovich, *De providentia Dei.*

28. Valentin, *Saint Prosper,* 687–713. M. Cappuyns, "L'auteur du *De vocatione omnium gentium,*" *RB* 39 (1927): 198–226.

29. J. J. Young, *Studies on the Style of the "De vocatione gentium,"* *PS* 87 (Washington, D.C.: The Catholic University of America Press, 1952), 179.

30. Dekkers, *Clavis patrum latinorum,* 186.

31. A. G. Hamman ("Introduction, notes et guide thématique," *L'appel de tous les*

was reached by R. A. Markus who held that Cappuyns had laid to rest the question of Prosper's authorship of the work.[32] The year 450 has been put forward as the likely date for the composition of the poem.[33] The text is in PL 51: 647–722 and was translated by Letter.[34]

Epistula ad Demetriadem de vera humilitate

This letter was addressed to Demetrias, daughter of one of the most illustrious families in the West, giving further instruction on the ascetic life.[35] The controversy over this letter's authorship was largely due to Quesnel, who suggested the same author for *De vocatione omnium gentium* and the *Epistula ad Demetriadem de vera humilitate*, whom Quesnel concluded was Pope Leo.[36] Valentin agreed with Quesnel's one author theory, but concluded Prosper was the author, based upon the similarity of the letter to the "authentic" works of Prosper in terms of language and style.[37]

M. Kathryn Krabbe edited and translated the letter along with an introduction in her 1965 dissertation.[38] Expanding on Valentin's initial study of the question, Krabbe examined the letter's internal evidence for Prosper's authorship. [39] After comparing the letter to five undisputed "authentic" works of Prosper, Krabbe concluded, "As in the matter of Scriptural quotations, as in the matter of prose rhythm the evidence points more directly to St. Prosper of Aquitaine."[40]

---

peuples /Prosper d'Aquitaine, trans. [French] F. Frémont-Verggobi and H. Throo [Paris: Migne, 1993], 12): "Affirmation aujourd'hui universallement reconnue."

32. Markus, "Chronicle and Theology," in *The Inheritance of Historiography 350–900*, ed. Christopher Holdsworth and T. P. Wiseman (Exeter, U.K.: Exeter University Press, 1986), 36.

33. Cappuyns, "L'auteur," 226; Young, *Studies*, 164; Hamman, "Introduction," 12.

34. *De vocatione omnium gentium* (PL 51: 647–722; *The Call of All Nations*, trans. P. De Letter, ACW 14 (Westminster, Md.: Newman Press, 1952).

35. *Epistula ad Demetriadem de vera humilitate: A Critical Text and Translation with Introduction and Commentary*, trans. M. Kathryn Clare Krabbe, *PS* 97 (Washington, D.C.: The Catholic University of America Press, 1965).

36. PL 55: 421.

37. Valentin, *Saint Prosper*, 714–37.

38. Krabbe, *Epistula ad Demtriadem*.

39. Krabbe, "Introduction," *Epistula ad Demetriadem*, 52.

40. Krabbe, "Introduction," 92.

Praeteritorum episcoporum sedis apostolicae auctoritates de gratia Dei et libero voluntatis arbitrio

This is the least controversial of the questionable works of Prosper. Though written toward the end of his life, the work found its way into the collection of Celestine's writings. The *Auctoritates* is composed of a series of papal pronouncements on grace selected and interpreted by Prosper, which was later determined to be the continuation of the *Apostolici verba* (431).[41]

The *Auctoritates* does not have a manuscript tradition apart from the *Apostolici verba*. The earliest preservation of the joined documents appears in the early-sixth-century collection of papal decretals by Dionysius Exiguus, under the decrees of Pope Celestine.[42] Thus, from at least the early sixth century, the *Auctoritates* and the *Apostolici verba* were assumed to be one decree from Celestine's pontificate.

Celestine's authorship of the *Auctoritates* was first questioned by the Ballerini brothers in 1756.[43] In 1900, Valentin was inclined to attribute the work to Prosper.[44] The question of authorship was effectively resolved in 1929 by Cappuyns, which has been followed by scholars ever since.[45] Dekkers included the work in the authentic list of Prosper's works.[46]

The text is in PL 51: 205–12 and in a slightly different edition in 67: 270–74, and translated by Letter.[47]

Works Falsely Attributed to Prosper

The following writings have the weight of scholarship against their Prosperian authorship and will be considered inauthentic works

41. Celestine, *Epistola* 21, *ad episcopos Galliarum* [*Apostolici verba*], PL 50: 528–30.

42. Lotte Kéry, *Canonical Collections of the Early Middle Ages (ca. 400–1140),* in History of Medieval Canon Law, 1 (Washington, D.C.: The Catholic University of America Press, 1999), 9–11. Dionysius Exiguus, *Decreta Coelestini papae* (PL 67: 267–74).

43. P. Ballerini and H. Ballerini, *S. Leonis opera,* 2 (Venice, 1756), 251–57.

44. Valentin, *Saint Prosper,* 741.

45. M. Cappuyns, "L'origine des capitula pseudo-Célestiniens contre le semi-pélagianisme," *RB* 41 (1929): 156–70.

46. Dekkers, *Clavis patrum latinorum,* 186.

47. *Praeteritorum episcoporum sedis apostolicae auctoritates de gratia Dei et libero voluntatis arbitrio* [*Apostolici verba*] (PL 51: 205–12; 67: 270–74; *Official Pronouncements of the Apostolic See on Divine Grace and Free Will,* in *Defense of St. Augustine,* 178–85).

of Prosper. Of these works, only one—the *Hypomnesticon*—has received any substantial support for Prosperian authorship, and therefore deserves special attention. In addition, the *Capitula sancti Augustini in urbem Romam transmissa* and *Poema coniugis ad uxorem*, which have received some arguments for Prosper's authorship, will be briefly discussed. The following texts are listed among the spurious works of Prosper in the bibliography.

Hypomnesticon

The question of the authorship of the *Hypomnesticon* has progressed in three phases.[48] The first phase (ninth century) was limited to the question of whether or not Augustine was the author, and ended with a denial of his authorship. The second phase (seventeenth to twentieth century) has sought to identify the author, but although several possible authors were proposed, the authorship remained unresolved. The third phase was initiated by John Edward Chisholm in 1967, when he presented a paper at the 1967 Oxford International Patristic Conference in support of Prosper's authorship, which was itself based on the first volume of his work on the *Hypomnesticon* published in that same year.[49] The long-promised second volume containing the critical edition of the *Hypomnesticon* was published in 1980.[50] Only one scholarly response to Chisholm's argument for Prosperian authorship has appeared since—Jean de Savignac's 1983 brief critique.[51] Dekkers listed the work under the Ps-Augustinian list and, quoting Savignac, concluded the *Hypomnesticon* "non est Prosperi Aqvitani, ut quidam proponunt."[52] Dekkers neglected to list the *Hypomnesticon* even among the spurious works of Prosper.

48. The first two phases in the debate on its authorship are detailed in Chisholm's first volume of his work on the *Hypomnesticon* (*The Pseudo-Augustinian Hypomnesticon against the Pelagians and Celestians,* vol. 1 [Fribourg, Switzerland: Fribourg University Press, 1967], 41–62), which contributes to the third stage.

49. Chisholm, "The Authorship of the pseudo-Augustinian *Hypomnesticon* against the Pelagians and Celestians," SP 11 (1972): 307–10; *Pseudo-Augustinian Hypomnesticon,* vol. 1.

50. Ed. Chisholm, *The Pseudo-Augustinian Hypomnesticon against the Pelagians and Celestians,* vol. 2 (Fribourg, Switzerland: Fribourg University Press, 1980).

51. Jean de Savignac, "Une attribution nouvelle et une édition critique de l'*Hypomnesticon,*" *Scriptorium* 37 (1983): 134–40.

52. Dekkers, *Clavis patrum latinorum,* 151.

Chisholm concluded in favor of Prosper's authorship for the work based on the similarities between the *Hypomnesticon* and Prosper's known works—in the title, doctrine, scriptural quotations, style, and vocabulary—and in light of the weak objections to Prosperian authorship.[53]

Savignac's two main arguments against Chisholm's conclusion was that Georges de Plinval—Chisholm's teacher—did not endorse his student's view, and that the author of *De vocatione omnium gentium,* which Chisholm believed was Prosper, cannot be the same as that of the *Hypomnesticon,* as Chisholm claimed. The latter critique has been resolved, but the former presents "an insurmountable difficulty."[54]

Savignac held that Chisholm's comparison of the *De vocatione omnium gentium* to the *Hypomnesticon* to establish Prosper's authorship of the *Hypomnesticon* is undermined by the fact that "[i]l est donc impossible d'attribuer au même auteur le *De vocatione gentium* et l'*Hypomnesticon.*"[55] However, as detailed above, Prosper's authorship of the *De vocatione omnium gentium* has since been firmly established.

Moreover, an argument in favor of Prosper's authorship for the *Hypomnesticon* is the similarity in the views on predestination in Prosper's *Pro Augustino responsiones ad capitula obiectionum Gallorum calumniantium* and *Pro Augustino responsiones ad capitula obiectionum Vincentiarum* with the *Hypomnesticon.* Oddly, these com-

53. Chisholm, *Pseudo-Augustinian Hypomnesticon,* vol. 1, 77–129. One argument Chisholm did not include in his arguments for Prosper's authorship of the *Hypomnesticon* is the similar phrase found in the *Hypomnesticon* and *De vocatione omnium gentium*—a work that Chisholm assumed was written by Prosper. The *Hypomnesticon* has "Habet gratia quod adoptet, non habet unda diluat" (2.24); *De vocatione omnium gentium* has "Habet enim in eis gratia quod adoptet, non habet unda quod diluat" (5.8). Chisholm made this comparison in a section dealing with the date of the composition of the *Hypomnesticon,* but not in the section dealing with Prosper's authorship. The reason Chisholm did not pursue this similarity in terms of authorship was, as Chisholm readily admitted, "the quotation because of its aphoristic nature could have been easily passed from mouth to mouth and could have found its way into the *De vocatione* independently of Hypomnesticon" (Chisholm, *Pseudo-Augustinian Hypomnesticon,* vol. 1, 28).

54. Savignac ("Une attribution nouvelle," 138): "Il est le premier à le faire, et apparement le seul, car son maître Georges de Plinval n'a pas ratifié cette opinion [cf. vol. 1, 129 n.]. Elle se heurte en effet à des difficultés insurmontables."

55. Savignac, "Une attribution nouvelle," 140.

parisons are not included in Chisholm's argument for Prosperian authorship, but in the section comparing the *Hypomnesticon* to Augustine's thoughts. The two responses, which are without doubt Prosper's, assert that God withholds predestination from those whom God foreknows will lead a sinful life. This same view is expressed in the *Hypomnesticon.*[56]

Still, there is Savignac's other critique. Chisholm was quick to point out that de Plinval came to agree with Chisholm's dating of the work, but Chisholm remained silent on whether de Plinval agreed with his conclusion of Prosperian authorship.[57] The weight of de Plinval's favorable opinion would have no doubt strengthened immeasurably Chisholm's conclusion. Savignac suggests that the absence of such an approval was indicative of an unfavorable response from de Plinval.

Thus, the question of Prosper's authorship seems unresolved. The argument in favor of Prosper's authorship for the *Hypomnesticon* based on similarities to Prosper's other known works is tenable, but textual similarities do not necessarily point to a single author. The implication of de Plinval's inferred disapproval carries considerable weight, but this alone is not conclusive. There is, however, one more argument that neither Chisholm nor Savignac fully considered. *Hypomnesticon*'s purpose and composition are not consistent with what is known about Prosper's concerns and method of argumentation.

The preface of the *Hypomnesticon* explicitly states that the work will answer five blasphemies from the heresy of the Pelagians and Caelestians.[58] A sixth response was later added to deal with a new situation, that of the objections to predestination.[59] Thus the work was originally limited to the refutation of the Pelagian heresy.

This could not have been the work of Prosper for three reasons.

56. Chisholm, *Pseudo-Augustinian Hypomnesticon,* vol. 1, 173–75.

57. Chisholm (*Pseudo-Augustinian Hypomnesticon,* vol. 1, 24 n. 5): "Since writing the above, I had the pleasure of meeting M. Georges de Plinval and of discussing with him the date of Hypomnesticon. I am happy to be able to say now [1965] M. de Plinval agrees with me in saying that Hypomnesticon was written prior to 435."

58. *Hypomnesticon,* Praef. (Ed. Chisholm, 101–3).

59. *Hypomnesticon* 6.1 (Ed. Chisholm, 191): "addere etiam hoc quam maxime huic operi oportet, ut et vestra calumnia . . . revincatur. . . ."

As it will become clear in the following chapters, Prosper never limited his attention to the Pelagians; he began his polemical writing career over the issue of predestination, which became his primary concern; and he was in the habit of prefacing his attacks on his Gallic opponents by first establishing the error of the Pelagians, thereby linking his opponents with the heresy. This was his consistent method of opposing his Gallic enemies, which is at odds with the approach taken by the author of the *Hypomnesticon.*

Savignac concluded that the author is unidentifiable, but conjectured, "qu'il fut probablement africain."[60] While the consensus among scholars is for the author's anonymity, there are good reasons to believe that the work may have come from another Augustinian. On the question of whether Prosper is the author of the *Hypomnesticon,* the weight of de Plinval's implied judgment, Savignac's criticisms, Dekkers's judgment, the reasons stated above, and the general scholarly consensus for anonymity, all together strongly suggest that Prosper was not the author of the *Hypomnesticon.*

The similarities between Prosper's responses and the *Hypomnesticon* suggest that the *Hypomnesticon* was written in the same period, between 433 and 435, roughly corresponding to Chisholm's dating of 430 to 435.[61]

Capitula sancti Augustini in urbem Romam transmissa

This work consists of twenty *capitula* drawn from Augustine's works and was first referred to in 520.[62] *Capitula* 3 to 10 were used for the first eight canons of the Second Council of Orange in 529.[63] In 1934, Cappuyns reviewed the question of authorship and con-

60. Savignac, "Une attribution nouvelle," 140.

61. See Chisholm, *Pseudo-Augustinian Hypomnesticon,* vol. 1, 24.

62. *Capitula sancti Augustini in urbem Romam transmissa* (CCL 85A: 243–73). Pope Hormisdas wrote to Possessor in Constantinople mentioning a set of capitula from the works of Augustine on the question of grace (*Epistula Papae Hormisdae ad Possessorem* 2.15 [CCL 85A: 120–21]). This letter was part of the controversy over Augustine's doctrine of grace in Constantinople, initiated by certain Scythian monks led by John Maxentius. For the conflict and the general history of the conflict over Augustine's doctrine of grace in the fifth and sixth century, see Weaver, *Divine Grace and Human Agency.*

63. *Concilium Arausicorum* (CCL 148A: 55–76; *The Synod of Orange,* A.D. 529, in *Theological Anthropology,* 109–28, trans. J. Patout Burns [Philadelphia: Fortress Press, 1981]).

cluded that the *Capitula* was written by John Maxentius, the leader of the Scythian monks in Constantinople, around 520.[64]

In 1978, Fr. Glorie edited the *Capitula* (CCL 85A: 243–73) and offered two new theories: the *Capitula* was probably composed in Gaul, and that Prosper was the author.[65] Glorie's theses were not fully elaborated in his four-page introduction to his edition of the *Capitula*, and he meekly ended with: "Sed ego dicam quod mihi in mentem venit: alii diiudicent."[66]

In 1989, R. A. Markus dismissed Glorie's proposal of Prosper as its author, but supported Glorie's contention for its Gallic origin.[67] Dekkers did not include the *Capitula* among the works of Prosper; instead, the work was listed under the spurious works of John Maxentius and with this description: "In Gallia confecta videntur, et quidem a Prospero Aquitano, iuxta novissimum editorem."[68] Neither Dekkers, nor anyone else, accepts Glorie's Prosperian authorship thesis. The possible identity of its author will be discussed in chapter 5.

Poema coniugis ad uxorem

The 122-line poem was addressed by a husband to his wife to encourage her to embrace the ascetic life together. The poem is contained in two surviving manuscripts, which name Prosper as the author.[69] The poem had been attributed to Paulinus of Nola, whose authorship has been effectively ruled out.[70] Le Brun and Mangeant,

64. M. Cappuyns, "L'origine des *Capitula* d'Orange 529," *Recherches de théologie ancienne et médiévale* 6 (1927): 126–40 (hereafter *RTAM*).

65. Fr. Glorie, "Prolegomena," in *Capitula sancti Augustini* (CCL 85A: 246): "Et probabilis nobis videtur recens sententia quae vult *Capitula s. Augustini* in Gallia fuisse composita. . . . *Capitula s. Augustini* a Prospero Aquitano inter a. 430–435 composita et ab illo ante a. 435 *in urbem Romam transmissa fuerint.*"

66. Glorie, "Prolegomena" (CCL 85A: 246).

67. R. A. Markus ("The Legacy of Pelagius: Orthodoxy, Heresy and Conciliation," in *The Making of Orthodoxy: Essays in Honor of Henry Chadwick*, ed. Rowan Williams [Cambridge: Cambridge University Press, 1989], 225): "We need not accept his conjecture (which is actually impossible) that their author was Prosper; but the evidence certainly points to Gaul as their home country."

68. Dekkers, "Ioannes Maxentius," *Clavis patrum latinorum*, 234.

69. G. Hartel, "Praefatio," in *Sancti Pontii Meropii Paulini Nolani Carmina* (CSEL 30: xxxiii–xxxv).

70. The question of Paulinus's authorship has long been settled; see R. P. H. Green,

in view of the diverse opinions regarding Prosper's authorship, concluded that such an attribution was dubious.[71] Dekkers judged the work spurious and Hamman concurs.[72]

Valentin concluded in favor of Prosper's authorship.[73] Only one scholar has followed Valentin's attribution. In 1911, Scott T. Holmes assumed the poem was Prosper's and proceeded to paint a rather sympathetic portrait of their struggles.[74] Scholars since Holmes have taken the cautious approach of Le Brun and Mangeant.

The strongest argument yet for excluding Prosper's authorship is what will become apparent in the following chapters—Prosper never revealed anything about his personal life. Such a deeply personal poem is completely uncharacteristic of Prosper.

The text is in PL 51: 611–16, 61: 737–42; and CSEL 30: 344–48.

De vita contemplativa libri tres

This work has been established as belonging to Julianus Pomerius, the native African who taught Caesarius of Arles. The text is in PL 59: 415–20 and was translated by Mary Suelzer in 1947.[75]

Confessio

This reflection on the suffering and redemption of its author seems to suggest the context of the barbarian invasions of Gaul in the early years of the fifth century, like that of the *Poema coniugis ad uxorem* and *De providentia Dei,* but written in allegorical language.[76]

The Poetry of Paulinus of Nola: A Study of His Latinity (Brussels: Latomus, 1971), 131–32. The question of Paulinus's authorship is not even entertained in the most recent work on Paulinus (Dennis Trout, *Paulinus of Nola: Life, Letters, Poems* [Berkeley and Los Angeles: University of California Press, 1999]).

71. Le Brun and Mangeant (PL 51: 611–12): "Quam si hoc opus nec inter veros, nec inter spurios suppositosque Prosperi fetus, sed inter dubios exhibeamus."

72. Dekkers, *Clavis patrum latinorum,* 531; Hamman, "Prosper Aquitanus," in *Supplementum* (PLS 3: 149).

73. Valentin, *Saint Prosper,* 755–66.

74. Scott T. Holmes did not provide any arguments in support of Prosper's authorship (*The Origin and Development of the Christian Church in Gaul during the First Six Centuries of the Christian Era* [London: Macmillan and Co., 1911], 385).

75. Julianus Pomerius, *The Contemplative Life,* trans. Mary Josephine Suelzer, ACW 4 (Westminster, Md.: Newman Bookshop, 1947).

76. PL 51: 607–10.

Valentin concluded, "[C]'est que l'authenticité de la Confessio n'est pas invraisemblable."[77] Apart from Valentin, the text has not received much attention and does not contribute significantly to the understanding of Prosper, even if it was written by Prosper. The text is in PL 51: 607–70.

De promissionibus et praeditionibus Dei

This lengthy treatise inspired by the theology of Augustine has been described as "un travail de speculation exégétique."[78] The absence of Prosper's characteristic polemical tone and the broader theological concerns expressed in the work led Valentin to conclude that Prosper was not the author and that the author could not be identified.[79] In 1976, R. Braun, the most recent editor of the text (CCL 60: 1–189) attributed the work to Quodvultdeus, and the attribution has been accepted.[80] The text is also in PL 51: 733–854.

Commonitorium quomodo sit agendum cum Manicheis qui confitentur pravitatem nefandi erroris

The work directed against the Manicheans has been associated more with Augustine than with Prosper. The text is printed among the Ps.-Augustinian works (PL 42: 1153–56) and in CSEL 25/2: 979–82.

"Prosperi" anathematismata seu Capitula S. Augustini

This work was written either in 515 or 526, which excludes the possibility of Prosper's authorship.[81] The text is in PL 65: 23–26 in the volume containing the works of Fulgentius of Ruspe.

Fragmentum de duobus testibus

This fragment, which has been appended to the end of Prosper's *Chronicon* in the manuscript tradition, was judged by Harnack to be

77. Valentin, *Saint Prosper*, 686.

78. Ibid., 658.

79. Ibid., 657–60.

80. R. Braun, "Introduction," in *Opera Qvodvultdeo Carthaginiensi episcopo tributa* (CCL 60: v–vii). Cf. Daniel Van Slyke, *Quodvultdeus of Carthage: The Apocalyptic Theology of a Roman African in Exile*, Early Christian Studies 5 (Strathfield, Australia: St. Pauls, 2003).

81. Dekkers, *Clavis patrum latinorum*, 188.

from Hippolytus or a member of his sect.[82] The text is in PLS 3: 150 and MGH, AA 9: 493.

Conclusion

There have been twenty-six works attributed to Prosper. Of these, seventeen are authentic, as argued above, not including the lost first letter to Augustine. The seventeen works are listed below in alphabetical order.

Pro Augustino responsiones ad capitula obiectionum Gallorum calumniantium
Pro Augustino responsiones ad capitula obiectionum Vincentiarum
Pro Augustino responsiones ad excerpta Genuensium
Carmen de ingratis
Epigrammata ex sententiis sancti Augustini
Epigrammata in obtrectatorem Augustini
Epistula ad Augustinum (*Ep.* 225)
Epistula ad Demetriadem de vera humilitate
Epistula ad Rufinum de gratia et libero arbitrio
Epitaphium Nestorianae et Pelagianae haereseon
Epitoma chronicorum
Expositio psalmorum a centesimo usque ad centesimum quinquagesimum
De gratia Dei et libero arbitrio liber contra collatorem
Liber sententiarum ex operibus sancti Augustini delibatarum
Praeteritorum episcoporum sedis apostolicae auctoritates de gratia Dei et libero voluntatis arbitrio
De providentia Dei
De vocatione omnium gentium

Literature on Prosper

The study of Prosper in the twentieth century began with L. Valentin's monumental dissertation, *Saint Prosper d'Aquitaine: Étude sur*

82. Theodore Mommsen (MHG, AA 9: 493 n. 1): "Harnackius noster, quem de hoc commentariolo consului, eum iudicat aut Hippolyti ipsius esse aut certe profectum ex secta Hippolytiana."

la littérature latine ecclésiastique au cinquième siècle en Gaule.[83] Valentin readily acknowledged the difficulty of writing about such a mysterious figure:

> Il naquit vers la fin du quartrième siècle, en Aquitaine, et mourut dans le dernier tiers du cinquième; c'est tout. Etait-il laïque, prêtre, évêque? Il était probablement simple laïque. Est-il saint? Le témoignage du martyrologe donne une grande force à l'opinion affirmative. Nous ne saurions aller plus loin.[84]

This did not prevent him, however, from writing nearly one thousand pages about Prosper. Published in 1900, the dissertation sought to establish the significance of Prosper as both a theologian and a significant literary figure. It has become the seminal work on Prosper, and considered the finest and most comprehensive study on Prosper to date.

As a theologian, Valentin argued, Prosper was able to maintain a certain "personnalité" while defending and expositing his master's ideas and, in due course, contributed some of his own ideas to the discussion on grace and free will.[85] Prosper was not a slave to all the details of Augustine's thoughts, but rather a faithful disciple to the spirit of his ideas. It was Prosper's treatment of the details of Augustine's doctrines that reveals his originality, according to Valentin, and ensured the acceptance of Augustine by the Church. Valentin summarized the relationship of Prosper to the thoughts of Augustine: "Sur quelques points il s'écarte du 'sentiér' trace par son maître; la foule croit qu'il marche derrière, quand il marche á côté, et quelquefois en avant."[86]

Whatever one may think of Prosper's theological dependence on Augustine, Valentin asserted, there remain other remarkable writings—history, poetry, and prose.[87] This part makes up the second half of the work and carefully details the style, language, characteristics, meter, translation, and imitation of the "authentic" texts

83. Valentin, *Saint Prosper.*
84. Ibid., 154–55.
85. Ibid., 1.
86. Ibid., 410.
87. Ibid., 1.

of Prosper. The book ends with a similar treatment for works whose Prosperian authorship is supposed, doubtful, or lost.

Valentin's book laid the groundwork for three issues that will be explored by others: the enduring question of Prosper's theological dependence on Augustine, his *Chronicon,* and the question of authorship of writings associated with Prosper's name. Scholarship on Prosper has explored these issues, but none has approached the breadth and depth of Valentin's study.

Immediately following Valentin's book, Léonce Couture reviewed Valentin's work. The first was published in 1900 and provided the textual history of the works of Prosper, which was not fully addressed by Valentin. The second article was a favorable book review.[88]

Beginning with M. Jacquin's 1906 article, a number of works explored the issue of Prosper's dependence upon Augustine's thoughts.[89] Jacquin was able to identify two distinct periods in Prosper's adhesion to the thoughts of the Bishop of Hippo: an earlier "pure" period marked by a reproduction of Augustine's doctrine, and a later one marked by an "interpretation" of the Augustinian system.[90] Following Valentin, Jacquin concluded that Prosper, despite deviating from "pure" adherence to Augustine's doctrines, remained a faithful disciple whose aim was to present Augustine in such a manner as to make him acceptable to his compatriots.[91]

Expanding the division made by Jacquin, M. Cappuyns added a third stage to Prosper's evolution.[92] Cappuyns identified three periods: intransigence (up to 432); first concessions (433–435); and grand concessions (after 435).[93] In tracing this evolution, Cappuyns detailed the circumstances that may have brought the changes, most notably the influence of Leo and the "theologically peaceful Roman sky."[94] Cappuyns understood Prosper as essentially a follower of Augustine,

88. Couture, "Saint Prosper d'Aquitaine," 269–82, and "Saint Prosper d'Aquitaine II," *Bulletin de littérature ecclésiastique* 3 (1901): 33–49.

89. M. Jacquin, "La question de la predestination aux V et VI siècles," *Revue d'histoire ecclésiastique* 7 (1906): 268–300.

90. Jacquin, "La predestination," 297.

91. Ibid., 299.

92. M. Cappuyns, "Le premier représentant de l'augustinisme médiéval, Prosper d'Aquitaine," *RTAM* 1 (1929): 309–37.

93. Cappuyns, "Le premier," 310.

94. Cappuyns, "Le premier," 336.

who incorporated the ideas of the Massilians, Leo, and his own to form a "catholic" view of grace and free will. Thus, argued Cappuyns, Prosper is the first representative of medieval Augustinianism.

Cappuyns's article exercised a great deal of influence on Prosperian scholarship that dealt with the issue of Prosper's dependence on Augustine. The division into the three periods became standard for addressing the question of Prosper's Augustianism.

The second book-length work to appear was Lionello Pelland's *S. Prosperi Aquitani: Doctrina de predestinatione et voluntate Dei salvifica.*[95] Published in 1936, the book, written entirely in Latin, addressed Prosper's doctrine of predestination and the salvific will of God in relation to Augustine's doctrine.

Pelland concluded, countering Cappuyns's thesis, "In his tribus epochis, Prosper suo magistro fidelis remansit."[96] According to Pelland, Prosper had discovered the "true mind" of Augustine and so was able to see through the exaggerations and ambiguous language to what Augustine truly meant.[97] Thus, Prosper only modified the doctrine of Augustine to make it acceptable, but his adhesion to Augustine's doctrine of grace did not undergo any fundamental change or transformation in the process.

Georges de Plinval in his 1958 article, "Prosper d'Aquitaine interprète de saint Augustin," shared Pelland's general thesis of Prosper's fidelity to Augustine's thoughts.[98] Like Pelland, Plinval rejected Valentin's and Cappuyns's assertions that Prosper "deviated quite strongly from the original Augustinianism."[99] While Plinval admitted Prosper's view of Augustine had changed, it was only in a certain measure.[100] Moreover, according to Plinval, Augustinianism was not "an expression of a 'system,' but a wide doctrine, living

95. Pelland, *S. Prosperi.*

96. Ibid., 183.

97. Pelland (*S. Prosperi,* 188): "eius tamen maxima laus fuit quod sub formulis aliquando exaggeratis vel ambiguis veram mentem Augustini invenerit."

98. Georges de Plinval, "Prosper d'Aquitaine interprète de saint Augustin," *Recherches Augustiniennes* 1 (1958): 339–55.

99. Plinval, "Prosper d'Aquitaine," 350.

100. Plinval ("Prosper d'Aquitaine," 354): "Est-il vrai qu'il ait dévié de la pure tradition augustinienne? . . . Oui, dans une certaine mesure."

and fertile, remaining in contact with the more open aspirations of its times."[101] In this regard, Plinval concluded Prosper was a faithful Augustinian.

In 1962, Rudolf Lorenz summarized much of the scholarship on the question of Prosper's Augustinianism in his article, "Der Augustinismus Prospers von Aquitanien."[102] After reviewing the current state of the question, Lorenz analyzed the Augustinianism of Prosper by examining Prosper's stand on the pertinent issues of predestination, reprobation, and the universal salvific will of God. Lorenz concluded that there were no fundamental differences between Prosper's and Augustine's positions on the above-mentioned issues, and that Prosper was independent only in form.[103]

In 1999, Arturo Elberti published the most recent of the three books on Prosper.[104] It is in many ways inspired by Valentin's book. Elberti followed Valentin's outline, shortened some parts and expanded others, but omitted the literary discussions. The influence of Augustine on Prosper was briefly examined, which closely followed Valentin's interpretation. Elberti concluded that Prosper was both a disciple of Augustine and a theologian, as indicated in the title of his book.

The focus of the book is on Prosper's later years in Rome. A great deal of attention is placed on *De vocatione omnium gentium.* The last part of the book deals with the question of Prosper's association with Leo the Great and finishes with a brief discussion on semi-Pelagianism and St. Benedict, and the influence of Prosper on Augustinianism.

On the issue of Prosper's Augustinianism, Elberti added nothing

101. Plinval ("Prosper d'Aquitaine," 355): "Non pas l'expression d'un 'système,' mais une doctrine large, vivante et féconde, restée en contact avec les aspirations plus ouvertes de ses contemporains."

102. Rudolf Lorenz, "Der Augustinismus Prospers von Aquitanien," *Zeitschrift für Kirchengeschichte* 73 (1962): 217–52.

103. Lorenz ("Augustinismus Prospers," 252): "Für die Geschichte des Augustinismus im 5. Jahrhundert muß berücksichtigt werden, daß eine Fortentwicklung Prospers von Augustin in der Gnaden- und Prädestinationslehre nicht stattgefunden hat. Er is nur im Formalen selbständiger geworden."

104. Elberti, *Prospero.*

new to the discussion. However, he contributed to the discussion on *De vocatione omnium gentium* as an authentic work of Prosper, and advanced the discussion on the question of Prosper's authorship of some works associated with Leo. Elberti's original contribution is in his discussion of Prosper and the Roman liturgy.[105]

In the summer of 2003, Fr. Roland Teske delivered a seminar paper at the 2003 Oxford International Conference on Patristic Studies entitled "The Augustinianism of Prosper of Aquitaine Revisited."[106] Teske, after discussing the authenticity of *De vocatione omnium gentium*, addressed the problems of attributing a work to Prosper that appears dramatically different from his earlier writings. Following the divisions of Cappuyns, Teske argued that the differences are attributable to Prosper's theological growth. While Teske does not provide any new arguments, he stressed the independence and genius of Prosper. This was the thought of Valentin a little over a century ago and it is worth repeating, for Prosper has yet to fully emerge from the wide shadow cast by Augustine.

The most recent treatment of Prosper to date was made by Augustine Casiday in his 2005 article entitled "Rehabilitating John Cassian: An Evaluation of Prosper of Aquitaine's Polemic against the 'Semipelagians.'"[107] After providing the background history for the conflict between Prosper and Cassian, Casiday turns to Prosper's disingenuous attack of Cassian's *Conlatio* 13. Casiday concludes that Prosper's "wilful distortion of evidence in furtherance of his bias . . . to be deeply and systematically flawed."[108] Despite the negative evaluation of Prosper, this recent treatment on Prosper is a welcome sign, perhaps of things to come.

The other issue that Valentin addressed was Prosper's *Chronicon*, but scholars have only recently explored this issue. R. A. Markus, in his 1986 article "Chronicle and Theology: Prosper of Aquitaine," pointed to the negative appraisal by Mommsen as a possible reason

105. Ibid., 231–52.

106. Roland Teske, "The Augustinianism of Prosper of Aquitaine Revisited," SP 43 (2003): 491–504.

107. Casiday, "Rehabilitating John Cassian," 270–84.

108. Ibid., 284.

for the neglect.[109] In this article, Markus addressed the question of Leo's influence on Prosper's later years, especially on his *Chronicon*. According to Markus, Augustine was the inspiration for Prosper's "sense of history as the theatre of God's hidden purposes," but it was Leo who provided the specific theological inspiration.[110] These were the universality of salvation and the spread of faith that extended even beyond the borders of the Empire.[111]

A fuller treatment of the *Chronicon* appeared in Steven Muhlberger's 1990 book *Fifth-Century Chroniclers: Prosper, Hydatius, and the Gallic Chronicler of 452*.[112] Muhlberger focused on the literary and historical aspects of the work, but only touched slightly on its theological inspirations. Prosper's theological treatment of Rome in his *Chronicon* is explored by Hervé Inglebert's 1996 work, *Les Romains chrétiens face à l'histoire de Rome*.[113]

An aspect of Prosper not fully addressed by Valentin was the influence of Leo in Prosper's later theological writings. This was initially addressed by Cappuyns and slightly explored by Elberti. In 1993, two articles presented very different views on the relationship between Leo and Prosper. Philip L. Barclift asserted that Leo and Prosper came to similar conclusions on predestination and divine foreknowledge, suggesting that they arrived at their conclusions independently.[114] N. W. James, expanding on Gaidioz's work, argued for Prosper's hand in the writings of Leo. These include the *Tome to Flavian*, Leo's anti-Pelagian letters, and the first five sermons of Leo, and the sermons that dealt with important theological details.[115]

109. R. A. Markus, "Chronicle and Theology: Prosper of Aquitaine"; Theodore Mommsen, "Introduction," *Epitoma chronicorum*, in *Chronica minora* 1 (MGH, AA 9: 348).

110. Markus, "Chronicle and Theology," 36.

111. Ibid., 39.

112. Steven Muhlberger, *The Fifth Century Chroniclers: Prosper, Hydatius, and the Gallic Chronicler of 452* (Leeds, U.K.: F. Cairns, 1990).

113. Hervé Inglebert, *Les Romains chrétiens face à l'histoire de Rome*, Collection des Études Augustiniennes, série antique 145 (Paris: Institut d'études augustiniennes, 1996).

114. Philip L. Barclift, "Predestination and Divine Foreknowledge in the Sermons of Pope Leo the Great," *Church History* 62 (1993): 5–21 (hereafter *CH*).

115. N. W. James, "Leo the Great and Prosper of Aquitaine," Journal of Theological Studies 44 (1993): 554–84 (hereafter JTS); J. Gaidioz, "Prosper d'Aquitaine et le Tome à

Barclift returned to the theme, in 1997, with "Shifting Tones of Pope Leo the Great's Christological Vocabulary," and concluded that the *Tome* was a cooperative work between Leo and his theological advisor, Prosper.[116]

The 2007 Oxford International Conference on Patristic Studies included a workshop dedicated to Prosper. Augustine Casiday presented on Prosper's polemics, Rebecca Harden Weaver on the legacy of Prosper in the early Middle Ages, and Alexander Hwang on a reevaluation of Prosper's Augustinianism. The papers from the workshop are expected to be published in *Studia Patristica.*

Flavien," *Revue des sciences religieuses* 23 (1949): 270–301. James's thesis had already been explored by Valentin, who concluded against Prosper's authorship in Leo's works (Valentin, *Saint Prosper,* 746–53).

116. Philip L. Barclift, "Shifting Tones of Pope Leo the Great's Christological Vocabulary," *CH* 66/2 (1997): 221–22.

~2

Prosper's Life to 416 and *De providentia Dei*

THERE IS LITTLE information about Prosper's personal life in general, but even less for his early years. It is possible, however, to reconstruct a general picture of Prosper's early life from inferences drawn from his writings, documented events of the time, and the details of life in late antiquity provided by his less taciturn contemporaries and compatriots. Based on the evidence, admittedly largely circumstantial, it appears that Prosper was born around 388 into the Gallo-Roman aristocracy in Aquitaine. He received the benefits associated with his class and region, including the finest education available in the West, until the barbarian invasions of Gaul, beginning in 406. Prosper eventually relocated to Marseilles, around 416, and shortly afterward wrote his first known work, *De providentia Dei.*

Historical Context

The Roman Empire that Prosper was born into was in the process of dramatic and lasting changes. During his early years, Prosper witnessed the reign of the last emperor to rule both East and West (Theodosius 379–395), the sack of Rome (410), and personally suffered from the invasion and occupation of Gaul by barbarians (406–416).[1]

1. Against the traditional view, Ralph Mathisen suggests the invasions were not as destructive as presented by contemporaries and eyewitnesses, who Mathisen asserts

Changes were taking place in the life of the Church as well. Asceticism was sweeping across the West, inspiring aristocratic Christians to move beyond the comfortable balance they maintained between their religious and worldly commitments.

The East was and will continue to be consumed with Christology. The West had its own theological conflict, but one involving issues related to grace. At the center of the controversy were the ideas associated with Pelagius. Augustine had yet to openly condemn Pelagius, and the conflict during this period was limited to Italy, Sicily, North Africa, and Palestine.

Prosper's Origin

The lack of historical and literary evidence for the date of Prosper's birth has led the majority of scholars to assign the late fourth century as a general period for Prosper's birth.[2] Some have ventured to put forward a more precise date. Among them, Valentin's approximate year of 390 has been the most influential. However, the literary and historical evidence suggests an earlier date of 388, at the latest.

Valentin arrived at the date of 390 after considering the necessary maturity required by certain later events in Prosper's life. Valentin cited Hilary's high estimation of Prosper in his letter to Augustine (429), the request made to Prosper by the Genoese priests for an interpretation of Augustine's difficult passages (431), and Prosper's attack of the illustrious John Cassian (439), all of which required a mature figure. Moreover, Valentin argued, Prosper's first works revealed qualities of a mature author.[3] A birth year around 390 then,

---

had exaggerated their accounts of the destruction (*Roman Aristocrats in Barbarian Gaul* [Austin: University of Texas Press, 1993], esp. 26–31); Peter Brown takes it even further and presents a rather benign portrait of what Brown labels "guests" of the local populations. Brown's view may apply at a general level, but at the local level, according to the testimony of eyewitnesses and contemporaries, even allowing for exaggerations, there appears to be a significant amount of violence and destruction. Also, such a view of the invaders as "guests" appears inconsistent with the evidence of the mass dislocation and flight of Gallo-Roman aristocrats (Peter Brown, *The Rise of Western Christendom,* 2nd ed. [Oxford: Blackwell, 2003], 101–6).

2. For an extensive discussion on the date of birth, see Valentin, *Saint Prosper,* 124–26.

3. Valentin, *Saint Prosper,* 125–26.

according to Valentin, provided enough time for Prosper to gain a level of maturity reflected in the events of his initial public life.

Kruger, Pelland, Muhlberger, and McHugh have deferred, rather uncritically, to Valentin's date.[4] Valentin's method of arriving at this birth year is reasonable; however, Valentin's maturity argument did not include the evidence of Prosper's earliest known writing, *De providentia Dei,* written in 416. Valentin did not consider the work in his birth year argument because the authenticity of the work was in question at that time. Valentin addressed the work of *De providentia Dei* in a later chapter, which was concerned with establishing the authenticity and dating of the work. Since Valentin, Prosper's authorship of *De providentia Dei* and its dating have been convincingly established by Duckworth and Marcovich, among others.[5] If then, according to Valentin's maturity argument, Hilary's high estimation of Prosper required a mature Prosper in 429, the same argument should also apply to an earlier period, 416, the date of *De providentia Dei.*

Would Prosper have been mature enough to write *De providentia Dei* at the age of twenty-six, a work Marcovich called a "gem of the Christianized Stoicism?"[6] Couture raised this very concern immediately after the publication of Valentin's study. Couture conceded that it was possible for Prosper to have written the work in 416 at age twenty-six, but cautioned that the work would be a marvel for someone of that age.[7] Although not a definitive judgment either way, Couture noted the problem that *De providentia Dei* posed on Valentin's dating scheme.

The concern with assigning *De providentia Dei* to Prosper at age twenty-six can easily be resolved by moving back Prosper's birth year. An earlier birth year would resolve the problem of maturity with *De providentia Dei,* and, more importantly, an earlier birth year corresponds with Prosper's education in the context of histori-

4. Following Valentin's date are: Muhlberger, *Fifth Century Chroniclers,* 48; Pelland, *S. Prosperi,* 23; and M. P. McHugh, "Prosper of Aquitaine," *ATA,* 685.

5. See chapter 1.

6. Marcovich, "Preface," *De providentia Dei,* xii.

7. Couture, "Saint Prosper d'Aquitaine II," 35.

cal events in early-fifth-century Gaul. Assigning an earlier date than 390 provides the necessary time for Prosper to have completed, or come near to completing, his education before the barbarian invasions, which began in 406 and lasted a decade.

Education in Gaul was supported by the Empire, and "their fate was bound up with the political structure of the Empire. And when the Empire collapsed, they [education] collapsed."[8] The political collapse in Gaul was most pronounced in Aquitaine and resulted in the end of the vitality of the educational system in Aquitaine.[9] Against this traditional view of the invasions' disastrous effects on education, Mathisen makes a convincing case for the transformation of the Roman secular schools in Gaul, including Aquitaine.[10] Even if that were the case, the argument for an earlier date than 390 is still viable. If Prosper was born in 390, he would only have been sixteen at the start of the invasions. Prosper would have had the beginnings of the last, but crucial, stage of education, rhetoric.[11] However, Prosper's writings reflect a fully, classically trained author. The possibility of Prosper finishing his education at his original school or elsewhere, or by means of a private tutor, according to Mathisen's scenario, are precluded by Prosper's own testimony in *De providentia Dei*—that he was a captive of the Goths and led into exile.[12] In addition, Prosper begins the work confessing that a greater part of the year had passed

8. H. I. Marrou, *A History of Education in Antiquity,* trans. George Lamb (Madison: University of Wisconsin Press, 1982), 344.

9. Nora Chadwick, *Poetry and Letters,* 122–41; and in Theodore Haarhoff, *Schools of Gaul: A Study of Pagan and Christian Education in the Last Century of the Western Empire* (London: Oxford University Press, 1920), 243–49.

10. Ralph W. Mathisen ("Bishops, Barbarians, and the 'Dark Ages': The Fate of Late Roman Educational Institutions in Late Antique Gaul," in *Medieval Education,* ed. Ronald B. Begley and Joseph W. Koterski [New York: Fordham University Press, 2005], 13): "Rather than disappearing, degenerating, or being submerged, the late Roman secular schools were transformed into institutions that reflected the social, religious, and political realities of their times."

11. A discussion on the age of students can be found in Alan D. Booth, "Date of Jerome's Birth," *Phoenix* 33 (1979): 347, 351 n. 18.

12. *De prov. Dei* 1 (ed. Marcovich, 6–7): "And you yourself, all covered with dust and carrying your pack, traveled the pitiless road amidst the wagons and arms of the Goths, when the holy bishop was driven from his burnt city, leading his mangled flock as a shepherd in exile." All citations of the poem will indicate both the pages of the Latin text and the facing English translation.

since he had written anything in verse.[13] Prosper's reference to composing in verse suggests he had attained his full education, and was in the practice of using it, before the writing of *De providentia Dei* in 416. The reference to his captive status alone indicates the opportunities for continued education were unavailable to Prosper.

Prosper's testimony and the quality of *De providentia Dei* lead to the conclusion that Prosper completed or was very near completing his education before the invasions of 406. According to the Roman educational system, the average age of graduates was eighteen at the earliest. Prosper had to have been born, at the latest, by 388, in order to finish his education by 406. Thus, 388 as a likely *terminus ante quem* for his birth year is consistent with the literary, educational, and historical evidence.

Prosper's connection with Aquitaine is one of the few details that are known with some measure of certainty about his personal life. Gennadius, writing in the 490s, established the link between Prosper and Aquitaine: *Prosper, homo Aquitanicae regionis,* and the association has been assumed ever since.[14] The particular references to events in Aquitaine in his *Chronicon,* and the eyewitness perspective of the events in Aquitaine in *De providentia Dei,* confirm this connection.

The place of his birth is unknown, but the evidence suggests he spent at least a significant period of his early life in Aquitaine. Prosper's familial background is equally unknown. The quality of Prosper's education and, to a lesser extent, his ability to reside in Marseilles and to travel to Rome, however, suggests a Gallo-Roman aristocratic background.[15] Prosper's initial relationship to Christianity is also unknown. The earliest evidence of Prosper's Christianity is *De providentia Dei.* The work, intended for beginners in the faith, assumes Prosper had reached a measure of Christian maturity some time before 416.[16]

13. *De prov. Dei* 1 (ed. Marcovich, 4–5): "Months run, the most part of the year has already passed away, and yet not a single page has been written in your verse."

14. Gennadius, *De viris inlustribus* 85 (TU 14/1: 90).

15. The Gallo-Roman aristocracy in this period is explored in Mathisen, *Roman Aristocrats,* 9–16.

16. *De prov. Dei* 12 (ed. Marcovich, 66–67): "What I have written in this brief pamphlet will do for the beginners."

Aquitaine

Prosper spent his early years in late-fourth-century Aquitaine. It was a fortunate time and place. Although Gaul suffered greatly from the wars of the third century, Aquitaine was able to rebuild and even enjoyed a measure of prosperity throughout the fourth century. The invasions of the mid-fourth century and the civil war resulting from the revolt of the usurper Magnentius did not affect Aquitaine as it had other parts of Gaul.[17] Trade with Britain continued, and the great West-East route, which connected Aquitaine to centers as far east as Constantinople, still functioned.[18]

Beside the benefits of peace and prosperity, Aquitainians enjoyed the natural beauty of the province. Salvian of Marseilles, a contemporary of Prosper, echoed the common praises of Aquitaine when he paid homage to that "best part of all Gaul" in *The Governance of God*:

> It is a land productive in its fertility, and not only fertility, but also pleasantness, beauty, and luxury, which are sometimes preferred to fertility. In that part of Gaul the whole region is, so to say, interwoven with vines. Its meadows are flowered. Its fields are ploughed, or planted with fruit trees, or filled with delightful woods. The land is well watered with fountains, interspersed with rivers, and rich in harvests. Truly, the holders and masters of that land seem to have possessed not so much a portion of that soil as an image of paradise.[19]

Aquitaine was also distinguished for its educational system. Gaul, in general, had a long tradition of education dating back to the Druids, and Gallic eloquence was renowned even before Roman occupation. Roman education, finding a receptive and fertile soil, flourished in Gallo-Roman Gaul, and by the second half of the fourth century Gaul became the principal center of intellectual ac-

17. Olwen Brogan, *Roman Gaul* (Cambridge, Mass.: Harvard University Press, 1953), 226.

18. Brogan, *Roman Gaul,* 225; Chadwick, *Poetry and Letters,* 15.

19. Salvian of Marseilles, *De gubernatione Dei* (CSEL 8: 157; *The Governance of God,* in *The Writings of Salvian, the Presbyter,* trans. Jeremiah F. O'Sullivan, FC 3 [New York: CIMA Publishing, 1947], 187–88).

tivity in the West, a status that it would enjoy through the fifth century.[20] Within Gaul, the province of Aquitaine was the preeminent center of learning.[21] The tranquility afforded to Aquitaine along with the imperial support of the schools helped advance the excellence of Aquitanian education.

Aquitaine's reputation in education was famous throughout the Empire. Jerome mentioned three rhetors from Aquitaine and noted that Alcimus and Delfidus "taught in Aquitaine most eloquently."[22] Ausonius, who was a product of the schools of Aquitaine and later taught there, catalogued no less than twenty-five distinguished professors of Bordeaux.[23] The schools produced, besides imperial administrators, professors for the schools of Rome and Constantinople.[24]

The pleasant atmosphere of Aquitaine during this period can be glimpsed in the person of Ausonius of Bordeaux.[25] His retirement to the idyllic countryside of Aquitaine was a welcome relief from the political strife and intrigue that had marked his service in the courts of Valentinian and Gratian. Ausonius spent these years living the life of leisure, cultivating his relationships through letter writing, lavish dinners, and the exchange of gifts—marks of the Gallo-Roman aristocracy.[26]

20. Chadwick, *Poetry and Letters,* 22–23.

21. Haarhoff, *Schools of Gaul,* 46.

22. Jerome, *Chronicon* (ed. Helm, 233, 239; *Chronicon,* 41, 47).

23. Ausonius, "Commemoratio Professorum Burdigalensium," in *Decimi Magni Ausonii Opera* (ed. R. P. H. Green [Oxford: Oxford University Press, 1999], 46–66; "Poems Commemorating the Professors of Bordeaux," in *Ausonius,* vol. 1, trans. Hugh Evelyn White [Cambridge, Mass.: Harvard University Press, 1919; repr. 1961], 97–139).

24. Samuel Dill, *Roman Society in the Last Century of the Western Empire,* 2nd ed. (London: Macmillan and Co., 1925), 168.

25. The works of Ausonius are in *Decimi Magni Ausonii Opera,* ed. R. P. H. Green (Oxford: Oxford University Press, 1999); *Ausonius,* trans. Hugh Evelyn White, 2 vols. (Cambridge, Mass.: Harvard University Press, 1919; repr. 1961). For a recent study of Ausonius, see Hagith Silvan, *Ausonius of Bordeaux: Genesis of a Gallic Aristocracy* (London: Routledge, 1993).

26. Chadwick, *Poetry and Letters,* 47–62; Samuel Dill, *Roman Society,* 167–86.

Asceticism

Ausonius was also to witness the religious changes sweeping across Gaul in the form of asceticism. Christianity had arrived in Gaul in the second half of the second century. The next two centuries saw the gradual movement away from paganism to Christianity. Around the mid-fourth century, Christianity began to make an impact on pagan Aquitaine. Hilary of Poitiers, noting this change, wrote: "Every day the believing people grow in numbers and multiply the profession of their faith. One abandons pagan superstition and the vanity of idols. Everyone moves along the road to salvation."[27] Hilary, however, could not have imagined the road would become so wide. The Christianity that the Gallo-Roman aristocracy adopted was perfectly compatible with their social and cultural identity.

This was the Christianity of Ausonius. His Christian faith was the reserved faith of an aristocrat still in the world, if not of it, a faith that was but one part of his life. This compartmentalized faith is perhaps best illustrated in Ausonius's description of his daily life. It began with morning prayers until he felt "God has been prayed to enough" and devoted the rest of the day to worldly matters.[28] Ausonius's commitment to Christianity, as with other Christian aristocrats, was in harmony with their cultured material world.[29]

A new Christian movement was spreading across the West. Asceticism, in its various expressions, carried with it a radical commitment to the life of devotion, above all else.[30] Martin of Tours personified the new ascetic movement in Gaul. Martin helped convert Gaul away from paganism through his mission work, but it was the example of his ascetic lifestyle, as recorded by Sulpicius Severus,

27. Hilary of Poitiers, "Psalmum 67," *Tractatus super Psalmos* (CSEL 22: 295), quotation in W. H. C. Frend, "The Two Worlds of Paulinus of Nola," in *Latin Literature of the Fourth Century*, ed. J. W. Binns (London: Routledge, 1974), 102.

28. Ausonius, "Ephemeris," *Decimi Magni Ausonii Opera* (ed. Green, 12; "Daily Round," in *Ausonius*, vol. 1, 23): "Satis precum datum deo."

29. Chadwick, *Poetry and Letters*, 60.

30. The ascetic movement found expression in a number of different ways, from the simple layperson to the bishop, and from individuals to communities.

where his influence was felt most.[31] *The Life* was widely read in Gaul, Italy, Illyria, and even in the deserts of Egypt and Cyrene.[32]

Asceticism was not a mass movement, nor was it universally held in high regard. In Gaul, the resistance to this movement came from the established and conservative-minded bishops of Gaul, at first. The eventual acceptance and triumph of asceticism was well underway, however, by the early decades of the fifth century. The success of the movement is most evident in the increasingly common practice of installing members of ascetic communities in important bishoprics in Gaul. The new movement failed to inspire Ausonius toward the ascetic life, but the movement affected Ausonius in a deeply personal way.

Comparing asceticism to a wildfire seems a helpful way to convey the power, spectacle, and volatility of asceticism as it moved across the West. Embers came from the deserts of the East and were carried by those who had witnessed and practiced the ascetic life at the feet of its masters. Embers were powerless in themselves, but under the right conditions, they had the potential to ignite a blazing fire. Such fires were being ignited throughout the West, some with spectacular effect. Not even the most verdant was immune. Paulinus of Nola, Ausonius's brilliant former student and intimate friend, a man of great wealth and distinction, was firmly rooted in the rich soil of the Gallo-Roman aristocracy, but became enflamed by the call of asceticism.[33] The news of Paulinus's "conversion" elicited reactions of amazement and delight, but also puzzlement and disapproval from some, perhaps none more so than his old teacher and friend.

Ausonius was never able to fathom Paulinus's new devotion to Christianity, which caused a rupture in their long and intimate

31. Sulpicius Severus, *Vita Martini* (SC 133: 248–316; *The Life of St. Martin,* trans. B. M. Peebles, in *Niceta of Remesiana, Sulpicius Severus, Prosper of Aquitaine,* FC 7 [New York: Fathers of the Church, 1949], 101–40). See Clare Standcliffe, *St. Martin and His Hagiographer* (Oxford: Clarendon Press, 1983).

32. Dill, *Roman Society,* 181.

33. The works of Paulinus are in CSEL 29–30; *Letters of St. Paulinus of Nola,* 2 vols. trans. P. G. Walsh, ACW 35–36 (Westminster, Md.: Newman Press, 1966/1967). *The Poems of St. Paulinus of Nola,* trans. P. G. Walsh, ACW 40 (New York: Newman Press, 1975). For studies of Paulinus, see Joseph T. Lienhard, *Paulinus of Nola and Early Western Monasticism* (Cologne: Hanstein, 1977) and Trout, *Paulinus of Nola.*

friendship. After years of mutual silence, Paulinus tried to explain the reason for the dramatic course his life had taken, along with an ultimatum:

> But now another power, a greater God, inspires my mind and demands another way of life. He asks back from man His own gift, so that we may live for the Father of life. He bids us not to spend our days on the emptiness of leisure and business, or on the fictions of literature. . . . I am resolved to end my worldly cares while life remains, to entrust my possessions to God against the age to come, and to await harsh death with untroubled heart. If you approve this, take pleasure in the rich hopes of your friend. If you disapprove, leave me to win approval from Christ alone.[34]

It turned out to be the final farewell from the devoted student to his long-time friend. The often-quoted passage speaks poignantly of asceticism's powerful attraction and its uncompromising demand to withdraw from the intellectual and material riches of the cultured world, from even loved ones, toward the simple and humble life of singular devotion to God.[35]

Similar "conversions" were taking place in the West. One notable example is Augustine. In 386, Augustine, who had come from humble and provincial origins, was about to realize his life's ambitions. The choice confronting him, as Frend put it, "had defined itself clearly as one between a great administrative career backed by an Italian wife and estates in north Italy, combined with a non-assertive commitment to Christianity, or dedication to lifelong service of the catholic Church in ascetic retreat in his native North Africa."[36] Augustine, along with his circle of friends, chose the latter, rejecting the life he had labored so long and hard to attain.

The Aquitaine of Prosper's early years was marked by peace and prosperity, as it had been for generations. The Gallo-Roman aristocracy had built up a sophisticated culture in an idyllic place, lauded throughout the Empire. Changes were on their way. Invasions, both physical and spiritual, would transform the Gallo-Roman aristocracy.

34. "Poem 10 to Ausonius," *Poems of St. Paulinus*, trans. Walsh, 59, 69.
35. Dill, *Roman Society*, 399.
36. Frend, "Two Worlds of Paulinus of Nola," 103.

Early Years

Education

The evidence for Prosper's education is circumstantial. That he was educated in one of the schools of Aquitaine is a reasonable conclusion. The quality of his writings is consistent with the high standards of education for which Aquitaine was famous.

Valentin, understandably, claimed Bordeaux, the most famous school of Aquitaine, as a probable site for Prosper's schooling, thereby linking Prosper to the illustrious tradition of learned men that included Ausonius, Sulpicius Severus, and Paulinus of Nola.[37] However, as Couture noted, there is no good reason to assign Bordeaux or any school to Prosper.[38] Moreover, Bordeaux was not the only distinguished school of learning in Aquitaine; Ausonius mentioned illustrious professors at Auch, Angouleme, Poitiers, and Toulouse.[39] Whatever the particular school, Prosper received an excellent education somewhere in the preeminent center of Western education.

The education Prosper received was still in accord with the Roman system, observed in continuity throughout the Empire.[40] It consisted of three stages: primary, grammar, and rhetoric.[41] Prosper began elementary instruction in the primary school, either through a hired teacher or his parents, as was the case for Paulinus of Pella, who recalled, with great fondness, the evenhanded nature of his parents' instruction.[42] Prosper then passed into the grammarian level at six or seven, learning Greek and Latin, and then onto the school of rhetoric at fifteen or so until about age eighteen.

37. Valentin, *Saint Prosper,* 127.

38. Couture, "Prosper d'Aquitaine," 34.

39. Haarhoff, *Schools of Gaul,* 46.

40. For a general discussion on education, see Marrou, *History of Education in Antiquity;* and S. F. Bonner, *Education in Ancient Rome* (Berkeley and Los Angeles: University of California Press, 1977). For schools in Gaul during this period, see Haarhoff, *Schools of Gaul.*

41. For a recent discussion on the tripartite school division, see Robert Kaster, "Notes on 'Primary' and 'Secondary' Schools in Late Antiquity," *Transactions of the American Philological Association* 113 (1983): 323–46.

42. Paulinus of Pella, *Eucharisticus* (CSEL 16: 294; *Ausonius,* vol. 2, trans. Hugh G. Evelyn White [Cambridge, Mass.: Harvard University Press, 1921; repr. 1985], 313): "And my parents' noble pains, skilled to season learning with mingled enticements."

Prosper went through the successive stages of his education, immersing himself in the classics, as had so many young Roman boys before him. Although Prosper neglected to mention anything about his school days, there is abundant testimony of student life, especially the suffering received at the hands of the harsh and punitive schoolmasters. This seems to have been a common trait in the educational system and left an indelible impression on the memory of not a few students.[43]

Less easy to construct are his contacts to Christian learning. If Prosper or his family desired a Christian education for Prosper, it would have been an informal arrangement. The schools of Aquitaine were pagan and the rise of anything resembling a formal Christian education would come later, in the first decades of the fifth century in southern Gaul.[44]

Under normal circumstances, there would have been several options open for Prosper at the completion of his formal education: imperial service, teaching, ecclesiastical service, the life of *otium,* or the ascetic life. However, the barbarian invasions and settlements in the early part of the fifth century, around the end of his education, severely restricted his choices.

The invasions and decline of imperial authority in Gaul resulted in the loss of opportunities for imperial officeholding.[45] The possibility of a teaching career in Aquitaine likewise vanished in the wake of the destruction, with the schools of Aquitaine giving way to the emerging new center of literary activity in Marseilles.[46] A career in ecclesiastical service, at least in Gaul, appeared an unfavorable option as the barbarian settlements disrupted the operation of the Gallic Church, and, at times, endangered the lives of its clerics.[47] The

43. Augustine recalled the harsh treatment he received at the hands of his instructors, especially in the learning of Greek (*Confessiones* 1.14.23 [CCL 27: 12–13]). Ausonius, "Epistle 22: A Book of Exhortations to His Grandson" (*Ausonius,* vol. 2, 73–75): "Learn readily, and loathe not, my grandson, the control of your grim teacher. A master's looks need never cause a shudder. Though he be grim with age and, ungentle of voice, threaten harsh outbursts with frowning brow. But to yourself be true, mocking at fear, and let no outcry, nor sound of stripes, nor dread, make you quake as the morning hours come on. Your father and mother went through all this in their day."

44. Haarhoff, *Schools of Gaul,* 175–80.

45. Mathisen, *Roman Aristocrats,* 32.

46. Chadwick, *Poetry and Letters,* 122.

47. Mathisen, *Roman Aristocrats,* 32.

destruction and occupation of the land definitively put an end to any hope for a life of leisure such as Ausonius enjoyed. Attempts to reclaim their lands and reestablish their former lives were to prove futile and even dangerous in the coming decades.[48] The ascetic life, in whatever form, was an option still available, but it would have to be lived out elsewhere.

The invasions and settlement provided little choice for the Gallo-Roman aristocracy but to flee, although some remained to stake out their future among the barbarians.[49] Popular destinations for Aquitanians were the Holy Land, Spain, Italy, and Marseilles.[50] For Prosper, however, the decision was not his to make as he was among the unfortunate group taken captive by the Goths.[51]

Marseilles

The circumstances surrounding his release from captivity are unknown. Prosper only briefly mentions the conditions of their captive status and does not provide any information about their release.[52] Prosper could have been released as the Visigoths made their way to Spain, or ransomed. There are examples of the role that Gallo-Roman bishops played in ransoming captives held by the barbarians.[53] Whatever the circumstances for Prosper's release, the latest date is early 415, when the Visigoths moved on to Spain. What is certain is that Prosper was in Marseilles by 416, the date of *De providentia Dei.*

Situated on the southern coastline of Provence, Marseilles with its sheltered deep-water harbor and access to interior Gaul made it a commercial center throughout the Roman period. The fortified walls and towers, which were not breached until the sixth century, ensured the port city exceptional prosperity and peace in late antiquity, while cities in the West, in general, were in decline.[54]

48. Ibid., 30.

49. Service in barbarian administrations was one of the strategies of coming to terms with the barbarians (Mathisen, *Roman Aristocrats,* esp. 125–31). Peter Brown asserts that it was the barbarians, at least in the first generations, who were invited to come and offer their services of protection (*Rise of Western Christendom,* 101–2).

50. Mathisen, *Roman Aristocrats,* 60–63.

51. *De prov. Dei* 1 (ed. Marcovich, 6–7).

52. Ibid.

53. Mathisen, *Roman Aristocrats,* 101.

54. S. T. Loseby, "Marseille: A Late Antique Success Story?" *Journal of Roman Studies* 82 (1992): 165.

Marseilles became a "reception area" for many exiled Gallo-Roman aristocrats seeking safety in the wake of the invasions and settlement by barbarians in the early fifth century.[55] The decline of Bordeaux and this influx of aristocrats helped establish Marseilles as the new intellectual center of Gaul—a "new Athens."

The circumstances of Prosper's life in Marseilles are unclear. In terms of his financial situation, it can be inferred that he had some access to wealth. Prosper had to have had material resources in order to enjoy the opportunity to read and write, travel to Rome, and time to partake in the intellectual milieu of Marseilles.

Prosper's wealth could have come from the sale of whatever family property he held in Aquitaine. While certainly possible, regaining land in Aquitaine appears to have been difficult if not dangerous, as was the experience of Paulinus of Nola and Paulinus of Pella. Paulinus of Nola had the resources to relocate to his estate in Italy, but Paulinus of Pella was not as fortunate.[56] The *Eucharisticus* tells of Paulinus of Pella's struggle to maintain his sense of dignity as he toiled with the humble piece of inherited land in Marseilles, while still finding the need to receive support from others.[57] There appears to have been some network of charity available to the exiles in Marseilles, which Paulinus was at pains to acknowledge.[58] It was only with the sale of that small estate to a Goth that Paulinus lived out the last years of his life in Marseilles with some measure of self-respect, but never fulfilled his desperate dream of returning to his beloved Aquitaine.[59]

Paulinus of Pella's description of his life in Marseilles provides a picture of the precarious situation some exiles must have found themselves in. Although Prosper seemed to have fared better than Paulinus, the *Eucharisticus* may indicate possible sources for Pros-

55. Chadwick, *Poetry and Letters,* 122.

56. N. B. McLynn, "Paulinus the Impenitent: A Study of the Eucharisticos," *Journal of Early Christian Studies* 3 (1995): 461–86.

57. Paulinus of Pella, "Eucharisticus," 347.

58. Paulinus of Pella ("Eucharisticus," 347): "All that can still be thought as my own, I suffer myself to be supported at others' charges."

59. McLynn ("Paulinus the Impenitent," 478) against the view of Mathisen, holds that Paulinus never returned to Aquitaine; cf. Mathisen, "Emigrants, Exiles and Survivors: Aristocratic Options in Visigothic Aquitainia," *Phoenix* 38 (1984): 162.

per's finances. Perhaps Prosper benefited from possessing an estate in Marseilles, or received support from friends or relatives, or the exiled community, none of which can be confirmed.

Conclusions

Prosper's familial details are even more difficult to ascertain. In an age of letter writing, in which the exchange of letters was indispensable for the maintenance and strengthening of social bonds, Prosper's letters reveal almost nothing about his personal life. Prosper never once revealed the identity of his parents, matrimonial status, any children, or relatives, in any of his letters or in any of his writings. Given the lack of evidence, the details of Prosper's personal life are, as he seemingly intended it to be, a mystery.

Prosper was among the last generation of Aquitanians to benefit fully from the material culture of Aquitaine. That rich culture suffered its demise under the barbarian incursions, but the ascetic movement, which Prosper was also witness to, continued toward its eventual triumph in the West in the wake of the invasions. Prosper lived through this transitional period that witnessed the beginning of the transformation of the West—from Roman to barbarian Europe, and from aristocratic to ascetic Christianity.

Events that would have profound effects on his later life were taking place in Italy, North Africa, and the East. Up to this point, Prosper had very little, if any at all, exposure to the Pelagian conflict, which was about to escalate into an all-out campaign of extermination led by Augustine and his allies.

De providentia Dei

Along with other refugees, Prosper set about the necessary tasks of making a new home in Marseilles in the wake of tragedy. They were safe within the protective walls of the city, but their sufferings lingered. The exiled community carried with them the painful memories of those traumatic years. Prosper expressed their shared pain when he wrote: "Each time the image of our fatherland, all in smoke, comes to our mind, and the whole range of destruction stands before our eyes, we break down, and the tears water our cheeks beyond restraint."[60] The tragic events also caused a crisis of faith—specifically, the seeming absence of God in their suffering. Prosper wrote *De providentia Dei* to assure the exiled community of God's existence, power, goodness, and care.

Prosper was not the only writer to respond to the invasions; there were three other immediate responses as well: Orientius's *Commonitorium,* the *Epigramma Paulini,* and the anonymous *Poema coniugis ad uxorem.*[61] Like the other responses, Prosper's *De providentia Dei* exhorts its readers to turn to the spiritual life in response to suffering. What distinguishes Prosper's *De providentia Dei* is its attempt to answer the difficult question of God's role in human suffering—in particular, the relationship of God to indiscriminate suffering, both those inflicted by human actions and those caused by natural disaster. It is this "force of fire [human destruction] and rain [natural destruction]" that Prosper sought to reconcile with God's power and care.[62]

De providentia Dei was Prosper's first known work and contains his initial view of grace, but also, more importantly, his general view of theology in relation to the Church. *De providentia Dei* does not draw significantly from other sources, save Scripture. The work is primarily Prosper's own theological expression, guided entirely by his own interpretation of contemporary events and Scripture.

60. *De prov. Dei* 1 (ed. Marcovich, 4–5).

61. Orientius, *Commonitorium* (PL 61: 977–1006). *Epigramma Paulini* (CSEL 16: 503–10) was wrongly attributed to Paulinus of Nola, see *Patrology,* vol. 4, ed. Angelo di Berardino, trans. Placid Solari (Westminster, Md.: Christian Classics, 1986), 336–37. *Poema coniugis ad uxorem* (CSEL 30: 344–48); a poem wrongly attributed to Prosper; see chapter 1. A brief comparison of the three poems is found in M. Roberts, "Barbarians in Gaul: The Response of the Poets," in *Fifth-Century Gaul: A Crisis of Identity?* ed. John Drinkwater and Hugh Elton (Cambridge: Cambridge University Press, 1992), 97–106. Salvian of Marseilles also wrote a response to these invasions, but the work was composed in the 440s and addresses the general fall of the Empire (Salvian, *De gubernatione Dei* [CSEL 8: 1–200; *Governance of God,* 23–232]).

62. *De prov. Dei* 1 (ed. Marcovich, 6–7). Prosper is the only one among the writers of the invasions to include the reference to a flood.

Contact with the Christian Tradition

By 416, the date of *De providentia Dei,* Prosper thought himself advanced enough in the Christian faith and tradition to be able to write a "pamphlet" for "beginners" in the faith that explained the difficult question of the relationship between God and human suffering.[63] In what context Prosper gained this level of theological competence is unknown, except that Prosper acquired it at some point before 416.

From 406 to 415, Aquitaine fell victim to the destruction caused by the Vandals and then by the Goths. The beginning of that period was around the time Prosper finished his education at age eighteen. When exactly Prosper was taken captive is uncertain, but the destruction of Aquitaine would have severely limited the opportunity to engage in any serious theological study. Thus, whether Prosper was taken captive the first year or in the later years, it is unlikely that Prosper had an opportunity for serious theological study in the years 406 to 415.

Any opportunity for Prosper to study would have been in Marseilles after his release from captivity, sometime before 416. The literary resources of Marseilles only improved as the intellectual center shifted to Marseilles from Aquitaine in the wake of the Goths' destruction. The latest date for Prosper's release is the early part of 415, when the Visigoths moved on to Spain. Arrival in Marseilles in 415 or shortly thereafter, if not earlier, would have provided Prosper with the adequate resources and time needed to gain the theological knowledge reflected in *De providentia Dei.* The exact date of Prosper's arrival and theological reading remains uncertain, but the sources of *De providentia Dei* indicate the availability of pagan, biblical, and Christian writings for Prosper in Marseilles.

With access to the resources available in Marseilles, Prosper would not have needed much time to acquire a basic level of theological competence, at least the level needed to write *De providentia Dei.* The work displays a firm grasp of Scripture and acquaintance with at least one Christian poet, Prudentius.[64] Acquiring such

63. *De prov. Dei* 12 (ed. Marcovich, 66–67).

64. The sources of *De providentia Dei* are detailed by Michael McHugh, "Introduction," in *Carmen de Providentia Dei,* 24–107. McHugh judged Paulinus's influence on

knowledge would have been within easy reach of a classically trained person such as Prosper. Like Paulinus of Nola and Augustine before him, Prosper appears to have gained an initial theological education through self-study of the Christian tradition after completing formal pagan schooling.

Given the circumstantial and direct evidence available, the chronology of events appears thus: after completing his education in Aquitaine, Prosper was taken captive by the Goths and then released. Prosper arrived in Marseilles around 415 and began his initial study of theological material. By 416, Prosper felt he had achieved the necessary maturity, both spiritual and theological, to be able to write his first work, *De providentia Dei.*

Sources

Prosper's sources for *De providentia Dei* reflect a poet well versed in Scripture, classical authors, and an awareness of at least one Christian poet.[65] Biblical allusions and similarities abound throughout the work. The use of Virgil, whose prominence is second only to biblical sources, and, to a lesser extent, of Ovid and Horace, is characteristic of a classically trained poet. Prosper also employs the Christian poetry of Prudentius.

Augustine's influence on the poem has been debated. Valentin argued for a similarity of ideas and expressions between *De providentia Dei* and Augustine's works, especially Book 1 of *De civitate Dei.*[66] McHugh provided a detailed analysis of the specific sources for the poem, but did not include one for Augustine's.[67] McHugh, however, insisted on Augustine's theological influence on the poem in a brief concluding remark, and referred the reader only to Valen-

De providentia Dei to be uncertain, based on the nature of the evidence (McHugh, "Introduction," 102).

65. McHugh, "Introduction," 24–158.

66. Valentin (*Saint Prosper,* 795–96): "L'auteur du *de Providentia* puise surtout des idées et même des expressions dans les livres I (principalement), II, V, IX, X, XI, XII, XIII, XIV, XXII. Des rapports analogues existent entre ce poème et les autres ouvrages de saint Augustin, par exemple ... *de Trinitate* ... *Enchiridion* ... *Tractatus in Joannem.*" (*De civitate Dei* (CCL 47–48; *The City of God against the Pagans,* trans. R. W. Dyson [Cambridge: Cambridge University Press, 1998]).

67. McHugh, "Introduction," 24–158.

tin's assessment.[68] Marcovich concluded the influence of Augustine to be insignificant.[69]

There is no evidence for a direct dependence on Augustine in *De providentia Dei,* and Valentin acknowledged as much, simply arguing for similarity in ideas and expression between Augustine and the poem. Furthermore, it does not appear that Prosper had even read Augustine's *De civitate Dei* before writing *De providentia Dei*—Books 1 and 2 of *De civitate Dei* would have been available by this time. The fact that there was a similarity between *De providentia Dei* and Book 1 of *De civitate Dei* should be taken as evidence of Prosper's independence of Augustine's writings, not a direct dependence. Augustine's treatment of the same issues Prosper dealt with in *De providentia Dei* is much more sophisticated and rigorous. It seems unlikely that, if Prosper had read *De civitate Dei,* he would have simply borrowed, and that rather poorly, similar ideas and expressions from Augustine, rather than quoting him directly. Had Prosper read *De civitate Dei,* Prosper would have quoted directly from the work, or perhaps not have written *De providentia Dei* in the first place, since *De civitate Dei* addressed the issues of *De providentia Dei* in substance and style that were well beyond the talent and knowledge of the young writer.

Prosper drew from his knowledge of Scripture, from classical education, and from one Christian writer, in composing *De providentia Dei.* Noticeably absent from the work are any explicit appeals or references to Church pronouncements or authorities besides Scripture.

Structure

De providentia Dei is a lengthy poem consisting of 972 lines. Since the Maurist edition of 1711, the poem has been divided into twelve sections.[70] The prologue recounts the devastation of Gaul that led to questions concerning the providence of God. Sections two through seven deal with God's creation and providential care in

68. McHugh, "Introduction," 158.

69. Marcovich, "Text of St. Prosper's *De Providentia Dei,*" 110.

70. Le Brun and Mangeant, *Sancti Prosperi Aquitanici . . . Opera* (Paris, 1711).

salvation history, culminating in the Incarnation and work of Christ. The relationship between free will and God's providence is explored in sections eight through nine. Sections ten and eleven address the arguments against God's providence that emerge when good people suffer. The last section explains the role of suffering in God's divine plan and ends with an admonition to struggle against Satan.

The poem is difficult to follow at times. Prosper's general outline seems straightforward enough, but the poem suffers from digressions and repetitions.[71] The expositions on some of the stories from the Old Testament, in relation to the whole work, are overly lengthy. The rhetorical questions, directed at times to his polemical opponents and other times to the exiles, and Prosper's insistence on answering each one, also detract from the main points, as does the high number of repetitions.[72]

The Force of Fire and Rain

After a long and meandering discussion of human wickedness and of God's omnipotence and goodness, Prosper finally arrives at the connection between God and human disaster toward the end of the work. Here, Prosper explains that the natural disaster caused by the flooding to Aquitaine was the result of God's punishment for evildoers. This punishment inevitably included the suffering of the young and the just. The deaths of the young are justified because they would only increase the numbers of evildoers, and it was better for them to have perished through the sins of their fathers rather than through their own guilt.[73] For the just persons who were swept up in the punishment of the wicked, death is no evil.[74] Furthermore, God intended that some of the just be included in the deaths of the

71. A detailed literary analysis of the poem is found in Valentin, *Saint Prosper,* 802–24. The list of repetitions is contained in McHugh, "Introduction," 134–37.

72. For example, Prosper spends the whole of section 9 raising and answering the question on Chaldaean astrology. In Prosper's defense, he was following the conventions of verse at the time. A literary appreciation of the poem can be found in McHugh, "Introduction," 156–58.

73. *De prov. Dei* 11 (ed. Marcovich, 58–59).

74. *De prov. Dei* 11 (ed. Marcovich, 58–59): "For there is no evil death for good men. After a long and manifold toil to them any exit leading to the eternal rest is good enough."

wicked for the purpose of granting the just an early exit from this life.[75]

The survivors are to view the flood's devastation to land and people as God's "paternal whip," which seeks to remove their own desires and pleasures. Their suffering is an opportunity "to taste of the cup of the cross and life" and "embrace salvation."[76] Thus, natural disaster is just punishment for the wicked who survived and those who perished, an act of mercy for the young who perished, and a corrective for the survivors.

As for disaster caused by human hands, Prosper bewails the complaints of his fellow Aquitanians who have suffered the loss of money, household goods, jewels, flocks, and wine; of homes to fire; and the pitiful conditions of their children and servants. They, as servants of God, should have been open to surrendering them, even before their losses, and thus would not have lost anything. Instead of bemoaning their material poverty, they are to bewail their sin of mourning for the perishable.[77]

Noticeably absent in this type of suffering is the explanation for why harm befell them at the hands of the Goths or of God's role in it. Prosper also does not include deaths in the list of losses suffered, and thus there is no discussion on God's role in their deaths. Nor does Prosper discuss any redemptive or didactic element in the destruction for the survivors.

While Prosper's explanation for God's role in natural disaster is complete, the explanation for God's role in human-made disaster is entirely lacking. Instead of addressing the issues involved with human-made disaster as he did with natural disaster, Prosper goes directly to spiritual admonitions, which mark the conclusion of the poem.

Theology of Grace

De providentia Dei is not a systematic treatment of grace, nor was it intended to be. It may even be argued that Prosper, given his age

75. *De prov. Dei* 11 (ed. Marcovich, 58–59): "Therefore, if punishment of evildoers involves some just men as well, have no doubt that God wanted it this way."

76. *De prov. Dei* 11 (ed. Marcovich, 60–61).

77. *De prov. Dei* 12 (ed. Marcovich, 60–63).

and theological maturity, was incapable of such a demanding task. Prosper's main intention was to persuade, comfort, and admonish his readers through his interpretation of God's role in the tragic events. Still, Prosper's view of grace, inconsistent as it may be, is expressed in a number of places throughout the work.

In section nine, Prosper traces human history from the Creation to the Exodus event. Man lived in paradise free from sin. Satan, having fallen from heaven, devised an evil plan against man. Satan "drove him to pluck a fruit from its forbidden branches."[78] Man, having been overcome by Satan, transmitted death and guilt to all humans.[79] The original seed of the first parent, through corruption from sins, has now only a seed of poor strength.[80] Although Prosper never mentions the term, Original Sin is acknowledged.

All humans bear the image of God, possess the seed of virtue, and are equally illuminated by the one light of God.[81] "Through a long and thorough exercise of the respect for justice this power [image] would have imitated and reflected the divine light as in a mirror."[82] This "long and thorough exercise" is a result of free will and reason.

Humanity possesses freedom and wisdom, and thus has the ability to distinguish and discern between right and wrong—to exercise respect for justice. The reasons for a wrong choice are pride—caused by the struggles and uncertainties of this life—and desires—caused by the need for immediate satisfaction without regard to the future.[83]

This freedom is not subject to any external forces. After citing Deuteronomy 6: 13–14, it is argued that the human will is not cap-

78. *De prov. Dei* 5 (ed. Marcovich, 20–21): "perpulit a vetitis pomum decerpere ramis." Prosper does not make a distinction between Eve and Adam, and thus "Adam" and "Man" implies both.

79. *De prov. Dei* 7 (ed. Marcovich, 34–35): "Victus enim terrenus Adam transfudit in omnes mortem homines, quoniam cuncti nascuntur ab illo et transgressoris decurrit causa parentis."

80. *De prov. Dei* 5 (ed. Marcovich, 20–21): "audiat a primis distare parentibus actum per delicta genus, multa et rubigine morum corruptum exigui semen superesse vigoris."

81. *De prov. Dei* 4, 6, 8 (ed. Marcovich, 18–19, 30–31, 40–41).

82. *De prov. Dei* 4 (ed. Marcovich, 18–19).

83. *De prov. Dei* 4, 8 (ed. Marcovich, 18–19, 38–39).

tive to any external force, but that the human will can freely choose between good and evil. The only thing that hinders or impedes the human will from doing what is good is its own will.[84] Prosper's interpretation of Pharaoh in the Exodus event highlights this assertion. According to Prosper's reading, it is Pharaoh who hardens his own heart, not God.[85] Prosper's Pharaoh had a free choice and decided on his own to harden his heart.

Children, according to Prosper, are innocent from sin, apparently from both actual and Original Sin: "But what crime have committed innocent boys and girls, when their short life span had given them no time to sin?"[86] In another place, concerning the deaths of children caused by natural disaster: "They [young children] received a great reward in their destruction; for they perished through the sins of their fathers, rather than falling down through their *own guilt*."[87] Prosper views children as innocent, who are without Original Sin or actual sins.

Prosper's view of humanity is incomplete, and not completely coherent. In describing the Fall, Prosper portrays the first parents in a completely passive role. Satan, according to Prosper's reading, is chiefly responsible for the downfall of humanity. What the relationship was between Adam and Eve's free will and the temptation is not elaborated, only that Satan "drove" man to take the forbidden fruit.[88] There is no description of Eve's moral struggle with the temptation of eating from the tree, or of them actually eating the forbidden fruit. The first parents appear to be unable to help themselves. The result is that the force of the culpability of the first parents and thus the transmitted guilt is lessened. They are portrayed more as helpless victims than as transgressors.

It was a crime according to Prosper, but it does not seem to car-

84. *De prov. Dei* 9 (ed. Marcovich, 44–47).

85. *De prov. Dei* 5 (ed. Marcovich, 28–29): "Sed clade remota duratur parcente Deo." Cf. Ex. 10.1.

86. *De prov. Dei* 1 (ed. Marcovich, 6–7).

87. Emphasis mine. *De prov. Dei* 11 (ed. Marcovich, 58–59): "cui multus in ipso exitio est collatus honos, quod crimine patrum occidit, ante sua caderet quam noxia culpa."

88. *De prov. Dei* 5 (ed. Marcovich , 20–21): "perpulit a vetitis pomum decerpere ramis."

ry any practical consequences other than death.[89] Although Prosper states guilt, death, and a seed of poor strength are inherited from the first parents, only death and guilt are mentioned again. It is only death that "tainted" human nature.[90] Guilt is mentioned again, but only in reference to its absence in children.[91] Guilt is apparently a result of actual sins, and thus only in adults.

Prosper's emphasis on the freedom of the human will removes anything that may encroach upon it. The Fall is acknowledged briefly, as well as its consequences, but does not figure into the larger discussion. Humanity has complete exercise of the freedom of the will, and in its postlapsarian nature, not even God can interfere with it.

The power that Prosper ascribes to God is omnipotence.[92] First, Prosper provides a description of God's omnipotence, from the Creation to governing the universe, including control over human lives.[93] Then Prosper answers those who admit God's omnipotence, but deny God's care to humans, which takes up the rest of the poem.[94]

According to Prosper, God's omnipotence includes being able to give and take away life, save the perishing, lift what has been cast down, bring down the lofty, prolong and shorten life, change hearts, and remit sins.[95] Just as Prosper had described the effects of the Fall only to give attention to just one of the effects, here also, after describing many of God's powers, Prosper only details God's role in giving and taking life, and the closely related role of prolonging and

89. *De prov. Dei* 5 (ed. Marcovich , 20–21): "His illata dolis, hoc crimine nata subegit."

90. *De prov. Dei* 5 (ed. Marcovich , 22–23): "in mortem vitiata tamen natura bona trahebat."

91. *De prov. Dei* 11 (ed. Marcovich, 58–59): "quod crimine patrum occidit, ante sua caderet quam noxia culpa."

92. *De prov. Dei* 4, 7, 8, 9, 10 (ed. Marcovich, 16–17, 34–35, 40–41, 46–47, 48–49, 50–51). Prosper used "omnipotens" and its derivatives six times instead of "providentia," a word that could not be used due to the restrictions of Latin hexameter.

93. *De prov. Dei* 2–3 (ed. Marcovich, 8–15).

94. *De prov. Dei* 4–12 (ed. Marcovich, 16–67).

95. *De prov. Dei* 3 (ed. Marcovich, 14–15): "det vitas adimatque datas, pereuntia salvet, deiecta attollat, premat ardua, proroget annos et minuat, mutet corda, et peccata remittat." Cf. Ex. 10.1.

shortening life. After mentioning God's ability to change hearts, nowhere in the poem is there an instance of God actually accomplishing this.

Although Prosper acknowledges the power of God to change hearts, the power to change human hearts is also available to humans, who appear solely responsible for the changing of their hearts. God's action, in relation to salvation, is limited to equally illuminating all men with one light, summoning, and waiting patiently for humans to repent.[96] God has the power to change hearts, but, for all intents and purposes, human hearts are changed by the power of humans, not by God. The word *gratia* appears just once and is understood as a reward for faith during the period before Jesus.[97]

God is omnipotent, but does not interfere in human lives, at least on a certain level. Humans have absolute control over their spiritual lives; whether they will choose to have faith in Christ or not is a decision that they alone make. God has graciously given humanity the power to choose salvation.[98] The possibility of salvation is available for everyone.[99] This gift in no way interferes with free choice. It is still entirely up to the person's desire to choose salvation: "You can be a son of God if you wish."[100] Salvation, like the choice between good and evil, is a choice made freely by the human will.

Christ's role is to grant salvation, but only after Christ has been received in the heart of the person.[101] In the order of salvation, it is

96. *De prov. Dei* 4, 8, 10 (ed. Marcovich, 16–17, 40–41, 52–53): "[Christus] qui vocat, et secum nos deducturus et in se." "aequa Creantis mensura est, uno qui lumine luminat omnes." "Et pia dum populis Domini patientia parcit."

97. *De prov. Dei* 7 (ed. Marcovich, 34–35): "Utque illos veterum complexa est gratia solos qui Christum videre fide."

98. *De prov. Dei* 7 (ed. Marcovich, 34–35): "homo, quanta tibi est gratia collata potestas!"

99. *De prov. Dei* 8 (ed. Marcovich, 38–39): "Iamne Dei compertus amor diffusaque in omnes cura patet, notum et cunctis astare salutem?"

100. *De prov. Dei* 7 (ed. Marcovich, 34–35): "filius esse Dei, si vis, potes."

101. *De prov. Dei* 7 (ed. Marcovich, 34–35): "non renovat quemquam Christus, nisi corde receptus." Marcovich has mistranslated the passage to read, "Christ renews no man unless he has been received in His [Christ's] heart." I believe it should read: "Christ renews no one unless He [Christ] has been received in his [person's] heart." This translation also contains the order of salvation that is consistent with the rest of the passages concerning human will and salvation.

the human desire to be saved that anticipates the aid of God.[102] Humans must make the first step of desiring salvation. Nothing, including God, can interfere with the human will in making that first step toward God: "For as no man is saved against his will, or while remaining quiet in a deep sleep; and as no one who has withdrawn of his own accord is being sought out by force, so also the halls of eternal life will open only to those who return to them and knock."[103]

After the initial step is made and salvation accomplished, a person is united with Christ. "For while Christ unites what is ours with what is His, He at the same time joins what is His with what is ours."[104]

Observations

Prosper's understanding of grace is dominated by his emphasis on human free will. God's grace is relegated to a secondary role in the order of salvation. Salvation is the result of human decision, followed by the movement of God. After salvation, there appears to be a cooperating grace, in which human wills and grace are enjoined.[105] There is also a sense of the universality of salvation, that is, the light of God's illumination and offer of salvation are given to all, equally.

Prosper's view of the freedom of the will, especially in regard to the Fall, is overly optimistic, but still within the acceptable limits of the prevailing theological views of southern Gaul.[106] Prosper's view of the order of salvation is none other than the *initium fidei,* a chief characteristic among the *doctores Gallicani,* which places the beginning of faith as a purely human act, without the aid of God.[107] The idea of cooperating grace and the theme of universal salvation are

102. *De prov. Dei* 12 (ed. Marcovich, 64–65): "si tamen Assertoris opem festina voluntas praeveniat."

103. *De prov. Dei* 12 (ed. Marcovich, 64–65).

104. *De prov. Dei* 12 (ed. Marcovich, 64–65): "Qui dum nostra Suis sociat, iunxit Sua nostris."

105. *De prov. Dei* 12 (ed. Marcovich, 64–65).

106. The perception of traces of Pelagianism in the poem is not without some merit. Still, a direct influence is not discernable and there is doubt that the Pelagian dispute reached Gaul during this period; see McHugh, "Introduction," 22–23.

107. For a summary of the term, see Marianne Djuth's article, "Initium Fidei," *ATA,* 447–51.

also common elements found among these *doctores Gallicani*. That Prosper shared these views can hardly suggest a direct influence, since Prosper had been in Marseilles only a very short time before writing the poem. Rather, these ideas were, at the least, uncontroversial for most of the Church. In general, in its moderate form, the optimistic view of human nature and ability, along with God's desire to save all of humanity, appear to be the norm. It was not until Augustine and his small group of supporters began to present a much different view of grace that these assumptions began to be questioned. Prosper's general view of grace in *De providentia Dei* merely reflected what Prosper and most of the Church assumed to be true about God's grace and human free will.

With his limited knowledge, Prosper made a bold attempt to tackle one of the most difficult theological questions. The results are not completely satisfactory, but for all of its flaws, the work as a whole is something of an achievement for a first work by a young writer, who only recently acquired theological knowledge.

Prosper's theological knowledge was not wholly sufficient for the task. *De providentia Dei* suffers primarily from his lack of awareness of Church tradition and theological writings. Prosper's theological method consisted of joining past events with perceived relevant scriptural passages. Prosper never explicitly mentioned a theologian, theological work, Church council or synod, or Rome anywhere in *De providentia Dei.* Most telling of all is the absence of the word *ecclesia,* be it in regard to the local or universal church, from the work. *De providentia Dei* is a theological work that attempted to explain God's actions without regard to the Church, its traditions, or its theologians.

De providentia Dei's Future

Prosper never alluded to *De providentia Dei* in any of his later writings. The poem was not listed among the works of Prosper by Gennadius.[108] The poem was considered significant enough to be copied, but it remained in obscurity for more than four hundred

108. Gennadius, *De viris inlustribus* 85 (TU 14/1: 90).

years until Hincmar of Rheims quoted sixty verses from it in his *De praedestinatione,* around 860.[109] The general obscurity of the poem may have something to do with the fact that Augustine's *De civitate Dei* dealt with the same issues, but with much better style and substance. Indeed, why read Prosper's answer when there is Augustine's?

The question remains as to why Prosper or his contemporaries, especially his later opponents, never referred to the work. Perhaps Prosper may not have wanted to acknowledge such a naïve first work, especially in light of reading Augustine's *De civitate Dei.* Prosper, more than anyone else, would have known all too well how unsophisticated and inadequate his poem was compared to the work of a master writer and theologian such as Augustine.

In what could have been a potentially embarrassing situation for Prosper, his opponents did not refer to *De providentia Dei* either. Prosper's opponents could have easily attacked him for holding a position earlier, which seemed to support their own, but which he now stood against. Such a tactic was never used against Prosper—which assumes his opponents were aware of *De providentia Dei*—nor was there any direct assault on Prosper. Perhaps the best explanation for the obscurity of the poem was the lack of interest in Prosper in general, especially by those living in Marseilles. Prosper was a layman of little social and religious importance in Marseilles. What attention Prosper received, which was mostly outside of Marseilles, was based solely on his role as a defender and expositor of Augustine's views. The focus of their concern was Augustine, not his "press agent."[110] The poem's obscurity may be the direct result of the obscurity of the author.

Conclusion

De providentia Dei is the work of a classically trained poet, who attempted to write a theological response to human disasters. Prosper's theological method consisted of interpreting contemporary

109. Hincmar of Rheims, *De praedestinatione* (PL 125: 442–45).

110. H. I. Marrou, *St. Augustine and His Influence through the Ages,* trans. Patrick Hepburne-Scott (New York: Harper Torchbooks, 1957), 149.

events through relevant Scripture. It was a method exclusively driven by his personal discernment of Scripture. For Prosper, scriptural knowledge alone was adequate for the task of theology. Prosper wrote as a Christian certainly, but as an "independent" Christian with no sense of belonging to or appreciating the Church and its role in theology. This is in complete contrast to all the works of Prosper after *De providentia Dei.* Prosper's other writings were written from the perspective of a fully committed catholic Christian, whose appreciation of the role of the Church in theology increases over time. *De providentia Dei,* when compared to the later writings of Prosper, reveals the radical degree of change that occurred in Prosper since writing the poem.

~3

Formative Period (417–425)

MARSEILLES IN THE FIFTH CENTURY experienced an unusual level of prosperity and peace, while other cities of Gaul suffered various degrees of decline. The destruction of the barbarian invasions of Gaul in the early fifth century, disastrous for many cities, did not reach Marseilles. In addition, Marseilles was largely immune to the consequences of internal political and ecclesial strife that plagued other cities of Gaul.

There were no fewer than seven imperial usurpers between 406 and 422—three of whom were in Gaul—allowing Honorius (395–423) only six years of uncontested rule in the last seventeen years of his reign. Along with their secular counterparts, some ecclesiastical Gallo-Roman aristocrats took part in the revolts of Constantine III and Jovinus.[1] Consequently, the fall of the usurpers in Gaul had repercussions for ecclesiastical leadership in Gaul, especially in Provence. The papacy also had a vested interest in Gallo-Roman Church affairs. A case in point was Lazarus and Heros—who, incidentally, will become relevant figures in the Pelagian controversy. With the defeat of Constantine III, his partisans, the bishops Lazarus and Heros, were exiled to the East. With the support of Constantius and Pope Zosimus, Remigius then regained his bishopric,

1. For the revolts in Gaul, see John F. Matthews, *Western Aristocracies and Imperial Court A. D. 364–425* (Oxford: Oxford Univeristy Press, 1975), 307–16.

and Patroculus became the bishop of Arles. The ecclesial landscape changed again with the death of Constantius in 421, most notably with the murder of Patroculus. It was a time of complex and intense struggles for power and influence involving secular and ecclesiastical alliances and factions played out in the bitterly competitive ecclesiastical hierarchy of the Gallic church.[2]

The ecclesiastical leadership in Marseilles during this period was remarkably stable.[3] Proculus, bishop of Marseilles for nearly half a century (381 to 428), and no stranger to controversy and conflict, nonetheless was able to maintain Marseilles's ecclesiastical prominence, independence, and stability—not a minor accomplishment in the treacherous world of ecclesial-political affairs in early fifth-century Gaul.[4]

In terms of economic, social, intellectual, and ecclesial prosperity and stability, Marseilles had no equal among the cities of Provence. Prosper spent the next twenty-three years of his life in this setting. It was in this period, the first decade of his life in Marseilles, in particular, that Prosper was exposed to the influences that would shape the rest of his life.

First Period of Reflection

After writing *De providentia Dei,* Prosper's next work was written nearly a decade later. There is no extant writing or anything that suggests Prosper wrote any work during this "silent" period. Although

2. A detailed account of the complicated struggles between these three groups and others are provided in Mathisen, *Ecclesiastical Factionalism.*

3. Jean-Rémy Palanque ("Les évêchés provençaux à l'époque romaine," *Provence historique* 1 [1951]: 105–43) provides a brief general introduction to the Church in Provence during this period, followed by a list of the bishops of the various cities in Provence.

4. The bishop of Marseilles had been the metropolitan bishop of its province by custom, but with the secular reorganization of the provinces in the late fourth century, the bishop of Aix assumed the title of metropolitan, not the bishop of Marseilles. However, the Council of Turin, in 398, granted conditional metropolitan privileges to Proculus by virtue of his authority, a privilege that would revert to the bishop of Aix after Proculus's death. Proculus remained bishop for nearly three more decades and exercised his metropolitan powers to the great consternation of Pope Zosimus, who attempted, but failed to revoke Proculus's privileges. See Mathisen, *Ecclesiastical Factionalism,* 22–74.

much of his life during these years remains a mystery, the writings that follow this period indicate that Prosper underwent a radical and lasting religious transformation. In the flourishing and dynamic intellectual milieu of Marseilles, between 417 and 425, Prosper was exposed to the three most significant influences that would transform his life: Augustine, the *doctores Gallicani,* and the Roman Church.

Prosper came into contact with these influences as a consequence of the Pelagian controversy. Among the theological issues of the day in the West, none was more prominent than Pelagianism. Prosper was an observer of these events, participating in the intellectual discussions while reading, discussing, and reflecting on the issues involved in the Pelagian controversy. Prosper emerged from this "study" period as a committed member of the catholic Church, broadly defined and which included the Roman Church, and joined in the Pelagian debate on the side of the catholic Church. In committing to the catholic Church, Prosper embraced Augustine because he had thought Augustine was authoritative and his teachings represented the Church. Not everyone, however, agreed with Prosper's assumptions about Augustine—the most prominent of whom were the *doctores Gallicani.*

Augustine and the Pelagian Controversy

Around the late fourth to the early fifth century, an interest in Latin Pauline exegesis was flourishing in Rome and in North Africa.[5] From the beginning, these two "schools" of thought took the meaning of Paul in two very different and conflicting directions concerning the issues related to grace. The Roman exegetes consisted of Pelagius, Ambrosiaster, and Rufinus of Syria.[6] On the other side, literally and figuratively, an African tradition was in the process of development, namely, by Augustine. The conflict between the two

5. Gerald Bonner, "Augustine, the Bible and the Pelagians," in *Augustine and the Bible,* ed. Pamela Bright (South Bend: Notre Dame University Press, 1999), 231.

6. The connection of the Roman exegetes, especially Rufinus's, to the Origenist controversy is taken up in Elizabeth Clark, *The Origenist Controversy: The Cultural Construction of an Early Christian Debate* (Princeton: Princeton University Press, 1992).

understandings of grace, both based on their respective interpretations of the Pauline texts, is the theological background to what has become known as the Pelagian controversy.[7] How these two approaches actually came into contact, then open conflict, and, finally, resolution, is a complex story involving not only the theological elements, but also the social and political.[8]

Brief Sketch of Events

Sometime around 405, Augustine's *Confessiones,* which had become well received and widely known, was read to a small group gathered in Rome. Pelagius, an ascetic from Britain, was in the audience and expressed his outrage when he heard: *Da quod iubes, et iube quod vis!*[9] Though not the actual beginning of the conflict, it was an event that anticipated the drama and passion of the conflict between Augustine and Pelagius and his supporters.

7. Comprehensive treatments of Augustine and his relationship with Pelagianism are found in Peter Brown's *Augustine of Hippo: A Biography,* 2nd ed. (Berkeley and Los Angeles: University of California Press, 2000) and Gerald Bonner's *St Augustine of Hippo.* Brown situates the conflict in the historical context, while Bonner takes a more theological approach. Eugene TeSelle's article "Pelagius, Pelagianism," *ATA,* 633–40, provides a succinct introduction to the controversy. Vittorino Grossi's "Adversaries and Friends of Augustine," in *Patrology,* vol. 4, 461–503, contains a thorough catalogue and brief discussion of the "Pelagian corpus," 469–71. Pelagius has recently enjoyed something of a sympathetic reevaluation; see B. R. Rees, *Pelagius: A Reluctant Heretic* (Suffolk, U.K.: Boydell Press, 1988) and R. A. Markus, "The Legacy of Pelagius," 214–34. Elizabeth Clark makes a case for the Pelagian and, by extension, the [Augustinian] controversies as continuances of the Origenist controversy: "The Pelagian controversy, I posit, provided an arena in which Origen's questions were answered in new and different ways" (*Origenist Controversy,* 195).

8. Gerald Bonner ("Pelagianism Reconsidered," SP 27 (1993): 237–41) views the Pelagian controversy as a succession of accidents, suggesting that the conflict between Augustine and Pelagius was not necessarily inevitable; Brown (*Augustine of Hippo,* 344) had previously shared a similar sentiment, implying that if Pelagius had actually met with the charming and aged bishop, things might have turned out differently between the two. Brown later retracted the suggestion that a meeting could have prevented the conflict: "I was probably wrong to speculate [in *Augustine of Hippo*] that Augustine would have had any effect on him [Pelagius] at all. They were on a collision course" (Alexander Hwang, "An Interview with Peter Brown: On Scholarship, Faith and Augustine," *Princeton Theological Review* 6 [1999]: 25).

9. The event was recounted in Augustine, *De dono perseverantiae* 20.53 (PL 45: 1026; *The Gift of Perseverance,* in *Answers to the Pelagians,* vol. 4, trans. Roland Teske, WSA I/26 [Hyde Park, N.Y: New City Press, 1999], 227–28). The quotation was from Augustine, *Confessiones* 10.31.45 (CCL 27: 179).

The first direct contact between the two groups came as a result of Alaric's invasion of Rome in 410. Pelagius and his younger and zealous disciple, Caelestius, fleeing the invasion, stopped in Carthage on their way to the East.[10] Pelagius soon left for Palestine, but Caelestius decided to remain, only to be put on trial by the Synod of Carthage (411/412) for espousing ideas contrary to grace and Original Sin.[11] Caelestius was excommunicated by the synod, and headed to Ephesus, where he was ordained.

Pelagius fared much better in Palestine, gaining the support of Bishop John of Jerusalem.[12] At the instigation of the exiled bishops, Heros and Lazarus, fourteen Eastern bishops examined Pelagius and, satisfied with his answers, declared him in conformity with the Church at the Council of Diospolis.[13]

The African bishops reacted, under the leadership of Augustine, by orchestrating a campaign, waged on both political and ecclesias-

10. *De gestis Pelagii* 22.46 (CSEL 42: 100; *On the Deeds of Pelagius,* in *Answer to the Pelagians,* vol. 1, trans. Roland Teske, WSA I/23 [Hyde Park, N.Y.: New City Press, 1997], 365). Pelagius and Caelestius landed at Hippo hoping to meet with Augustine, who, unfortunately, was absent for their visit. All three were present in Carthage for the Synod of Carthage in 411, where Augustine recalled seeing Pelagius "once or twice," but was too busy to meet with him.

11. An account of the proceedings of this council is contained in Augustine's *De peccato originali* 3–4.3 (CSEL 42: 168–69; *The Grace of Christ and Original Sin,* in *Answers to the Pelagians,* vol. 1, 404). There were six counts charged against Caelestius, as summarized in Bonner (*St Augustine,* 321): "Adam was created mortal and would have died even if he had not sinned; that his sin injured only himself and not the human race; that infants at the time of their birth are in the same state that Adam was in before the Fall; that mankind as a whole did not die through Adam's death or transgression, nor would it rise again through Christ's resurrection; that the Law had the same effect as the Gospel in bringing men into the Kingdom of Heaven; and that even before the coming of Christ there had been sinless men."

12. The optimism at the heart of Pelagianism found a sympathetic audience in the East. For a discussion on the theological differences between the Latin and Greek traditions concerning salvation, see J. Patout Burns, "The Economy of Salvation: Two Patristic Traditions," *Theological Studies* 37 (1976): 598–619 (hereafter *TS*); Peter Brown approaches the matter of the Eastern support for Pelagius within the wider world of Roman social relations, "The Patrons of Pelagius: The Roman Aristocracy between East and West," *JTS* 21 (1970): 56–72.

13. *De gestis Pelagii* 20.44 (CSEL 42: 99): "Synodus dixit: 'nunc quoniam satisfactum est nobis prosecutionibus praesentis Pelagii monachi, qui quidem piis doctrinis consentit, contraria uero ecclesiasticae fidei reprobat et anathematizat, communionis ecclesiasticae eum esse et catholicae confitemur.'"

tical fronts, which was to prove efficient and effective against the Pelagians. In 416, Pelagius and Caelestius were condemned at provincial synods at Carthage and Milevis. A letter from each synod was sent to Pope Innocent.[14] In addition, the leading figures of the African Church, including Augustine, wrote a separate, more detailed letter to the pope.[15] Upon receiving the African documents, Innocent condemned Pelagius and Caelestius, but died shortly afterward in 417.[16] However, the new pope, Zosimus, examined Caelestius and Pelagius and declared them innocent.[17] The African bishops, helped by the alarming news of rioting by Pelagians in Rome, gained the support of the Imperial Court, which effectively outlawed Pelagianism.[18] A few days later, the Africans convened a council at Carthage (418) condemning Pelagian teachings in a series of nine canons.[19] Zosimus, with the pressure of the African Church and the imperial edict, issued the *Epistola tractoria,* condemning and excommunicating Caelestius and Pelagius, which was to be signed by all the Italian bishops.[20] A group of eighteen bishops led by Julian of Eclanum, in support of Pelagius, refused to sign and attempted to have their case heard at Ravenna.[21] Augustine's allies at court blocked the appeal

14. *Epp.* 175, 176 (CSEL 44: 652–668; *Letters* 175, 176, in *Letters* 156–210, vol. 3, trans. Roland Teske, WSA II/3 [Hyde Park, N.Y.: New City Press, 2004], 134–40).

15. *Ep.* 177 (CSEL 44: 669–88; *Letter* 177, 141–50).

16. Innocent responded to the three separate letters of the Africans. Found in Augustine, *Epp.* 181, 182, 183 (CSEL 44: 701–30; *Letters* 181, 182, 183, 161–72).

17. Zosimus, *Ep. de causa Pelagii, "Postquam a nobis"* (PL 45: 1721–23).

18. In PL 48: 379–97. Brown suggests Augustine may have played a role in the imperial condemnation by his influence on certain court officials (*Augustine of Hippo,* 362); see also J. P. Burns, "Augustine's Role in the Imperial Action against the Pelagius," *JTS* 30 (1979): 77–83.

19. *Concilium Carthaginense* (CCL 149: 67–73; *The Canons of the Council of Carthage, A. D. 418,* in *Theological Anthropology,* trans. J. Patout Burns [Philadelphia: Fortress Press, 1981], 67–70).

20. The *Tractoria* exists only in fragments. Its contents are discussed in Otto Wermelinger, *Rom und Pelagius: Die theologische Position der römischen Bischöfe im pelagianischen Streit in den Jahren 411–432* (Stuttgart: Anton Hiersemann, 1975), 209–18. The scholarly disagreements over the *Epistola Tractoria*'s fidelity to the African canons are detailed in Ogliari, *Gratia et Certamen,* 22–23 n. 7.

21. See Mathijs Lamberigts's article, "Julian of Eclanum," in *ATA,* 478–79; and J. Lössl, *Julian von Aeclanum: Studien zu seinem Leben, seinem Werk, seiner Lehre und ihrer Überlieferung* (Leiden: Brill, 2001).

and helped to obtain an edict, not only against Pelagius and Caelestius, but against anyone who offered them any support.[22] The exiled Julian now became the leader of the Pelagian movement and proved to be a formidable opponent of Augustine. His theological battle with Julian would occupy him to his last days, but Augustine's cause enjoyed the ultimate victory: at the ecumenical Council of Ephesus (431), Pelagius, Caelestius, and Julian were condemned, although Augustine did not live to see that day, having died in August 430.[23]

Pelagianism Defined

The Pelagian movement, which consisted of various and varied expressions, was defined by its opponents, who lumped the members of the movement into a single group and reduced their ideas to a series of crude propositions. These beliefs were formulated and condemned at the Council of Carthage in 418 and promulgated throughout the Empire. In summary, the nine canons of the council defined and condemned Pelagianism for holding the following beliefs:

Canon 1. Adam was created mortal and death came naturally, not as a result of sin.
2. Original Sin is not hereditary, and baptism is only for the forgiveness of sins.
3. A place in heaven is reserved for children not baptized before death.
4. The grace of God, through Christ, forgives past sins, but is no help in not sinning.
5. That same grace reveals the divine commandments, but does not provide the desire and strength to follow them.
6. Fulfilling the divine commands can be accomplished by the free will, without grace, but not as easily.
7–9. One can live a sinless life.

22. Edict in Augustine, *Ep.* 201 (CSEL 57: 296–99; *Letter* 201, 357–58).

23. *Council of Ephesus,* in *Decrees of the Ecumenical Councils,* vol. 1, ed. Norman P. Tanner (London: Sheed & Ward, 1990), 37–74 [Includes the original text reproduced from *Conciliorum Oecumenicorum Decreta,* ed. G. Alberigo et al., 3rd ed. (Bologna: Istituto per le Scienze Religiose, 1973)].

The efforts of the African Church, led by Augustine, with the help of Rome and Ravenna, ensured that Pelagianism was rejected as heretical. On that point, there was consensus in the West. However, in the course of Augustine's campaign against Pelagianism, the Bishop of Hippo developed a controversial doctrine of grace.

Augustine Defined

Augustine's doctrine of grace, with its emphasis on the grace of God and its pessimistic anthropology, had been taking shape before any contact with the Pelagians.[24] Between 395 and 410, there were three experiences that helped shape his doctrine of grace: continued exploration of Scripture, especially the Pauline epistles, the writing of the *Confessiones,* and the experiences of parish life. Taken together these were powerful elements that tainted his view of human nature and expanded his awareness of the sovereignty of God.

In writing the *Confessiones,* reflecting back on his life, he realized "the burning problem of the apparent permanence of evil in human actions."[25] As a pastor, he was entrusted with the care of lay Christians who lived their lives in the world, if not of the world. If he had earlier believed in the best of people, he was now inclined to expect the worst. Augustine's further study of Romans only confirmed what he experienced in his own life and what he witnessed in his flock. In *De diversis quaestionibus ad Simplicianum* (397) Augustine's rudimentary form of his doctrine of predestination emerged.[26] No longer are the elect predestined based on foreknowledge of future belief, which he held earlier, but now election was based solely on God's act of mercy, not whether God foreknows the faith of the person.[27] Augustine's answers to the second question in Book 1 con-

24. For an in-depth study on the development of Augustine's theology, see Eugene TeSelle, *Augustine the Theologian* (New York: Herder & Herder, 1970).

25. Brown, *Augustine of Hippo,* 148.

26. *De diversis quaestionibus ad Simplicianum* (CCL 44; *To Simplician—On Various Questions. Book I,* in *Augustine: Earlier Writings,* trans. John Burleigh [Philadelphia: Westminster Press, 1953], 376–406).

27. In 394, Augustine held that God's predestination was based on foreknowledge of a person's faith: "Nec praedestinavit aliquem, nisi quem praescivit crediturum et secuturum vocationem suam, quos et electos dicit" (*Expositio quarundam propositionum ex*

cerning the interpretation of Romans 9: 10–29 contains the essential elements of his doctrine of predestination.

Augustine uses the example of Jacob and Esau to illustrate the absolute sovereignty of God in the economy of salvation and the utter inability of humans to contribute to this process. The highlights of Augustine's understanding of grace can be summarized as follows: Faith is a gift of grace, and the merits of faith follow from God's calling;[28] God elected Jacob because God made Jacob loveable, not because God foresaw Jacob would be faithful;[29] from Adam there is but one *massa peccatorum,* out of which some receive mercy and others wrath.[30] God elects and prepares the will of the human, and humans have no power in election or in the preparation of their will for salvation.[31]

Augustine's doctrine of grace had taken a dramatic turn with his answers in *ad Simplicianum.* The elements of his later doctrine of predestination were in the mind of Augustine by 396. Augustine employed the word "predestination" only in one place—a hypothetical explanation for predestination based upon foreknowledge, which he refuted.[32] Augustine explicitly defined only what predestination was not, but did not positively define what predestination was. Instead, Augustine employed the terms *electio* and *vocatio* and their cognates to describe his understanding of grace. The Pelagian conflict served

---

epistula Apostoli ad Romanos; [text and facing translation in] *Propositions from the Epistle to the Romans,* in *Augustine on Romans: Propositions from the Epistle to the Romans, Unfinished Commentary on the Epistle to the Romans,* trans. Paula Fredrick Landes [Chico, Cal.: Scholars Press, 1982], 28–29).

28. *Ad Simplicianum* 1.2.7 (CCL 44: 32): "Nisi ergo vocando praecedat misericordia dei, nec credere quisquam potest, ut ex hoc incipiat iustificari et accipere facultatem bene operandi. Ergo ante omne meritum est gratia."

29. *Ad Simplicianum* 1.2.8 (CCL 44: 32–33): "Quod enim fecit deus ea quae diligeret, nulla questio est."

30. *Ad Simplicianum* 1.2.19 (CCL 44: 48): "una est enim ex Adam massa peccatorum et impiorum."

31. *Ad Simplicianum* 1.2.22 (CCL 44: 55): "Restat ergo ut voluntates eligantur. Sed voluntas ipsa, nisi aliquid occurrerit quod delectet atque inuitet animum, moveri nullo modo potest. Hoc autem occurrat, non est in hominis potestate."

32. *Ad Simplicianum* 1.2.8 (CCL 44: 32): "Si enim quia praesciebat deus futura eius opera mala, propterea eum praedestinavit ut seruiret minori, propterea praedestinavit et Iacob ut ei maior seriuret."

to expand and refine the elements of his doctrine of grace already in place.

Augustine was not present at the Synod of Carthage (411) that condemned Caelestius and his teachings. Augustine's writings against Pelagianism up to 416 are "marked by a curious reserve."[33] Although Augustine was aware of the proceedings of the synod and had read Pelagius's *De natura,* he had yet to attack Pelagius directly during this period.

In time, however, Augustine came to realize Pelagius was a dangerous heretic and needed to be treated as such. Shortly following his participation in the Council of Milevis, Augustine wrote *De gestis Pelagii,* in which he attacked Pelagius directly. Pelagius proved to be an easy target and was never able to recover from the African Church's campaign against him. Julian of Eclanum, however, was a much more difficult opponent. Augustine's *Contra Iulianum,* written in 421, was his most extensive work against the Pelagians.[34] Augustine refuted Julian's interpretation of 1 Timothy 2: 4, "God wills that all be saved and come to the knowledge of the truth," a key passage in the Pelagian conflict as well as in the later Augustinian conflict.[35] Julian interpreted the passage in support of his assertion that the reason why people are not saved was due to their own fault of not asking, seeking, or knocking at the door of salvation that would be opened if they were, in fact, to ask, seek, and knock.[36] Augustine refuted this assertion with the example of infants who, although they cannot ask, seek, or knock, nonetheless enter the doors of salvation if they are baptized.[37] Augustine then explained the reason why some people are saved and others are not.

33. Gerald Bonner, "Augustine and Pelagianism in the Light of Modern Research," in *God's Decree and Man's Destiny: Studies on the Thought of Augustine of Hippo* (London: Variorum Reprints, 1987), 38.

34. *Contra Iulianum* (PL 44: 641–874; *Answer to Julian,* in *Answer to the Pelagians,* vol. 2, trans. Roland Teske, WSA I/24 [Hyde Park, N.Y.: New City Press, 1998], 268–534).

35. For Augustine's numerous and varied interpretations of the seeming universal salvific will of God expressed in 1 Tim. 2: 4, see Athanase Sage, "La volonté salvifique universelle de Dieu dans la pensée de saint Augustin," *Recherches augustiniennes* 3 (1965): 107–31, and Alexander Hwang, "Augustine's Interpretations of 1 Tim. 2: 4," SP 43 (2006): 137–42.

36. *Contra Iulianum* 4.8.42 (PL 44: 759; *Answer to Julian,* 405).

37. *Contra Iulianum* 4.8.42 (PL 44: 759; *Answer to Julian,* 405).

In the course of his explanation, Augustine interpreted 1 Timothy 2: 4 as the reason for what causes the salvation of people. People are saved because God wills it to happen; thus God's will or desire to save is only true for those whom God will save. "All" means only those whom God saves. As for those who are not, they "have themselves to blame for it."[38] God does not will their salvation, but neither does God will their damnation. And God punishes with damnation only those who deserve it.[39] God is just in condemning and God is good when he saves.[40]

The terms "free choice" and "freedom of the will" are not used, and in further writings, the use of these terms and Augustine's explanations of them are noticeably absent. Augustine still maintained that people have the use of the choice of their will, but God prepares the will of a saved person.[41] As for the will of those whom God does not will to be saved, it appears that God leaves these alone.

In Book 5 of the same work, Augustine interpreted 2 Peter 3: 9b, "God not wanting any to perish, but all to come to repentance," in the course of explaining the mystery of predestination. God's plan of salvation involves God's patience toward "even those who have lived very bad lives."[42] God does not want them to perish, who are chosen and predestined to salvation—those whom God wills to save—and so allows time for them to be saved.

Augustine used the same twin attributes of God, "just" and "good," that he used in Book 4: "He [God] is, nonetheless, just and good."[43] This goodness and justice of God are the fundamental differences between a saved and a condemned person: "But by his merciful goodness God draws some of them to repentance, and by his just judgment he does not draw others."[44]

Both interpretations reveal the same understanding of God's will and human involvement in salvation and damnation. Both re-

38. *Contra Iulianum* 4.8.43 (PL 44: 760; *Answer to Julian,* 406).
39. *Contra Iulianum* 4.8.45 (PL 44: 761; *Answer to Julian,* 406).
40. *Contra Iulianum* 4.8.46 (PL 44: 761; *Answer to Julian,* 407).
41. *Contra Iulianum* 4.8.45 (PL 44: 761; *Answer to Julian,* 406).
42. *Contra Iulianum* 5.4.14 (PL 44: 792; *Answer to Julian,* 442).
43. *Contra Iulianum* 4.8.46 (PL 44: 761; *Answer to Julian,* 407).
44. *Contra Iulianum* 5.4.14 (PL 44: 792–93; *Answer to Julian,* 443).

veal a firm predestination to salvation, and a clear insistence on complete human responsibility for damnation. Both interpret God's will to save as absolutely effective, and "all" to mean only those who will actually be saved.

Contra Iulianum reveals not only Augustine's doctrine of predestination but also Augustine's most emphatic attempt to situate this doctrine within the catholic faith. Augustine viewed his doctrine to be in clear conformity with the Church's teaching, and used the first two books to gather the teachings of the Church against the Pelagian heresy.[45]

Shortly after the work against Julian, Augustine wrote the *Enchiridion* in 422 as a sort of handbook for Christians.[46] Augustine interpreted 1 Timothy 2: 4 in two places in the work. In the first interpretation of 1 Timothy 2: 4, Augustine was more concerned about asserting the omnipotence of God's will than actually interpreting the passage. That God's will to save "all" seems to be thwarted by the will of those who choose not be saved, and so make God's will less than omnipotent, is proven false by the example of infants who have no place in choosing or not choosing to be saved.[47] Augustine did not directly define "all" but assumed that since God's will is omnipotent, "all" can refer only to those whom God wills to save. The emphasis in this writing is placed on God's omnipotence and further illustrates Augustine's growing awareness of God's absolute role in salvation.

Augustine treated the passage in another place, but this time more attention is given to the interpretation of 1 Timothy 2: 4 than anywhere else in his previous writings. Augustine first established the assertion that God's will is omnipotent and then proceeded to understand this passage within that assumption. Since what God wills necessarily occurs and what God does not will does not occur, it follows that if God wills the salvation of anyone, it will necessar-

45. *Contra Iulianum* 1–2 (PL 44: 641–702; *Answer to Julian*, 268–335).

46. *Enchiridion ad Laurentium* (CCL 46: 49–114; *The Enchiridion on Faith, Hope, and Charity*, in *On Christian Belief*, trans. Bruce Harbert, WSA I/8 [Hyde Park, N.Y.: New City Press, 2005], 273–343).

47. *Enchiridion* 24.97 (CCL 46: 100; *Enchiridion*, 328–29).

ily happen. Thus, Augustine instructed his readers to pray to God to will our salvation, since God's willing our salvation is the only way we can obtain it.[48]

Augustine situates the passage within the passages that precede it and draws from these passages Paul's meaning of "all." People are not only to pray for their own salvation but also offer up prayers for the salvation of "all": "The whole race of humankind in all its diversity."[49] Augustine interpreted 1 Timothy 2: 4 as belonging to Paul's instructions for prayers to be made for the salvation of all *kinds* of people, and, in particular, those in positions of power. Thus, Augustine interprets 1 Timothy 2: 4 in the context of 1 Timothy 2: 1–3.

The effect of the prayers or their role in the process of salvation is not exactly clear, but only that "God has judged it good that he should deign to give salvation to important people through the prayers of the humble."[50] That prayers are involved somehow in the process of other people's salvation is evident, however, at least in 422.

In summary, Augustine's doctrine of predestination grew out of his initial understanding of grace, and developed in the course of the Pelagian conflict. God predestines those whom God chooses, and human beings have no role in the economy of salvation, apart from an undefined notion of the potential of human prayer. Yet even that role is overshadowed by Augustine's overall emphasis on God's role in choosing and preparing the will of the saved person. In a few years, even the ambiguous role of prayer in salvation will be eliminated from his doctrine of predestination.

Augustine had been the leader in the campaign to eradicate Pelagianism, on both the political-ecclesiastical and the theological fronts. The West was aware of Augustine's activities in the controversy, and while there was wide agreement in terms of his condemnation of Pelagianism, there were some in the West who were concerned with Augustine's alternative to Pelagian grace.

48. *Enchiridion* 27.103 (CCL 46: 104; *Enchiridion,* 332–35)
49. *Enchiridion* 27.103 (CCL 46: 105; *Enchiridion,* 333).
50. *Enchiridion* 27.103 (CCL 46: 105; *Enchiridion,* 333).

The Roman Church

The papacy from the late fourth to the early fifth centuries began to assert more of its authority among the churches of the West.[51] From Siricius to Leo, Roman pontiffs began claiming and defining the one unique power it held over the churches of the West—that of being Peter's heir. Although the churches of North Africa and Gaul showed some measure of deference to the pope, the growing papal claims of overall authority were met with resistance.

From the perspective of North Africa, the relationship between Rome and the African Church had been close since the late second century.[52] Both could claim a rich and long history for their respective churches, but the Africans acknowledged that it was the Roman Church that brought Christianity to Africa, and that Rome was the only Apostolic See in the West. This did not mean, however, that the Africans readily accepted all of Rome's pronouncements. Rome was its mother church, an apt term since the tie that bound them remained despite the most vociferous disagreements. The African Church appealed to Rome for support in confirming their decisions against the Pelagians and also in enforcing them.[53] When Zosimus took a different direction, the Africans took matters into their own hands. The Africans recognized the importance of papal support in a campaign that went beyond their own jurisdiction, but when the ecclesiastical approach failed, they appealed to Ravenna. Yet they did not openly confront the Roman decision or appeal to another church.

The Church of Gaul viewed the authority of Rome in a different manner. Although the Gauls recognized Rome's prestige, only a few Gauls accepted the full authority of the pope. The Gauls, for

51. The development of the Church of Rome can be found in Charles Pietri, *Roma Christiana: Recherches sur l'Église de Rome, son organisation, sa politique, son idéologie de Miltiade à Sixte (311–440),* 2 vols. (Rome: École française de Rome, 1976).

52. For the relationship between Rome and the African Church, see J. E. Merdinger, *Rome and the African Church in the Time of Augustine* (New Haven: Yale University Press, 1997).

53. For Rome's theological position in the Pelagian controversy, see Wermelinger, *Rom und Pelagius.*

the most part, looked to themselves for leadership and judgment.[54] The highly factional nature of the Gallic Church, however, provided the Roman pontiffs opportunities to begin encroaching on Gallic ecclesiastical independence. Rome functioned as a court of appeals for Gauls, as it did for Africans, who sought redress of local judgments. Rome's intervention in such cases "served their purpose over the long term in establishing precedents for the jurisdiction of the bishop of Rome in Gaul."[55]

Throughout the Pelagian conflict, Rome's concern was for a peaceful solution. It was reactionary and conservative in its actions. Rome made a definitive declaration on Pelagianism only after the interventions of the imperial court forced their hand. Rome's preferred policy, in terms of dealing with conflict within the Church, was to act the part of a disinterested arbiter, whose goal was to promote peace and unity as far as this was possible. When Rome finally condemned Pelagianism through the *Tractoria,* the decision was final, and at least for Zosimus and his successors the matter was settled.[56] Rome, however, had yet to make a definitive pronouncement on what grace was, especially in light of the new controversy between Augustine and the powerful and influential members of the Gallic Church. If Rome was hesitant to get involved in the Pelagian conflict, how much more care would be taken in a conflict between unquestionably orthodox Gauls and Augustine? It was in the practice and interest of Rome to wait and see.

Roman pontiffs were far from exercising preeminent authority in the West; yet Rome had an undeniable claim to apostolicity. The churches of Gaul and North Africa, rooted in tradition and importance, were, in the end, only provincial; and the influence of the church of North Africa would soon come to an end with the death of Augustine and the fall of North Africa to the barbarians. Although

54. Mathisen, *Ecclesiastical Factionalism,* 46.

55. Ibid., 68.

56. The phrase, "Roma locuta est; causa finita est," has been traditionally but falsely attributed to Augustine. Augustine actually wrote, "Jam enim de hac causa duo concilia missa sunt ad Sedem Apostolicam: inde etiam rescripta venerunt. Causa finita est uninam." See *Sermo* 131.10 (PL 38: 734; *Sermon* 131, in *Sermons,* vol. 4, trans. Edmund Hill, WSA III/4 [Brooklyn: New City Press, 1992], 322).

both churches resisted the new claims of apostolic power and its authority, especially when Rome's decisions conflicted with their own, the Roman pontiffs' continual and persistent claims to universal authority were slowly becoming accepted and on its way toward the full realization of papal claims.

Doctores Gallicani

The first instance of monasticism in Gaul is identified with Martin of Tours, as stated earlier, who, around the middle of the fourth century, established monasteries in Tours and Poitiers. Martin's connection to Hilary of Poitiers, who was exiled to the East and was familiar with Eastern monasticism, along with the influence of Athanasius's *Vita Antonii* on Severus's *Vita Martini,* suggests the first Gallic monastic communities were inspired by Eastern monasticism.[57] Furthermore, the *Vita Martini* became widely known throughout the West, and thus, with it, the spread of Eastern monastic ideas.

Monasticism in southern Provence began around the early fifth century with the founding of monasteries on Lérins and in Marseilles, and they too had a connection to the East. Provence, especially Marseilles and Lérins, were havens for Gallo-Roman aristocratic refugees who sought to devote themselves to God. Some joined or identified themselves with monasteries, while others belonged to still less defined groups of ascetics. These monastic communities drew much of their inspiration from the Eastern monastic model. Their founders had received monastic training in the East, and both monasteries proudly acknowledged their debt and connection to Eastern monasticism.

The traditional view has assumed that these monastic communities in the south were organized, regulated, and unified; thus a

57. Athanasius, *Vita Antonii* (PG 26: 837–976; *Athanasius: The Life of Anthony and the Letter to Marcellinus,* trans. Robert C. Gregg [New York: Paulist Press, 1980]). Sulpicius Severus, *Vita Martini.* See Philip Rousseau, *Ascetics, Authority, and the Church in the Age of Jerome and Cassian* (Oxford: Oxford University Press, 1978), 143–65; Weaver, *Divine Grace,* 73.

"South-Gallic monasticism" was identified.[58] In recent years, scholars have questioned these views, presenting a less formal and much more disjointed picture of these communities.[59] It is the latter view that best corresponds to the situation in Provence. Likewise, the traditional Benedictine connotations of "monk" and "monastery" do not apply to the situation on Lérins and in Marseilles, which appear less regulated and much less isolated than previously thought.[60]

In and around Marseilles men lived out the ascetic life in various ways and in various circles: lay married and celibate ascetics, monks, hermits, and clergy. Through a shared interest in literary activities and theological discussions, these various ascetic circles, led by the *doctores Gallicani,* remained in close contact with each other. Among the most important in Prosper's life were the monasteries on Lérins and in Marseilles, and his own circle of lay ascetics in and around Marseilles.

Lérins

Situated off the coast of modern-day Cannes, the island of Lérins became home to a monastic community sometime in the beginning of the fifth century.[61] Little is known about the organization of the

58. Among the traditional views, see A. de Vogüé, *Les Règles des saint Pères,* SC 297–98 (Paris: Cerf, 1982); Salvatore Pricoco, *L'isola dei santi: Il cenobio de Lerino e le origini del monachesimo gallico* (Rome: Edizioni dell'Ateneo and Bizzarri, 1978); Friedrich Prinz, *Mönchtum im Frankenreich* (Munich: R. Oldenbourg, 1965); Columba Stewart, *Cassian the Monk* (Oxford: Oxford University Press, 1998); and most recently, Ogliari, *Gratia et Certamen,* 91–130.

59. Against the traditional views, see Conrad Leyser, "'This Sainted Isle': Panegyric, Nostalgia, and the Invention of Lerinian Monasticism," in *The Limits of Ancient Christianity: Essays in Honor of R. A. Markus,* ed. William Klingshirn and Mark Vessey (Ann Arbor: University of Michigan Press, 1999), 188–206, and, idem, "*Lectio divina, oratio pura*: Rhetoric and the Techniques of Asceticism in the Conferences of John Cassian," in *Modelli di santità, modelli di comportamento,* ed. G. Barone et al. (Turin: Rosenberg and Sellier, 1994), 79–105; and Philip Rousseau, "Cassian: Monastery and the World," in *The Certainty of Doubt: Tributes to Peter Munz,* ed. Miles Fairburn and Bill Oliver (Wellington: Victoria University Press, 1996), 68–89.

60. Rousseau's candid remark is indicative of the new perspective ("Cassian: Monastery and World," 78): "In my earlier study [*Ascetics, Authority, and the Church*] I took it for granted that Cassian was a monk, and I took it for granted that I knew what 'monk' meant."

61. The founding and early history of the monastic community on Lérins are known primarily through Hilary's biography of the community's founder, Honoratus, the future

community, but Eucherius's *De laude eremi* provides the inspiration behind and some of details of the community: "Holy old men in separate cells who introduced the fathers of Egypt to us Gauls."[62] Eucherius's situation of still being attached to his wife and two sons also sheds some light on the makeup of the monastery.[63]

Though the island was nothing like the Eastern deserts, the first generation of monks sought to live and struggle on their figurative desert.[64] Lérins was a desert in bloom for the first generations of monks, and a desert as the spiritual battlefield for the later monks.[65] The imagery appears to have been an ideal not wholly followed, however. The Eastern model's influence did not appear to extend beyond a general and yet undefined pursuit of holy living in isolation. The community remained open to the outside world, especially to ecclesiastical and monastic centers, through correspondence and the practice of monks becoming bishops. Lérins soon became a center of recruitment for bishops, a kind of "seminary for aristocratic monk-bishops," a practice initiated by Honoratus himself.[66]

---

bishop of Arles. See Hilary, *Sermo de vita sancti Honorati* (SC 235; *Sermon on the Life of Honoratus*, in *The Western Fathers*, trans. F. R. Hoare [New York: Sheed & Ward, 1954]).

62. Eucherius of Lyons, *De laude eremi* 42 (PL 50: 711; trans. in Weaver, *Divine Grace*, 75–6). The existence of a "rule of Lérins" put forth most notably by Adalbert de Vogüé remains uncertain; "Les 'Règles des saints Pères' à Lérins," *Lérins* 287 (1980): 4–10, and, idem, "Les débuts de la vie monastique à Lérins: Remarques sur un ouvrage recent," *Revue d'histoire ecclésiastique* 88 (1993): 5–53. For a review of the scholarship on this issue, see Ogliari, *Gratia et Certamen*, 113–15.

63. As referenced in Trout, *Paulinus of Nola*, 260. See A. Gouilloud, *Saint Eucher, Lérins et l'église de Lyon au Ve siècle* (Lyon: Librairie Briday, 1881); Germain de Montauzen, "Saint-Eucher, évêque de Lyon et l'école de Lérins," *Bulletin historique du diocèse de Lyon* 2 (1923): 81–96.

64. R. A. Markus contrasts the monasticism of southern Gaul and the monasticism of Augustine as two different models based on different images. The former built in the image of the Desert and the latter in the image of the City (*The End of Ancient Christianity* [Cambridge: Cambridge University Press, 1990], 160). See also Owen Chadwick, "The Ascetic Ideal in Church History," in *Studies in Church History* 22 (1985): 1–23.

65. Markus, *Ancient Christianity*, 162.

66. Markus, "The Legacy of Pelagius," 222; Adalbert Hamman, noting the practical aspect of Lerins and Marseilles, compared them to "seminaries," which functioned as training schools for future bishops ("The Turnabout of the Fourth Century: A Political, Geographical, Social, Ecclesiastical, and Doctrinal Framework of the Century," in *Patrology*, vol. 4, 26). See also Pierre Courcelle, "Nouveaux aspects de la culture lérinienne," *Revue des etudes latines* 46 (1968): 379–409.

Lérins, despite the fact that a number of its members pursued ecclesiastical careers, remained an important center of asceticism, whose prestige, in fact, benefited from its well-placed alumni.[67] Among its notable literary figures were Salvian of Marseilles and Vincent, although Salvian eventually moved on to the monastery at Marseilles. This learned community was and continued to be a place of ascetical theological reflection in constant contact with the outside world, including the events of the Pelagian controversy.

John Cassian

Around the same time that Prosper made his way from the West to Marseilles, John Cassian was heading for Marseilles from the East, eventually arriving around 415.[68] The reasons for his move to Marseilles are unclear, only that he established twin monasteries in Marseilles shortly after arriving.[69]

Cassian was also to provide a "more detailed and lasting guidance on the daily conduct of asceticism" for his community, and serve as a mentor for Gallic ascetics in general.[70] In that regard, Cassian's importance to the development of Gallic and Benedictine monasticism has been well articulated.[71] However, Cassian's im-

67. Leyser makes an interesting case for the "invention" of Lerinian monasticism as a reaction against the instability of the community as a result of the "culture of leaving" ("'This Sainted Isle,'" 189).

68. According to Gennadius: "Cassianus, natione Scytha, Constantinopolim a Iohanne Mago episcopo diaconus ordinatus, apud Massiliam presbyter, condidit duo id est virorum ac mulierum monasteria, quae usque hodie extant" (*De viris inlustribus* 62 [TU 14/1: 82]). For recent studies, see K. Suso Frank, "John Cassian on John Cassian," SP 33 (1997): 418–33; Stewart, *Cassian the Monk;* and Casiday, *Tradition and Theology.*

69. The tradition of identifying Cassian's monastery with St. Victor abbey go back only to the eleventh century, which was based on the claims of the abbey during a time of restoring the order. See Michel Fixot, "Saint-Victor, saint Victor, à propos d'un livre récent," in *Marseille: Trames et paysages urbains de Gyptis au Roi René. Actes du colloque de Marseille* 1999, Études Massaliètes 7 [Aix-en-Provence, 2001], 235–54). My thanks to Dr. Simon Loseby of Oxford University, who kindly brought the article and issue to my attention.

70. Rousseau, *Ascetics,* 169. For a discussion on Cassian's role as a monastic reformer in Gaul, see Conrad Leyser, *Authority and Asceticism from Augustine to Gregory the Great* (Oxford: Clarendon Press, 2000), esp. 33–61; and Stewart, *Cassian,* 16–19.

71. Recent works include Stewart, *Cassian;* Owen Chadwick, *John Cassian;* Rousseau, *Ascetics;* and Leyser, *Authority and Asceticism.*

portance, in this present work, is restricted to his opposition to Augustine's doctrine of grace. In this role, Cassian was not a spokesman or the leader of the *doctores Gallicani*. Instead, Cassian was one of the many distinct dissenting voices. Cassian's role in the Augustinian conflict has been greatly exaggerated due to his fame and the convenience afforded by his body of works, which present the most comprehensive treatment on grace among Augustine's opponents in the Augustinian conflict. From these writings, scholars, working on the false assumption of a cohesive south-Gallic monasticism, have presented Cassian as the representative and main opponent of Augustine's doctrine of grace.[72] What follows is a brief account of Cassian, one that is more proportional to his actual role in the conflict.

Before his arrival in Marseilles, Cassian had spent more than twenty years among the monastic communities in the East, in Bethlehem and then in Egypt. During these years Cassian became acquainted with the Eastern monastic tradition, primarily through Evagrius of Pontus, who was the chief expositor of Origen's ascetic theology in Egypt. It was an ascetic theology that held a deeply optimistic view of human nature. Cassian came across this Origenist view, "explicitly or implicitly, in all the sources of the Egyptian desert."[73] It was a view of human nature that was dominant in parts of the East and served as a foundation for the Eastern monastic tradition. It was this tradition that Cassian brought to Gaul, but modified to the context of Marseilles and by his own appropriation of that tradition.[74]

Cassian detailed this monastic life in the celebrated *De institutis coenobiorum* and *Conlationes*.[75] The goal of these works was to "facil-

72. Scholars from Valentin (1900) to Ogliari (2003) have overestimated Cassian's role in the Augustinian conflict.

73. Chadwick, *John Cassian*, 110.

74. On the extent and limits of Cassian's use of Evagrius, see Salvatore Marsili, *Giovanni Cassiano ed Evagrio Pontico: dottrina sulla carità e contemplazione*, Studia Anselmiana philosophica theologica 5 (Rome: Herder, 1936); and Stewart, *Cassian*, 11–12, 36–37, 42–43, 90–94, 115–22, as referenced in Leyser, *Authority and Asceticism*, 36 n. 12. See also Steven Driver, *John Cassian and the Reading of Egyptian Monastic Culture* (New York: Routledge, 2002).

75. *Conlationes* (CSEL 13; *Conferences*); *De institutis coenobiorum* (CSEL 17; *The Institutes*, trans. Boniface Ramsey, ACW 58 [New York: Newman Press, 2000]).

itate moral and spiritual instruction. His tropological intention was to give monks of southern Gaul—and their bishops, many of them monks as well—an overview of the monastic life, explaining where to begin, what to do, what to expect along the way, and where it all leads."[76] Where it all led was the vision of God, achieved through what Cassian termed the "purity of heart," a phrase that he used more than fifty times.[77] To gain this purity of heart, monks must undergo the process of spiritual cleansing, which involves the systematic expurgation of sins.[78] Then the monk who is perfect, having the "purity of heart," can contemplate God.

Cassian's purpose in establishing a monastery was to provide a place in which earnest and sincere men could practice the instructions set forth in his monastic writings. The ultimate goal was the vision of God, but this was possible, according to Cassian, only when the monk had reached perfection in the "quality of life and purity of heart."[79]

Cassian was primarily concerned with the practical aspects of the monastic life, but there are limited discussions on grace. *De institutis coenobiorum,* written between 419 and 426, contains initial remarks on the role of grace in the process of perfection, which anticipates *Conlatio* 13, written after this period.[80]

Cassian's initial statements on grace were not put forward in a systematic manner. In *De institutis* 12.10, Cassian asserted that human effort was not sufficient for "perfection and the palm of integrity and purity, unless he were protected by the divine mercy."[81] Cassian then ended with James 1: 17 and 1 Corinthians 4: 7—passages that seem to emphasize human effort. However, in 12.14.2, Cassian asserted "[f]or he [God] is ready, so long as we have offered him

76. Stewart, *Cassian,* 29.

77. Stewart (*Cassian,* 42): "While *puritas cordis* is undoubtedly Cassian's favorite way of characterizing monastic perfection, the addition of synonymous expressions such as purity of mind *(puritas mentis)* and purity of soul *(puritas animae),* and of similar concepts like purity of body or pure prayer, quadruples the total number of such phrases."

78. The expurgation of the eight sins is detailed in books 5–12 of *De institutis coenobiorum* (CSEL 17: 78–231).

79. *Conlationes* 1.15.3 (CSEL 13: 25–26); as quoted in Stewart, *Cassian,* 47.

80. *Conlationes* was written between 425/426 and 428; on the dating of the works, see Ogliari, *Gratia et Certamen,* 125–26 n. 155.

81. *Insititutis* 12.10 (CSEL 17: 213; *Institutes,* 259).

our good will, to grant all these things, inasmuch as he desires and longs for our perfection and salvation more than we do ourselves."[82] In 12.18, Cassian notes that humans were created "rational" and with the "power of free will," but that the exercise of "daily divine providence" works with and protects and helps humanity.[83] Then Cassian proclaimed that "we are often even against our will drawn to salvation by him, and lastly, that, when he visits and moves us, he turns even our free will itself, which is readily inclined to vice, to better things and to the path of virtue."[84]

When taken together, Cassian's disparate and conflicting remarks on the nature and role of the human will in the economy of salvation are unclear and not a little confusing. Cassian suggests that there were no inherent conflicts in insisting on irresistible grace, *initium fidei,* exercise of free will, tainted will, and cooperative grace.

Cassian approached the problem of grace and free will from a different perspective than the Pelagians or Augustine, who saw the issue as *either* grace *or* free will. Instead, Cassian believed it was grace *and* free will—a relationship of cooperation between the two—even at the cost of consistency. Like Augustine, Cassian claimed the necessity of grace in the economy of salvation, but not to the exclusion of human responsibility.[85] Like Pelagius, Cassian insisted on free will, but not to the point that it operated completely independent of grace.

Cassian was aware of the Pelagian conflict prior to the *De institutis,* as well as the discussions about Augustine's doctrine of predestination that were taking place in Provence.[86] Knowing that his

82. *Insititutis* 12.14.2 (CSEL 17: 215; *Institutes,* 261).

83. *Insititutis* 12.18. (CSEL 17: 219; *Institutes,* 264–65): "The daily exercise of his providence—namely, that he frees us from the snares of our adversaries, that he works with [*cooperatur*] us in order that we may be able to overcome the vices of the flesh, that he protects us from dangers even unbeknownst to us, that he guards us from falling into sin, that helps and enlightens us."

84. *Insititutis* 12.18 (CSEL 17: 219–20; *Institutes,* 265).

85. On the reevaluation of Cassian's relationship to Augustine, which presents Cassian as a discriminating student of Augustine, see Boniface Ramsey, "John Cassian: Student of Augustine," *Cistercian Studies Quarterly* 28 (1993): 5–15 (hereafter *CSQ*).

86. "[Cassian's] allusions [in the *De institutis*] to other perspectives indicate that he was aware of the hardline views of the Augustinian party" (Stewart, *Cassian,* 79).

monks were being exposed to two opposing views, equally in error in his opinion, Cassian informed them of the proper view on grace and free will, but in a limited and cursory manner. At least for the moment, Cassian restricted his opposition to Augustine's doctrine of predestination in a very limited and indirect literary response, but which contributed to the discussions on Augustine's doctrine already taking place among the *doctores Gallicani.*

Reactions to Augustine

The general view of the *doctores Gallicani* was that the Pelagians were clearly in error. The evidence about the reactions in Provence to Augustine's doctrine during this period comes from Prosper's *Epistula ad Rufinum,* his letter to Augustine, and Hilary's letter to Augustine, which were written approximately between 426 and 427.[87]

In regards to Augustine, they held him in respect, and sided with Augustine, insofar as he represented the Church's condemnation of Pelagianism. It was on Augustine's doctrine of predestination that many of the Gauls parted company.[88] This doctrine aroused controversy, and there were several levels of reactions, not one unified voice of opposition as has been traditionally maintained. There were some who zealously admired and defended Augustine and his doctrine, some who became convinced in the course of discussions, and then there were those opposed to the doctrine.[89] This last group was the largest and consisted of three varying levels of opposition: those adamant in their opposition, those who simply followed the opinions of the powerful and respected *doctores Gallicani,* and those

87. Prosper, *Ep. ad Rufinum* (PL 51: 77–90; *Letter to Rufinus,* 21–37); Prosper, *Ep.* 225 (CSEL 57: 454–68; *Letter* 225, 87–94); Hilary, *Ep.* 226 [among Augustine's letters] (CSEL 57: 468–81; *Letter* 226, in *Letters 211–270, 1*–29*,* vol. 4, 95–102).

88. There was one bishop (the identity of whom is discussed in chapter one) in particular whom Prosper identified as especially respectful of Augustine (*Ep.* 225.9 [CSEL 57: 467]): "sciat beatitudo tua admiratorem sectatoremque in aliis omnibus tuae esse doctrinae." Mathisen has gone so far as to describe the Gallic view of Augustine as "schizophrenic" (*Ecclesiastical Factionalism,* 124).

89. Prosper mentioned that in those places where these discussions were taking place, there are "many people who learn from his [Augustine's] enlightening tracts how to understand the teaching of the gospel and of the apostles and who rejoice in seeing his [Augustine's] writings spread" (*Ep. ad Rufinum* PL 51: 79; *Letter to Rufinus,* 24).

who raised objections, but wished to remain silent on what is a mystery.[90]

The intellectually sophisticated *doctores Gallicani* that opposed the doctrine had not blindly acquiesced to Rome's or Africa's decisions on Pelagianism. They did their own theological inquiry and familiarized themselves with Augustine's writings, including his earlier writings. Their opposition to the doctrine of predestination was essentially centered on three objections—it was novel, fatalistic, and removed free will—all of which seemed to undermine their pursuit of perfection.[91]

In addition to the theological reasons, there were other possible reasons. Augustine was merely the bishop of an unimportant provincial town in North Africa. Moreover, Augustine's political and ecclesiastical victories against the Pelagians may not have been as impressive a victory for the cultured Gallo-Roman aristocratic ascetics, who were well aware that such victories were results of successful political power plays, a game the Gauls knew all too well. The cultured Italian bishops who refused to sign the *Tractoria* viewed Augustine's appeal to the secular sword as a "confession of intellec-

90. Prosper, *Ep.* 225.2–4 (CSEL 57: 456, 459, 460; *Letter* 225, 88, 90): "That certain more simple people, who have great reverence for these men from having observed their goodness, may judge that what they hear these men maintain, whose authority they follow without question. . . . Ultimately, their whole obstinacy comes down to the point at which they declare that our belief is something opposed to the edification of those who hear it, and so, even if it is true, it should not be brought into the open. For it is dangerous to hand on teachings that should not be accepted, and it involves no danger to pass over in silence ideas that cannot be understood. . . . Certain of them, however, do not wander very far from the paths of the Pelagians." Hilary, *Ep.* 226.8 (CSEL 57: 478, *Letter* 226, 100): "With the agreement even of those who do not dare to disapprove of this position, to ask, 'What need is there that the hearts of so many simple people be disturbed by the uncertainty of such an argument? For the Catholic faith has been defended no less effectively for so many years without this doctrine.'"

91. Prosper, *Ep. ad Rufinum* 3 (PL 51: 79; *Letter to Rufinus*, 23): "They say he completely sets aside free will and under cover of grace upholds fatalism." Prosper, *Ep.* 225.2 (CSEL 57: 455; *Letter* 225, 88): "Many of the servants of Christ who dwell in the city of Marseilles think that whatever you discussed in them concerning the calling of the elect according to God's plan is opposed to the opinion of the Fathers and to the mind of the Church." Hilary, *Ep.* 226.2 (CSEL 57: 469; *Letter* 226, 96): "These, therefore, are the ideas which are being discussed at Marseilles . . . that it is a new idea and one opposed to the usefulness of preaching that it said that some people will be chosen according to God's plan in such a way that they can neither acquire this election nor hold onto it unless they have been given the will to believe."

tual impotence."[92] Their aristocratic counterparts in Gaul may very well have shared similar sentiments. Cassian, especially, knew from personal experience that truth was not necessarily served by those in power, a painful lesson he learned in Constantinople, having been on the receiving end of the destructive and undiscriminating power of a theological argument joined by secular force.[93]

It should then come as little surprise that Augustine's doctrine of predestination had a poor reaction in Provence. Most were naturally opposed to it. During this period, those who opposed Augustine's doctrine remained rather unconcerned, if not unimpressed. Apart from Cassian's rather benign rebuttal in the *De institutis,* the discussions on Augustine's doctrine in Provence were restricted to debates within and among the various ascetic circles. Such a novel and speculative doctrine would have fueled a lively debate among intellectually minded ascetics. It was a doctrine worthy of discussion, but not important enough to elevate it to a literary debate. It may also have been, at least in Cassian's mind, potentially dangerous to directly challenge the powerfully connected Augustine. In general, those who opposed Augustine's doctrine of grace—bishops and other ecclesiastics, as well as monks—appear to have been secure enough in their positions and tradition to tolerate Augustine and his supporters in Provence, while engaging with them and among themselves in a lively, but still restrained, oral debate, at least for now.[94]

Prosper and the Augustinian Faction

From the limited amount that is known about his life during this period, Prosper, along with other like-minded men, was an out-

92. Brown, *Augustine of Hippo,* 364.

93. On Cassian's careful omission of the events in Constantinople, see Stewart, *Cassian,* 12–15.

94. Both Hilary and Prosper mentioned the high ecclesiastical position of some of the opponents of Augustine in Gaul; Hilary, *Ep.* 226.9 (CSEL 57: 478): "Sunt ex parte tales personae, ut his consuetudine ecclesiastica laicos summam reverentiam necesse sit exhibere." Prosper, *Ep.* 225.7 (CSEL 57: 465): "Sed auctoritatem talia sentientium non sumus pares, quia multum nos et vitae meritis antecellunt et aliqui eorum adepto nuper summi sacerdotii honore supereminent."

sider, not only because he was not part of one of the powerful monastic circles, but also because of his differing views. Like others in Gaul, Prosper was aware of the events unfolding in the Pelagian conflict and became acquainted with Augustine's writings. Prosper, unlike many of his fellow ascetics, was fully convinced on three related points: the correctness and authority of Augustine *in toto,* the catholicity of Augustine's doctrine of predestination, and the authority of the catholic Church, still broadly defined.

In the course of following the events of the Pelagian conflict and reading Augustine's works on grace, Prosper became convinced of Augustine's authority and his doctrine of predestination. Prosper's theology of grace had changed dramatically from *De providentia Dei.* Although Prosper never admitted this change, or any further changes he would make, Prosper was refuting those very same views he previously held.[95] How exactly Prosper came to this conclusion about Augustine is uncertain, but it may have had something to do with the deacon Leontius. In Prosper's second letter to Augustine (*Ep.* 225), Prosper mentioned Leontius's role as the mediator for his first letter to Augustine and the response from the bishop (both lost).[96] Perhaps it was Leontius who introduced Augustine's writings to Prosper. Although Leontius's role in Prosper's appreciation of Augustine is uncertain, at the very least, Prosper must have found encouragement from a likeminded admirer of Augustine. Whatever the catalyst, Prosper, like so many after him in the history of the Church, became enamored of the eloquence and charisma of the old bishop. What Prosper saw in Augustine was a man of immense authority, wisdom, and power. Prosper became an enthusiastically devoted disciple and spared no compliments in describing him:

95. A fuller analysis will be provided in the next chapter. Cf., e.g.: *De prov. Dei* 7 (ed. Marcovich, 34–35): "Non renovat quemquam Christus, nisi corde receptus. En, Homo, quanta tibi est gratia collata potestas. Filius esse Dei, si vis, potes." *Ep. ad Rufinum* 2.3 (PL 51: 78): "[Prosper's opponents hold] Ut qui voluerint credant, et qui crediderint, justificationem merito fidei et bonae voluntatis accipiant: ac sic gratia Dei secundum hominum meritum tribuatur."

96. Prosper, *Ep.* 225.1 (CSEL 57: 454–55): "Nam per sanctum fratrem meum Leontium diaconum misi epistula et recepi."

Augustine also, at the time the first and foremost among the bishops of the Lord.... Among many other divine gifts showered on him by the Spirit of truth, he excelled particularly in the gifts of knowledge and wisdom flowing from his love of God, which enabled him to slay with the unconquerable sword of the word.... Resplendent with the glory of so many palms and so many crowns which he gained for the exaltation of the Church and the glory of Christ.... The greatest man in the Church today.[97]

Any suggestion to the contrary, in Prosper's view, was akin to heresy. Prosper was so utterly convinced by Augustine that he assumed Augustine was synonymous with authority and orthodoxy—that Augustine's doctrines were the expressions of the catholic Church. In defending Augustine, Prosper believed he was defending the Church. Prosper naively thought the Church's endorsement of Augustine's anti-Pelagianism extended equally to Augustine's alternative doctrine to Pelagianism. This was the result of Prosper's poor ecclesiology.

Prosper's appreciation of Augustine and the Church, the latter broadly and vaguely defined, appears to have come together during this same period. How Prosper came to an appreciation of the Church also remains unclear, but here, also, Prosper had changed dramatically from *De providentia Dei,* where there was no awareness or attention given to the role of the Church. From Prosper's first work after *De providentia Dei, Epistula ad Rufinum,* and in all of his later works, the Church takes a consistent and increasingly important place, and becomes more narrowly defined over time.

Prosper was convinced of the authority of the Church, but he had only a vague sense of what that meant. The Church, for Prosper, was conceived in the broadest terms: the whole of the Church, East and West. In his list of authorities involved in the Pelagian condemnation, Prosper named the Eastern bishops, the authority of the Apostolic See, and the African councils.[98] The authority of the Apostolic See, however, seems at odds with what Prosper then stated about Augustine: "At the time the first and foremost among the

97. *Ep. ad Rufinum* 3, 18 (PL 51: 78–79, 89; *Letter to Rufinus,* 23, 36).
98. *Ep. ad Rufinum* 3 (PL 51: 78; *Letter to Rufinus,* 22–23).

bishops of the Lord."[99] What exact authority the Apostolic See has in the Church is unclear.

Prosper was not alone in his enthusiasm for Augustine. Among the ascetic circles in Provence, there was a group of men united by their common admiration for Augustine, *perfectae gratiae intrepidi amatores.*[100] By 427, when Prosper wrote his second letter to Augustine, the circle consisted of at least three acquaintances: Prosper, Hilary, and Leontius.[101] Nothing is known about the deacon Leontius except that he was an admirer of Augustine and knew him personally, and was close to Prosper and Hilary.[102]

The exact relationship of Prosper and Hilary is unknown, but from the evidence of the two letters, it appears that they were not as close as previously thought, at least initially. Traditionally it has been held that Hilary was Prosper's only associate, which is based on Hilary's introduction of Prosper in his letter and their joint trip to Rome after Augustine's death. However, a careful look at the two letters reveal they were far from close friends, at the time. Hilary's awareness of Augustine's opposition went beyond Marseilles, whereas Prosper's awareness was restricted to the city of Marseilles.[103] Furthermore, Hilary made the mistake of introducing Prosper to Augustine when Prosper had already written to Augustine.[104] The evidence suggests that Hilary and Prosper moved about in differ-

99. *Ep. ad Rufinum* 3 (PL 51: 78; *Letter to Rufinus,* 23).

100. Prosper, *Ep.* 225.7 (CSEL 57: 465).

101. It is uncertain if this was the same Hilary who wrote to Augustine in 414–15 from Sicily; *Ep.* 156 (Aug.) (CSEL 44: 448–49). Tillemont (*Mémoires pour sevir à l'histoire ecclésiastique des six premiers siècles,* 13 [Paris: Chez Charles Robustel, 1702], 640) argued in favor of the identification. Prosper's personal circle of associates included Rufinus, to whom he wrote a letter, and an unnamed mutual associate mentioned in the same letter. These two figures do not appear to have been part of Prosper's Augustinian circle. *Ep. ad Rufinum* 1.1 (PL 51:77; *Letter to Rufinus,* 21).

102. *Ep. ad Rufinum* 1.1 (PL 51:77; *Letter to Rufinus,* 21).

103. Cf. Hilary, *Ep.* 226.2 (CSEL 57: 469): "Haec sunt itaque, quae Massiliae vel etiam aliquibus locis in Gallia ventilantur." Prosper, *Ep.* 225.2 (CSEL 57: 455): "Multi ergo servorum Christi, qui Massiliensi urbe consistent."

104. Hilary, *Ep.* 226.10 (CSEL 57: 480). Apparently, Hilary was not aware that Prosper had already sent a letter (not extant) to Augustine through the deacon Leontius. See Prosper, *Ep.* 225.10 (CSEL 57: 454–55): "nam per sanctum fratrem meum Leontium diaconum misi epistulas et recepi."

ent circles and had only recently met. It appears that their meeting did not entail significant conversation—it is difficult to imagine that Prosper's correspondence to Augustine would have gone unmentioned in an extended conversation. If anything, Prosper appears to have been closer to Leontius than Hilary, at least initially. The joint trip to Rome, around 431, with Hilary may be evidence of their later close association, which occurred sometime after their letters to Augustine. Still, it is plausible that Leontius may have died or was unable to travel, and that Hilary was the only one available for the trip. Speculations aside, the perception of a unified and uniform Augustinian faction in Marseilles appears just as faulty and misleading as a unified and uniform doctores Gallicani faction.

Conclusion

Prosper had undergone a transformation during this period. He was now a committed member of the Church and as such felt compelled to confront what he considered a new heresy. Prosper's hypersensitivity to anything remotely differing from Augustine's doctrine of predestination, which he took to be the Church's teaching on grace, resulted in his participation in discussions occurring in and around Marseilles over the controversial doctrine. Together with at least two other Augustinians, Prosper defended Augustine's doctrine of predestination against the arguments put forth by the powerful *doctores Gallicani*.

~4

Servus Dei I (426–430)

In Defense of the Catholic Church

PROSPER ARRIVED in Marseilles having witnessed the destruction of life and property as well as extended captivity by the Goths. Prosper then wrote *De providentia Dei* as a Christian poet relying on his classical training and his own interpretation of Scripture to explain why they had suffered. After a decade of study, reflection, and participation in the intellectual milieu of Marseilles, Prosper emerged as a committed member of the Church—a *servus Dei:* an "ill defined" but "baptized, dedicated layman, determined to live, in the company of bishops, priests and noble patrons, the full life of a Christian."[1] Prosper at this time understood the Church broadly as the collection of churches, both East and West, who together defined the content and limits of catholicity. Prosper was convinced that Augustine was the most authoritative figure in the Church and his teaching on grace was in conformity with catholic teaching. In defending Augustine and his doctrine of grace, Prosper believed he was defending the Church's view and vigorously opposed those who attacked, what was in Prosper's estimation, a catholic doctor and the catholic understanding of grace. Prosper should be viewed not so much as a disciple of Augustine as he was a disciple of the Church.

1. Brown, *Augustine of Hippo,* 132.

This chapter details the beginning of the conflict over Augustine's alternative to Pelagian teaching on grace. In Provence and even in his native North Africa, Augustine's doctrine of predestination began to encounter criticisms. The first formal opposition came from an otherwise unknown person by the name of Rufinus, presumably from Gaul, but it was Augustine's treatises addressed to the monks of Hadrumetum that caused some of the *doctores Galliani*, already critical of Augustine's doctrine of predestination, to virulently oppose the bishop of Hippo. Augustine was informed of the situation in southern Gaul through the letters from his ardent supporters, Hilary and Prosper, and responded to their requests for his involvement by writing a treatise, which was among his last works.

Epistula ad Rufinum

The news of Prosper's participation in the discussions on Augustine's doctrine of predestination reached a friend of Prosper's by the name of Rufinus. Through a mutual friend, Prosper became aware of Rufinus's concern for Prosper and wrote a letter (now lost) to give his side of the conflict, around 426. The letter also elevated the level of the conflict to a public literary debate.

Summary

The *Epistula ad Rufinum* begins with a summary of the condemnation of the Pelagian heresy by adherents of the catholic faith, expressed by the "Oriental bishops, the authority of the Apostolic See, and the African councils."[2] Augustine is introduced as "first and foremost among the bishops of the Lord," and the principal agent in the eradication of the heresy. Prosper later points out the Church's endorsement of Augustine: "that not only the Church of Rome and of Africa and all the sons of the promise the world over agree with the teaching of this doctor both in the faith as a whole and in particular in the doctrine on grace."[3] In the conclusion to the letter, Prosper again reiterates his opinions of Augustine and his doctrine of

2. *Ep. ad Rufinum* 1–3 (PL 51: 77–79; *Letter to Rufinus*, 21–24).
3. *Ep. ad Rufinum* 3 (PL 51: 79; *Letter to Rufinus*, 23–24).

grace: "Augustine, the greatest man in the Church today. . . . Concerning the Catholic doctrine on grace, you will draw from them salutary insight into the teaching of the gospel and of the apostles."[4] It is against this Augustine that Prosper claims "some of ours. . . . speak and murmur in secret," and "are displeased when we [Prosper's faction] oppose the assertions they make in many a conference against a man of the highest authority."[5] The conference was none other than Cassian's, whose *Conlationes* 1–10 had recently been completed. Their criticisms became known to Prosper, which he characterizes as follows: Augustine sets aside free will, upholds fatalism, and ascribes two different substances and natures to humanity.[6]

According to Prosper's view, the conflict is the result of the improper interpretation of Scripture. Prosper explains that his opponents have grounded their objections to Augustine's teaching on the "strength of some texts of Holy Scripture." However, Prosper insists, "they do not explain these texts in the proper way." "To prove a proposition," Prosper counters, "such texts should be quoted as cannot be understood in another meaning opposed to that proposition." According to Prosper's hermeneutical principle, a proposition drawn from a text that is susceptible to an opposing interpretation is invalid. A valid proposition can only be drawn from a text that cannot be interpreted in opposition to the proposition.[7]

Prosper lists three scriptural quotations (Matt. 11: 28–30, Acts 10: 1–48, and 1 Tim. 2: 4) that his opponents use to support their view of free will: salvation or damnation is dependent on the choice of the free will to accept or reject Christ's invitation; grace is a result of good works done by free will; and God wills the salvation of all equally. For each text Prosper counters with several scriptural quotations that are "irreformable and cannot be twisted and interpreted in another sense."[8] Thus, Prosper's propositions are valid because they are drawn from texts that have only one meaning, whereas his opponents' propositions are invalid because they are drawn

4. *Ep. ad Rufinum* 18 (PL 51: 83; *Letter to Rufinus,* 36).
5. *Ep. ad Rufinum* 3–4 (PL 51: 79–80; *Letter to Rufinus,* 23–24).
6. *Ep. ad Rufinum* 3 (PL 51: 79; *Letter to Rufinus,* 23).
7. *Ep. ad Rufinum* 5 (PL 51: 80; *Letter to Rufinus,* 25).
8. *Ep. ad Rufinum* 5, 6, 13 (PL 51: 80–81, 83; *Letter to Rufinus,* 25–26, 31–32).

from texts that can be interpreted in another manner. The ambiguous texts of his opponents are to be interpreted according to the valid propositions, drawn from the clearer places in Scripture.[9]

According to Prosper's view, Scripture teaches that grace precedes the free will's desire to believe and obey the invitation to salvation; grace is not the result of good works, but good works are the result of grace; and that God's universal salvific will applies only to those whom God actually saves.[10] Prosper spends little effort in refuting the charges that Augustine teaches fatalism and divides humanity into two substances and natures. Prosper simply states at the end of the letter that fatalism cannot be found in any of the writings of Augustine or those who support Augustine, and that humanity is of one nature and one substance.[11]

Despite the letter's relative brevity and limited scope, Prosper's newfound appreciation of Augustine's doctrine of predestination is evident in the work. Prosper details the essential Augustinian elements with remarkable efficiency.

Prosper's Doctrine of Grace

All humans, because of Adam's sin, are condemned to a state of death, blindness, ungodliness, exile, and abandonment.[12] Human nature, having fallen through the first man, is captive to the debt of eternal death.[13] Fallen humanity does not practice justice, walk toward God, love God, or have faith; rather, humanity falls into ever-deeper error.[14]

For Prosper, free will is the vehicle by which one exercises good

9. Compare Augustine's *De doctrina Christiana* 3.27.38 (CCL 32: 99–100; *Teaching Christianity,* trans. Edmund Hill, WSA I/11 [Hyde Park, N.Y.: New City Press, 1996], 185–86): "But when from the same words of scripture not just one, but two or more meanings may be extracted, even if you cannot tell which of them the writer intended, there is no risk if they can all be shown from other places of the holy scriptures to correspond with the truth."

10. *Ep. ad Rufinum* 5, 6–12, 13–16 (PL 51: 80–81, 81–84, 85–87; *Letter to Rufinus,* 25–26, 26–31, 31–34).

11. *Ep. ad Rufinum* 18 (PL 51: 83; *Letter to Rufinus,* 35–36).

12. *Ep. ad Rufinum* 7–8 (PL 51: 82; *Letter to Rufinus,* 27–28).

13. *Ep. ad Rufinum* 13 (PL 51: 82; *Letter to Rufinus,* 31).

14. *Ep. ad Rufinum* 7–8 (PL 51: 82; *Letter to Rufinus,* 27–28).

or evil. There is an evil free will and a good free will, never a neutral free will as his opponents assert. Free will, apart from grace, is dead to justice, lives for sin, dwells in the kingdom of the devil, and will act only for its own perdition. Free will, enlightened by grace, is freed from the kingdom of the devil and brought to the kingdom of God.[15] Free will is not taken away or destroyed in the process, but set free to turn back to God. The free will is then given new desires, tastes, and actions. The free will is turned from evil to good.[16] This good, liberated free will cannot remain in this blessed state by itself unless it is also given perseverance.[17]

A liberated good will is a will that is under the complete control of grace, and thus a recipient of salvation. Salvation is possible only for those whose wills are liberated and are good. Those who have been liberated and are good were elected, predestined, and foreknown, according to God's counsel, before the creation of the world.[18] Salvation is not offered literally to "all" as 1 Timothy 2: 4 seems to suggest; rather, "all" can only mean "all" those actually saved.[19] Prosper warns that those who deny this view of grace and free will go against holy religion and grace itself.[20] As for the question of divine discrimination, Prosper acknowledges human ignorance, while insisting that God saves, but is not responsible for damnation.[21]

15. *Ep. ad Rufinum* 9 (PL 51: 83; *Letter to Rufinus,* 28–29): "Postea per profectum, ex bonis factura meliores; non adempto libero arbitrio, sed liberato." This is an Augustinian view, expressed as early as *Ad Simplicianum* 1.1.11 (CCL 44: 15–16) and developed more fully in *De spiritu et littera* 30.52–34.60 (CSEL 60: 208–21).

16. *Ep. ad Rufinum* 17 (PL 51: 87; *Letter to Rufinus,* 34–35): "Nunc autem idem arbitrium conversum est, non eversum, et donatum est ei aliter velle, aliter sapere, aliter agere, et incolumitatem suam non in se, sed in medico collocare."

17. *Ep. ad Rufinum* 9 (PL 51: 83; *Letter to Rufinus,* 29): "In quo ut permanere possit, ne ea quidem facultate sufficit sibi, nisi inde accipiat perseverantiam, unde accepit industriam."

18. *Ep. ad Rufinum* 15 (PL 51: 86; *Letter to Rufinus,* 33): "Non enim alii venient in consortium haereditatis Christi, quam qui ante constitutionem mundi electi sunt, et praedestinati atque praesciti."

19. Cf. Augustine, *Contra Iulianum* 4.8.42–46 (PL 44: 759–61; *Answer to Julian,* 405–7).

20. *Ep. ad Rufinum* 11 (PL 51: 84; *Letter to Rufinus,* 30): "Quod quidem tam impium est negare, quam ipsi gratiae contraire."

21. *Ep. ad Rufinum* 13 (PL 51: 85; *Letter to Rufinus,* 31).

Observations

The differences between *De providentia Dei* and *Epistula ad Rufinum* are remarkable. When compared to each other, they almost appear to be works written by two different authors. *De providentia Dei* was written by a relatively young Christian, whose theological views reflected a limited and independent understanding of Scripture and little awareness of the Christian tradition. Prosper relied a great deal on classical authors. His views on grace were closer to those of his opponents whom he now refutes. The *Epistula ad Rufinum* is the work of a writer who identifies himself firmly with the Church, as a *servus Dei*. Prosper does not rely on his own interpretations or those of pagan authors; instead, he situates his views within the Church—the churches of the East, Rome, and Africa, but especially with Augustine.

This appreciation of the Church is inextricably linked with Augustine. Prosper was wholly convinced that Augustine was the most authoritative figure in the Church, whose doctrine of grace was the expression of catholic doctrine. Prosper's answers are drawn from elements of Augustine's doctrine of grace, namely, Original Sin, free will, and predestination, because he equated Augustine with unequaled authority and catholicity.

Prosper presented the conflict in no uncertain terms; it was a polemical work whose purpose was to present the struggle as one between truth and error. Augustine's doctrine expressed the truth because it represented the Church's view. The disingenuous gossiping whisperers, who talk proudly among themselves, having no humility and integrity, were in error.

Prosper's true intention was to provoke a literary response from his opponents, which was unsuccessful. Despite Prosper's polemical prompting—"If what they say is true, why are they so remiss, not to say ungodly, as not to remove from the Church such a pernicious bane and to oppose such insane preaching, or even to counter in some writing or other the author of such teaching?"—Prosper's opponents did not respond. They would eventually take up the pen, not because of anything Prosper wrote, but because of what Augustine would later write—writings that had nothing directly related to the situation in Provence.

Hadrumetum

Provence was not the only place where Augustine's doctrine of predestination found resistance. Around 427, Augustine wrote a letter to a certain layman of Carthage by the name of Vitalis, whose views on grace concerned Augustine.[22] From what can be gathered from Augustine's response, Vitalis did not directly oppose Augustine's doctrine of predestination, but held a view of grace that was, according to Augustine's estimation, Pelagian. The effect of this letter on Vitalis is unknown, but the absence of further documents on this matter suggests the letter achieved its objective of correcting Vitalis, or, at the least, kept Vitalis quiet.[23]

Around the same time, there was a direct reaction to Augustine's doctrine of predestination at the monastery of Hadrumetum, which required much more attention by Augustine.[24] Florus, a monk of that monastery, came across Augustine's letter to Sixtus (*Ep.* 194) while in Evodius's monastery in Uzalis, and sent it back to Hadrumetum.[25] The letter was read to the community and caused disagreements among certain monks over Augustine's views on predestination. When Florus returned to Hadrumetum, the disagreements increased to the point that it caught the attention of the abbot, Valentine, who sent a delegation to Evodius, whom Valentine knew was Augustine's friend.

The delegation carried a letter (now lost) from Valentine to Evodius asking for clarification of Augustine's letter to Sixtus, specifically on the view of grace expressed in the letter. Evodius replied with a short letter that merely reiterated Augustine's doctrine. Humanity has free choice, but an injured choice, which is sufficient only for

22. Aug. *Ep.* 217 (CSEL 57: 403–25; *Letter* 217, 51–66). For the dating of the letter, see Ogliari, *Gratia et Certamen*, 26–27 n. 21.

23. One of Augustine's arguments used against Vitalis was that the Church prayed for the conversion of nonbelievers, *Ep.* 217.29 (CSEL 57: 423–24; *Letter* 217, 65). Augustine was referring to the "Prayers of the Faithful," found in the liturgy, and which will be referenced again in Augustine's response to Hilary's and Prosper's letters; see below, n. 195.

24. Hadrumetum (modern day Sousse, Tunisia) was a small coastal town about 120 km south of Carthage and about 300 km to the east of Hippo. See Rebecca Harden Weaver, "Hadrumetum," *ATA*, 411–12.

25. Aug. *Ep.* 194 (CSEL 57: 176–214; *Letter* 194, 287–308).

perdition. It is the gift of divine grace, without any preceding merits, that daily sets human beings free to live well, and gives them the will to pray well and the will to understand well.[26] Evodius would rather these monks focus on their piety than occupy their minds on contentious issues.[27] If they do not understand or had questions about Augustine's views on grace, Evodius exhorts them to submit to the grace taught in the books of the *sancti ecclesiae magistri,* as well as the decisions of a plenary council (Council of Carthage, 418).[28] Evodius's rebuke failed to satisfy Valentine, who next appealed to a respected priest by the name of Sabinus, whose response, which, though according to Valentine was a clear explanation of Augustine's letter, was equally unsuccessful in resolving the debate.[29]

Finally, Valentine allowed two monks, Cresconius and Felix, and another monk named Felix who would arrive a little after the other two, to appeal directly to Augustine. Augustine welcomed the monks, shortly before Easter of 426 or 427, who informed him about the disagreements in the monastery. It was reported to Augustine that some of the monks at Hadrumetum denied that human beings have free choice and that God will reward according to an individual's works on the day of judgment. Most, however, admit that free choice is helped by grace, and that good works are prepared by God, who will reward these works on the day of judgment.[30]

The monks were anxious to get back to their monastery in time for Easter, and so Augustine composed a brief letter to Valentine explaining that those monks who believed that free choice is helped by grace were correct, and summarized the intent and main issue involved in his letter to Sixtus.[31] The monks, however, decided to remain in Hippo for Easter, which gave Augustine the opportunity to

26. Evodius, *Epistula ad abbatem Valentinum* (PLS 2: 332; *A Letter of Bishop Evodius to Abbot Valentine,* in *Answer to the Pelagians,* vol. 4, trans. Roland Teske, WSA I/26 [Hyde Park, N.Y.: New City Press, 1999], 42–43).

27. Evodius, *Ep. ad Valentinum* (PLS 2: 332; *Letter to Valentine,* 42): "Laudamus quidem studium vestrum, sed nolumus esse contentiosum; contentio enim perturbationem excitat, studium pietatem requirit."

28. Evodius, *Ep. ad Valentinum* (PLS 2: 332; *Letter to Valentine,* 42–43).

29. Valentine (Aug.), *Ep.* 216.3 (CSEL 57: 399; *Letter* 216, 47).

30. Aug., *Ep.* 214.1 (CSEL 57: 380–81; *Letter* 214, 36–37).

31. Aug., *Ep.* 214.1–3 (CSEL 57: 380–83; *Letter* 214, 36–37.

instruct the monks further. Augustine read and explained to them some of the documents from the Pelagian controversy, Cyprian's *De dominica oratione* and the book *De gratia et libero arbitrio,* which he had written specifically for the monks at Hadrumetum.[32] Along with these documents—except Cyprian's work, which was already held in the library at Hadrumetum—Augustine sent two letters to Valentine with the monks for their return journey.

Valentine responded with a letter informing Augustine that they had "received with gratitude the medicine of your letters, which bring healing with their piety."[33] Valentine also sent Florus, whom Augustine had asked in the second letter to see in person so as to instruct him.[34]

Augustine met with Florus, who informed the bishop of the unrest caused by *De gratia et libero arbitrio* among some of the monks at Hadrumetum. Someone in the monastery drew the conclusion from *De gratia* that one should not rebuke another for not keeping God's commandments, but should only pray for him that he keep them, since it is God who produces in the person the power to will and to act.[35] Augustine responded with a second book to the monks of Hadrumetum entitled *De correptione et gratia.*[36]

De correptione et gratia

The aim of the book was much broader and comprehensive than the title of the work suggests. Augustine answered the objec-

32. Aug., *Ep.* 215.2 (CSEL 57: 389–90; *Letter* 215, 41). Cyprian, *De dominica oratione* (CCL 3A: 87–113); Aug., *De gratia et libero arbitrio* (PL 44: 881–912; *Grace and Free Choice,* in *Answer to the Pelagians,* vol. 4, trans. Roland Teske, WSA I/26 [Hyde Park, N.Y.: New City Press, 1999], 71–106).

33. Valentine (Aug.), *Ep.* 216.4 (CSEL 57: 399; *Letter* 216, 48).

34. Florus arrived after Augustine's first request (*Ep.* 215.8), but was unable to meet due to the bishop's poor health. Augustine requested the presence of Florus again (*Ep.* 215A), and this time he was able to meet him.

35. Aug. *Retractationes* 2.67 (CCL 57: 14; *The Retractations,* trans. Mary Inez Bogan, FC 60 [Washington, D.C.: The Catholic University of America Press, 1968], 270): "Rursus ad eosdem scripsi alterum librum quem *De correptione et gratia* praenotavi, cum mihi nuntiatum esset dixisse ibi quendam, neminem corripiendum si Dei praecepta non facit, sed pro illo ut faciat tantummodo orandum."

36. *De correptione et gratia* (CSEL 92: 219–80; *Rebuke and Grace,* in *Answer to the Pelagians,* vol. 4, 109–45).

tion raised by the anonymous monk on the issue of rebuke by situating his answers in the larger context of his doctrine of predestination. As a result, it is a clear and succinct explanation of the difficult aspects of his doctrine of predestination, which has been regarded as the essential explication of Augustine's doctrine of grace.[37] The work can be divided into three sections: the first section (1.1–6.9) introduces the issue of rebuke; the second section (6.10–13.42) deals with rebuke in the context of the grace of perseverance and predestination; and the last section (14.43–15.49) provides instructions concerning rebuke in light of grace.

Adam was created with a good will and the free choice to will it.[38] Adam needed God's help to maintain the good will, for without God's help Adam's willing to remain in that good will would prove unsuccessful.[39] Adam chose evil and he along with all his descendants were condemned.[40] All human beings became evil as a result of Adam's sin, and live under the dominion of sin and the judgment of condemnation.[41] Humans have the free choice to do good or evil, but in doing evil one is devoid of righteousness and enslaved to sin.[42]

37. Jean Chéné ("Les origines de la controverse semi-pélagienne," *Année théologique augustinienne* 13 [1953]: 100 n. 15): "Nous avons donc dans ce livre de la correction et de la grâce, la vision augustinienne de la grâce en son originalité irréductible et sous sa forme intégrale. Nous ne remercierons jamais assez le moine inconnu dont l'objection futile nous a valu une oeuvre de ce prix"; quotation in Ogliari (*Gratia et Certamen*, 71 n. 200). Ogliari claims Augustine expressed this in *De dono preseverantiae:* "Augustine himself affirms that nowhere has he stressed the all-encompassing power of grace so clearly and decisively as in this work" (*Gratia et Certamen*, 71). However, Augustine referred specifically to perseverance and not to the power of grace in general (*De dono perseverantiae* 21.55 [PL 45: 1027; *Perseverance*, 229]): "Et ego quidem in illo libro, cujus est titulus, *De Correptione et Gratia,* qui sufficere non potuit omnibus dilectoribus nostris, puto me ita posuisse donum Dei esse, etiam perseverare usque in finem, ut hoc antea, si me non fallit oblivio, tam expresse atque evidenter, vel nusquam, vel pene nusquam scripserim."

38. *De corr. et gr.* 11.32 (CSEL 92: 257; *Rebuke and Grace,* 131): "Tunc ergo dederat homini deus bonam voluntatem . . . ut autem vellet in eius libero reliquit arbitrio."

39. *De corr. et gr.* 11.32 (CSEL 92: 257; *Rebuke and Grace,* 131).

40. *De corr. et gr.* 10.28 (CSEL 92: 252; *Rebuke and Grace,* 128).

41. *De corr. et gr.* 1.2, 6.9, 10.28 (CSEL 92: 219–20, 226, 252; *Rebuke and Grace,* 110–11, 113, 128).

42. *De corr. et gr.* 1.2 (CSEL 92: 220; *Rebuke and Grace,* 109): "Liberum itaque arbitrium et ad malum et ad bonum faciendum confitendum est nos habere, sed in malo faciendo liber est quisque iustitiae servusque peccati."

One cannot be free to do the good unless set free by God.[43] Those set free have recovered the lost freedom. They are, like Adam, free to remain, with God's help, in the good, or to abandon it.[44] These are the Christians who have been given the gift of regeneration through the grace of baptism. Among these Christians, some will be given the help of not only receiving the good, but also holding onto it—the gift of perseverance. It is the grace of Christ that makes possible the ability to will the good and the willing itself.[45] Others will abandon it through their own will and go back to an evil life.[46] Thus all of humanity has free choice to do good or evil. Those not reborn through Christ are enslaved to sin and cannot do the good. Those reborn through Christ are no longer enslaved to sin and can do good or evil. Of the latter, some will choose the evil through their own will, and others will continue in the good through the gift of grace (perseverance), which provides the will and willing itself.

What distinguishes the grace of Adam and the grace of Christ is the type of perseverance. Adam was given the first power of perseverance, whereby he was able not to sin—*posse non peccare.* The grace of Christ provides the final blessedness of perseverance, which is the inability to sin—*non posse peccare.*[47] However, in the present life, those who have been given this perseverance still fight against the desires of sin, and sometimes succumb to it, but not to the sin, which leads to death.[48] Thus, although Augustine does not clearly distinguish the difference, there is the final blessed perseverance enjoyed in heaven, and the perseverance enjoyed on earth, which ensures faithfulness to the end, but does not ensure a life free from sinning.

This gift of perseverance is given only to those whom God foreknew, predestined, and called according to the divine plan of salvation.[49] God's predestination, foreknowledge, calling, and persever-

43. *De corr. et gr.* 1.2 (CSEL 92: 220; *Rebuke and Grace,* 109): "in bono autem liber esse nullus potest, nisi fuerit libertatus ab eo."

44. *De corr. et gr.* 11.31 (CSEL 92: 256; *Rebuke and Grace,* 130).

45. *De corr. et gr.* 11.32 (CSEL 92: 258; *Rebuke and Grace,* 131).

46. *De corr. et gr.* 6.9 (CSEL 92: 227; *Rebuke and Grace,* 114).

47. *De corr. et gr.* 12.33 (CSEL 92: 259; *Rebuke and Grace,* 132).

48. *De corr. et gr.* 12.35 (CSEL 92: 262; *Rebuke and Grace,* 133).

49. *De corr. et gr.* 12.35 (CSEL 92: 262; *Rebuke and Grace,* 134).

ance are inseparable. Perseverance is not given according to God's foreknowledge of the good one will accomplish on one's own; rather, perseverance is given in order that one will produce good works.[50] This gift takes away any place for human pride, since without God's help humans would not be able to persevere.[51] Human merits are taken into account in the process of salvation. Eternal life is a recompense owed to good works, but these good works are bestowed on a person by grace.[52]

The number of those who have been predestined is certain, but those who are predestined cannot know for certain if they are of the predestined lot. The reason for this uncertainty is to instill fear, which prevents the pride of confidence that believes they will never fall away.[53]

Not all who are reborn through the grace of baptism are given the gift of perseverance, because not all have been predestined, foreknown, and called according to God's plan of salvation. Although they may be spoken of as children of God, disciples of Christ, or those called by God, unless they are given perseverance, they are not the true children of God, true disciples of Christ, or those chosen by God.[54] God's true children, true disciples, and chosen are those who have been given the grace of perseverance. Those who have been baptized but do not receive perseverance belong to the mass of perdition—*massa damnata*—which also includes those who refuse to come to Christ after hearing the gospel and infants who die without receiving baptism.[55]

This divine discrimination is not opposed to 1 Timothy 2: 4. "All" should be understood as all the predestined, of which there is every kind of human being. The "all" cannot be taken literally to mean everyone, but only everyone who has been predestined.[56]

50. *De corr. et gr.* 12.36 (CSEL 92: 263; *Rebuke and Grace,* 134).

51. *De corr. et gr.* 12.37–38 (CSEL 92: 264–67; *Rebuke and Grace,* 134–36).

52. *De corr. et gr.* 13.42 (CSEL 92: 271; *Rebuke and Grace,* 138). Along with free choice, the monks of Hadrumetum were also concerned with the issue of salvation as a recompense for good works; see above.

53. *De corr. et gr.* 13.40 (CSEL 92: 268–69; *Rebuke and Grace,* 137).

54. *De corr. et gr.* 9.20–22 (CSEL 92: 241–45; *Rebuke and Grace,* 121–24).

55. *De corr. et gr.* 7.12, 16 (CSEL 92: 232, 236–37; *Rebuke and Grace,* 116–17, 119).

56. Augustine here cites one of his many interpretations of 1 Tim. 2:4. *De corr. et gr.*

As for why some were given the grace of baptism, but not the gift of perseverance, Augustine first acknowledges his ignorance and refers to Romans 9: 20 and 11: 33.[57] Augustine then goes on to acknowledge the peculiarity of this divine discrimination, but quickly notes that it is no less strange that infants of baptized and good believers, because these infants have not been baptized and die, are kept away from God's kingdom, when God could have willed their baptisms; or the case of children of non-Christians who are baptized through contact with Christians.[58]

The process of salvation works out in either of two ways. Some, having been predestined to eternal salvation, after having received the grace of baptism are taken to heaven by a sudden death. Others, having been predestined to eternal life, are baptized and then hear the gospel, which God has arranged for them to hear. Upon hearing the gospel, they believe and persevere in the faith to the end. If at some point in their lives they fall away, they will inevitably correct their lives through human rebuke or through God directly.[59]

Human rebuke is proper since it points out the bad in the person, which is due to the fault of that person.[60] Such a person may be of the predestined, and the rebuke may be salutary medicine.[61] The human rebuke, however, can only become beneficial if God wills the rebuke to be such.[62] Since those who are predestined cannot be distinguished from those not predestined by human discernment, rebuke must be given to all. God, through human rebuke, can make the rebuke beneficial for those who have been predestined. Thus, grace does not prevent rebuke, nor does rebuke exclude grace.[63] Grace, according to God's predestination, may work through rebuke. This rebuke is to be made along with prayer and done with love.[64]

14.44 (CCL 92: 272; *Rebuke and Grace*, 139): "Ex quibus in aliis opusculis nostris aliquos commemoravimus, sed his unum dicam."

57. *De corr. et gr.* 9.17 (CSEL 92: 237; *Rebuke and Grace*, 119).

58. *De corr. et gr.* 9.18 (CSEL 92: 239; *Rebuke and Grace*, 120).

59. *De corr. et gr.* 7.13 (CSEL 92: 233; *Rebuke and Grace*, 117).

60. *De corr. et gr.* 5.7 (CSEL 92: 223–24; *Rebuke and Grace*, 112).

61. *De corr. et gr.* 14.43 (CSEL 92: 272; *Rebuke and Grace*, 139).

62. *De corr. et gr.* 15.46, 16.49 (CSEL 92: 275, 279; *Rebuke and Grace*, 141, 143).

63. *De corr. et gr.* 16.49 (CSEL 92: 279; *Rebuke and Grace*, 143).

64. *De corr. et gr.* 16.49 (CSEL 92: 280; *Rebuke and Grace*, 143).

Observations

De correptione et gratia answered the question of rebuke, but also provided a clear exposition of the essential elements of Augustine's doctrine of predestination. *De correptione et gratia* was the final act of Augustine's intense and lengthy involvement in the affair. In all, Augustine wrote three letters and two treatises, and spent time conversing with and instructing these monks on two separate occasions. There was good reason for this concern. The situation with the monks of Hadrumetum came at a time when Augustine was still engaged in his struggle against Julian of Eclanum, and had recently been made aware of Vitalis's Pelagian ideas. Pelagianism was not completely eradicated, and the alarming news that monks who shared his native soil held Pelagian ideas had to be carefully and thoroughly dealt with.

The monastery of Hadrumetum was not affiliated with Augustine.[65] There is also no evidence that the two parties had any contact with each other before the affair.[66] The monastery certainly knew of Augustine and had deference for his authority, but it appears that Augustine's works were not in their library, and neither were any documents related to the Pelagian conflict. The monastery included some learned men (Florus, the two Felix's, and Cresconius) among its members, and others with little education.[67] The rather unsophisticated but practical issues raised by the monks of Hadrumetum, along with what is known about the library, suggests a community composed mostly of humble and simple-minded ascetics.[68] The one book that is known to have been available in their library was, in keeping with the African context, Cyprian's *De dominica ora-*

65. For a treatment of the monastery of Hadrumetum and the context of African monasticism, see Ogliari, *Gratia et Certamen,* 41–57.

66. Augustine never traveled to Hadrumetum or even to its region, Byzacena. The nearest he came to Hadrumetum was the town of Vallis, which was about 100 km away. For Augustine's travels in North Africa, see Othmar Perler, *Les voyages de saint Augustin* (Paris: Études Augustiniennes, 1969), 205–405, which also has helpful maps (following p. 22) of Augustine's journeys both in North Africa and Italy.

67. Valentine (Aug.), *Ep.* 216.2 (CSEL 57: 398; *Letter* 216, 47).

68. The issues raised by the monks of Hadrumetum were primarily concerned with practical matters related to grace: prayer, rebuke, and merits.

tione, which figured prominently in Augustine's strategy in dealing with the affair.[69]

Augustine was keenly aware of the mistakes he made in his life. The *Confessiones* is filled with details of his misspent past, and the *Retractationes* is the work of a man who humbly goes back into his past to correct and clarify his views. It is not difficult to imagine that Augustine was conscious of the mistakes he made in the Pelagian controversy. Augustine had failed to recognize the danger of Pelagius early on. And, perhaps most regrettably, Augustine did not take advantage of the opportunity to meet personally with Pelagius, Caelestius, or Julian. The battle with Pelagianism had become a battle of words with no end in sight, and Augustine had become all too aware that written words were open to misinterpretations and bitter polemic. Such sentiments are evident in Augustine's "touching" remark when he sought to correct a young man on the origin of the soul: "I only wish that I could read your writings in company with yourself, and point out the necessary emendations in conversation rather than writing. This is a matter which could be more easily accomplished by oral communication between ourselves than in letters."[70]

Writing was indispensable in resolving conflict for Augustine, but Augustine recognized that correction was more efficient and successful in person. This attitude is reflected in Augustine's welcoming and keeping the monks of Hadrumetum beyond their intended stay.[71] It is even more evident in the case of Florus. Augustine was unable to meet with Florus during his first visit, due to the bishop's illness, but Florus was immediately called back once Augustine's illness subsided. Augustine found it necessary, even though Valentine had written of the success of the documents sent back with the

69. Aug., *Ep.* 215.3 (CSEL 57: 390; *Letter* 215, 41–42).

70. Aug., *De anima et eius origine* 3.14.21 (CSEL 60: 377; *The Nature and Origin of the Soul,* in *Answer to the Pelagians,* vol. 1, trans. Roland Teske, WSA I/23 [Hyde Park, N.Y.: New City Press, 1997], 528). Quotation in Brown (*Augustine of Hippo,* 365), but with the wrong reference: 3.14.21, not 3.14.20.

71. Aug., *Ep.* 215.1 (CSEL 57: 387; *Letter* 215, 40): "Cresconium, Felicem et alium Felicem dei servos, qui ex vestra congregatione ad nos venerunt, nobis cum egisse pascha noverit caritas vestra. Quos ideo tenuimus aliquanto diutius . . . ."

monks, to see Florus in person to make sure he fully and accurately understood the doctrine of predestination.

Augustine was also aware of his lack of direct authority over this monastery.[72] Augustine included the documents related to the Pelagian controversy to make clear to them the catholicity of his position. As a further insurance, Augustine cited Cyprian in *Epp.* 215 and 217, and in *De gratia et libero arbitrio* and *De correptione et gratia.*[73] Augustine knew the weight of Cyprian's authority among all North African Christians and exploited this to his advantage.[74]

Augustine clearly did not want this affair to turn into a controversy. If the lack of any further documents is any proof, the affair ended with *De correptione et gratia.* Ironically, it was precisely this work, which was intended to end the affair, that served as the occasion for the eruption of another. This time, Augustine had neither the resolve nor the time to fully engage it, and the affair escalated into a full-blown controversy.

Reactions in Marseilles

Objections to Augustine's doctrine of predestination had already been taking place among certain ascetic circles in and around Marseilles. Hilary had written a letter (now lost) to Augustine in which he detailed these disagreements, but the furor caused by the appearance of *De correptione et gratia* in Marseilles and other parts of Gaul prompted Hilary to write a second letter to inform Augustine of the present situation (*Ep.* 226).[75] It was at this time that Hilary became acquainted with Prosper, who may have been introduced to him by

72. Cf. the authoritative tone of Augustine's *Ep.* 211 (CSEL 57: 356–71; *Letter* 211, 19–28), a letter to the nuns in the monastery at Hippo.

73. *Epp.* 215.3, 217.3; *De gratia et libero arbitrio* 13.26; and *De corr. et gr.* 6.10.

74. J. Patout Burns, *Cyprian the Bishop* (London: Routledge, 2002), 174, 176: "Yet Cyprian's writings, like the relics of his body, were precious to North African Christians.... The Christians of Africa—Catholic and Donatists alike—held him their father in faith and celebrated his triumph each year, with singing and dancing."

75. Hilary, *Ep.* 226.9 (CSEL 57: 479; *Letter* 226, 101): "Do not be surprised that I have expressed some other things otherwise in this letter and added other things that I wrote in my previous letter, for this is their position at present."

Leontius.[76] Hilary asked Prosper to write a separate letter to Augustine from his own particular social context that Hilary would include with his own.[77]

The dating of the two letters has been traditionally assigned to the year 429, based on Prosper's reference to Hilary, the bishop of Arles.[78] In 1945, Owen Chadwick argued, based on manuscript evidence, that Prosper referred to Helladius not Hilary.[79] Palanque and Griffe have followed Chadwick's thesis.[80] Expanding on their work, Ogliari has concluded that the letters were written in 427, during Helladius's episcopate.[81] Ogliari's argument is persuasive, but does not alter the general history of events. Hilary and Prosper wrote to Augustine, and Augustine responded before his death. The difference in the dates only results in giving Augustine more or less time to respond.

Prosper's Letter (*Epistula* 225)

Prosper informs Augustine that "many of the servants of Christ who dwell in the city of Marseilles" have objected to his teaching of predestination found in his writings against the Pelagians. Prosper had hoped that the appearance of *De correptione et gratia* in Marseilles would answer their objections, but it caused even more dissent.[82] These servants objected to Augustine's teaching on the grounds that it is "opposed to the opinion of the Fathers and to the mind of the Church."

Prosper begins by describing what these servants of Christ, the *doctores Gallicani,* believe about grace and their objections to Augus-

76. Leontius was mentioned by both Prosper (*Ep.* 225.1) and Hilary (*Ep.* 226.10).

77. *Ep.* 226.10 (CSEL 57: 480; *Letter* 226, 102): "I persuaded a man renowned for his morals, his eloquence, and his zeal to convey to you by his letter all the information he could gather, and I have taken care to send you his letter along with mine."

78. Prosper, *Ep.* 225.9 (CSEL 57: 467; *Letter* 225, 94).

79. Owen Chadwick, "Euladius of Arles," *JTS* 46 (1945): 200–205; repeated in his book, *John Cassian,* 128. A detailed summary of the debate is in Ogliari, *Gratia et Certamen,* 93–95. See also Augustine Casiday's discussion of Helladius in *Tradition and Theology,* 112–15.

80. Palanque, "Les Évêchés Provençaux," 132; Griffe, *La Gaule chrétienne à l'époque romaine,* vol. 2 (Paris: Letouzey et Ané, 1965), 239–41.

81. Ogliari, *Gratia et Certamen,* 96–97.

82. Prosper, *Ep.* 225.2 (CSEL 57: 455–56; *Letter* 225, 88).

tine's teaching on predestination. Correctly, they hold that all humans have sinned in Adam; that no one can be saved by his own works, but only by rebirth through the grace of God; and all human beings have been offered reconciliation with God through the blood of Christ. However, it is at this point that Prosper identifies their errors, when they state that salvation is possible for whoever chooses to come to faith and baptism; God foreknew who would believe and continue in that faith; the help of grace is necessary after this choice of belief is made; and God predestined those who were foreseen by God to be worthy of the call and election of God.[83]

What they find objectionable about Augustine's version of predestination is that God has made the decision of who will be and not be saved, creating two separate groups of people. If God's decision to save precedes human willing, then all human effort and virtue are removed from the process of salvation. This type of predestination creates two different natures whereby humans are fated to one or the other.[84]

According to Prosper, these objectors claim Julian of Eclanum's position is consistent with theirs, but when Prosper challenged them with Augustine's writings, they invoked tradition. They claimed that Augustine's interpretations of Romans are not found in anyone else in the Church. However, they cannot come up with a satisfactory example of this, at least according to Prosper's account, and thus claim ignorance and desire to be silent on such a mysterious issue.[85]

It is at this point that Prosper identifies two different groups of objectors to Augustine's teaching on predestination: those who have objected, but conceded ignorance and prefer silence on the issue, and those who continue to raise objections.[86]

The latter group Prosper labels *Pelagianae reliquiae pravitatis,* and who *a Pelagianis semitis non declinant.*[87] This group acknowledg-

83. *Ep.* 225.3 (CSEL 57: 457; *Letter* 225, 88–89).

84. *Ep.* 225.3 (CSEL 57: 457–58; *Letter* 225, 89).

85. *Ep.* 225.3 (CSEL 57: 458–60; *Letter* 225, 89–90).

86. Jean Chéné, "Le semipélagianisme du midi de la Gaule d'après les lettres de Prosper d'Aquitaine et d'Hilaire à saint Augustin," *Recherches de science religieuse* 43 (1955): 321–41 (hereafter *RechScRel).*

87. *Ep.* 225.4, 7 (CSEL 57: 460, 465; *Letter* 225, 90, 93.

es that the grace of Christ anticipates human merits, but defines this grace as God's act of creating every human being. This grace of the creator endows each person with free choice and rationality.[88] They define free choice as the power to choose good or evil with equal force.[89] Rationality is the ability to distinguish between good and evil.[90] It is up to the person whether to make a good use of his natural abilities or not. A good use of this initial grace entails asking, seeking, and knocking, in order to receive, to find, and to enter (Mt. 7:7). By doing this, a person will merit the grace of salvation.[91] This view of grace and salvation is consistent with God's universal call of salvation (1 Tim. 2:4). God's universal call is the grace of creation, whereby every human being was created with free choice and rationality. God's justice is upheld since it is strictly up to the individual to exercise his natural abilities to merit salvation, and God's goodness is evident in that God grants everyone the ability to come to salvation.

When the case of infants who die is raised in objection to this view of grace, they respond that the reason why some infants are saved or condemned before they had any will or actions is because of God's foreknowledge. God granted those infants, whom God foreknew would have merited salvation had they lived, the grace of baptism. Those whom God foreknew would not have merited salvation, God did not grant baptism. In the same way, foreknowledge explains why everyone is not given the grace of salvation. God foreknew that they would not have the will to be renewed by it. God's role in salvation is to prepare the possibility of eternal life for everyone, and humans are responsible for actualizing this possibility through the merit of belief.[92]

88. *Ep.* 225.4 (CSEL 57: 460; *Letter* 225, 90): "in qua eum nihil prius merentem quia nec existentem liberi arbitrii et rationalem gratia creatoris instituat."

89. *Ep.* 225.4 (CSEL 57: 461; *Letter* 225, 90–91): "et quantum quisque ad malum tantum habeat facultatis ad bonum parique momento animum se vel ad vitia vel ad virtutes movere."

90. *Ep.* 225.4 (CSEL 57: 460; *Letter* 225, 90).

91. *Ep.* 225.4 (CSEL 57: 460; *Letter* 225, 90): "bono naturae bene usus ad istam saluantem gratiam initialis gratiae ope meruerit pervenire."

92. *Ep.* 225.5–6 (CSEL 57: 461–63; *Letter* 225, 91–92).

In Prosper's view, this group denies that God, according to God's plan and counsel, creates one vessel for an honorable purpose and another for a dishonorable purpose (Rom. 9: 21).[93] And they do not accept the teaching that the predestined number of the elect is fixed and unchangeable. Such a belief would make exhortations to lead a good life useless. It also goes against their view of the process of salvation. For those who have reached the "age of free will," salvation is the result of two factors: the grace of God and human obedience.[94] Human obedience comes first, followed by the help of divine grace.

Prosper then makes an appeal to Augustine for assistance. Prosper and his circle of "a few intrepid lovers of perfect grace" had opposed these beliefs as best they could with the knowledge they attained from Augustine's works, but their opponents exceeded them in authority and merit—one of them had recently become a bishop, whom he identifies later in the letter. Prosper claims that these views are becoming more dangerous as those who advocate them have become more powerful and influential.[95]

Prosper begins by labeling his opponents *Pelagianae reliquiae pravitatis,* and then lists, in summary form, the errors of these opponents, but in a way that subtly challenges Augustine to respond. In a series of counterfactual conditional clauses, Prosper lists the errors of his opponents, followed by an appeal for help in clarifying these errors.[96] In other words, if all these statements about grace are wrong, which they are, then Augustine should respond, and in the manner suggested by Prosper. Prosper instructs Augustine to write

93. *Ep.* 225.6 (CSEL 57: 463; *Letter* 225, 92).

94. *Ep.* 225.6 (CSEL 57: 464; *Letter* 225, 92): "qui tempus acceperunt liberae voluntatis, duo sint, quae humanam operentur salutem, dei scilicet gratia et hominis oboedientia."

95. *Ep.* 225.7 (CSEL 57: 465; *Letter* 225, 92): "nec facile quisquam praeter paucos perfectae gratiae intrepidos amatores tanto superiorum disputationibus ausus est contra ire."

96. *Ep.* 225.7 (CSEL 57: 465; *Letter* 225, 93): "If the beginning of salvation is wrongly located in a human being; if the human will is impiously preferred to the will of God, so that a person is helped because he has willed to be and not so that he has such a will because he is helped; if one who is evil from his origin is wrongly believed to initiate the reception of the good not from the highest good but from himself; and if God is pleased by something other than what he himself is given—then grant us the care of Your Piety in this matter."

as clearly as possible on these specific issues: the danger of his opponents' dissent from Augustine's doctrine of predestination; how free choice is not impeded by grace; the exact relationship between God's foreknowledge and God's plan; how the preaching of God's plan is to be understood relative to those who have not been predestined; and why all the *priorum opiniones* accepted the *propositum et praedestinatio dei secundum praescientiam.*[97]

Before Prosper ends his letter, he makes one last appeal for Augustine to respond. Prosper, with no regard for tact, names the recently appointed bishop Helladius as one of the opponents of Augustine's doctrine of predestination.[98] And he presents Helladius in a less than complimentary manner. Prosper claims that Helladius, an admirer and follower of Augustine except on the issue of grace, had wanted to write to Augustine on this issue. However, according to Prosper, it is uncertain whether Helladius will write this letter or to what purpose.[99] The implication is that Prosper questions whether Helladius can be trusted to write directly to Augustine or to present an accurate portrayal of the situation if he were to extend the courtesy of writing directly to Augustine. Thus, it was not merely monks and clerics who opposed Augustine's doctrine of predestination, but also the powerful bishop of Arles. The inclusion of Helladius only added to Prosper's depiction of the dangerous threat.[100]

Prosper had viewed the opponents of Augustine's doctrine of predestination, in his letter to Rufinus, as being in error, but their reactions to *De correptione et gratia* convinced Prosper that they were *Pelagianae reliquiae pravitatis,* and men who *a Pelagianis semitis non declinant.*[101]

How much of Prosper's description of the situation can be trust-

97. *Ep.* 225.8 (CSEL 57: 466–67; *Letter* 225, 93–94). Prosper did not specify who the "predecessors" were.

98. See above for the debate on the name of the bishop.

99. *Ep.* 225.9 (CSEL 57: 467; *Letter* 225, 94).

100. Weaver (*Divine Grace,* 45) views the inclusion of Helladius as part of Prosper's desire for Augustine to respond to his episcopal counterpart. However, it is more likely that Prosper wanted a response from Augustine to address all those who opposed Augustine's doctrine of grace, not just the bishop of Arles. The inclusion of Helladius was meant to heighten the threat of these objectors.

101. *Ep.* 225.4, 7 (CSEL 57: 460, 465; *Letter* 225, 90, 93).

ed is difficult to determine. Clearly Prosper had a vested interest in portraying the situation as gravely as possible to Augustine. Prosper's purpose was to provoke a response from Augustine by describing the situation in terms that he hoped would rouse the old bishop to action. According to Prosper, there were many servants of Christ in Marseilles who opposed Augustine's doctrine of predestination. Among them were powerful men holding Pelagian ideas, and who identified themselves with Julian of Eclanum. And the movement was getting more powerful and pervasive, with only a few true believers in grace who are helpless to oppose them. Prosper appealed to Augustine's fears: a possible new Pelagian movement within the Church.

Prosper and his circle needed a clearer and direct explanation of the difficult questions raised by their opponents. What was at stake, in Prosper's view, was the purity of the Church. Augustine was the *specialis patronus fidei,* whose doctrine of predestination was the doctrine of the Church, and Prosper felt compelled to seek Augustine's assistance in resolving the *valde perniciosa* views of the opponents of Catholic grace.[102]

Hilary's Letter (*Epistula* 226)

Hilary's letter informs Augustine about his perceptions of the negative reactions to Augustine's doctrine of predestination in Marseilles and in other places in Gaul.[103] The disagreement was over the novelty and uselessness of predestination and perseverance.[104] However, unlike Prosper's assessment, Hilary does not suggest a connection between these men and Pelagianism.

According to Hilary, the opponents seem to agree with Augustine that all human beings perished in Adam; that they cannot be set free from this perdition by their own choice; that no one is sufficient by himself to begin or to complete any good work; and that the ability to believe has been damaged.[105] However, they interpret

102. *Ep.* 225.1 (CSEL 57: 455; *Letter* 225, 88).
103. *Ep.* 226.2 (CSEL 57: 469; *Letter* 226, 96).
104. *Ep.* 226.2 (CSEL 57: 469; *Letter* 226, 96).
105. *Ep.* 226.2, 4 (CSEL 57: 469, 473; *Letter* 226, 96, 98).

these statements in a way contrary to Augustine's. While they acknowledge the damage of the will, they claim it has not been so corrupted or destroyed as to remove the ability, given by God to human nature, to reject or obey God's call.[106] Accordingly, those chosen or rejected by God have received the merit of their own will.[107] Thus, the statement "one cannot be set free from this perdition by one's own choice" is interpreted to mean that the choice to be helped or set free is insufficient by itself because it needs the necessary help of grace that follows choice.[108] And one is insufficient to begin or complete any good work because good works are the result of the gift of the Holy Spirit by which one can do good works. However, the gift of the Holy Spirit, and thus good works, is given to those who will to believe, which is entirely a work of the human will.[109] According to Hilary, although they profess what is correct, their interpretations of these statements are at odds with Augustine's.

The reason why not all have been able to hear the preaching of the Gospel and respond through their will is that the truth of the Gospel has been preached only where God foreknew it would be believed.[110] Hilary points out that these opponents find support for this view not only among *aliorum catholicorum testimonia,* but also in Augustine's earlier works, *Epistula* 102 and *Expositio quarundam propositionum ex epistula ad Romanos,* where, in fact, Augustine expressed their view of salvation based on God's foreknowledge of future belief or unbelief.[111] Thus, "they insist that God's foreknowledge, predestination, or plan means only that God foreknew, predestined, or planned to choose those who were going to believe."[112]

106. *Ep.* 226.2 (CSEL 57: 470; *Letter* 226, 96).

107. *Ep.* 226.2 (CSEL 57: 470; *Letter* 226, 96): "de compendio putant rationem redidi electorum vel reiectorum in eo, quod unicuique meritum propriae voluntatis adiungitur."

108. *Ep.* 226.2 (CSEL 57: 470; *Letter* 226, 96).

109. *Ep.* 226.3 (CSEL 57: 472; *Letter* 226, 97).

110. *Ep.* 226.3 (CSEL 57: 471; *Letter* 226, 97): "ut eo tempore et ibi et illis veritas adnuntiaretur vel adnuntietur, quando et ubi praesciebatur esse credenda."

111. *Ep.* 226.3 (CSEL 57: 471; *Letter* 226, 97). Aug. *Ep.* 102.2.14 (CSEL 34: 556; *Letter* 102, 27); *Expositio quarundam propositionum ex epistula ad Romanos* 60, 62 (ed. Landes, 30–33, 34–37).

112. *Ep.* 226.4 (CSEL 57: 472; *Letter* 226, 97–98): "Ceterum praescientiam et praedes-

These opponents agree with Augustine that perseverance is a received power, but claim that perseverance can be gained only if one chooses to accept it, that it is merited by prayer, and that it can be lost or retained by the human will.[113]

They reject the idea of a fixed number of the chosen and reprobate because of the universal will to save all in 1 Timothy 2: 4, which is interpreted as applying to all human beings, even if it is the case that not all human beings are saved.[114] When the argument for infants is presented, Hilary claims that they counter by referring to Augustine's earlier work, *De libero arbitrio,* where Augustine did not make a definitive judgment on the fate of unbaptized infants.[115]

According to Hilary, their arguments eventually come down to the usefulness of such a doctrine for the life of faith. Even those who do not voice their disapproval of Augustine's doctrine question the need for such an uncertain doctrine that troubles so many simple people. The catholic faith, they add, has been defended from heretics, including the Pelagians, without this doctrine.[116]

Hilary and his associates have done what they could to oppose these opponents, but in a way befitting their lay status, for their opponents "are of such rank that the laity must pay them the highest reverence in accord with the custom of the Church."[117] In light of their lay status, Hilary admonishes Augustine to respond to these men. Although Hilary leaves it up to Augustine's judgment on how to respond to them, Hilary suggests that an explanation of Augustine's views may do little in persuading their *infatigabiliter contentiosa corda,* unless *addatur auctoritas.*[118] In other words, Hilary is seeking

---

tinationem vel propositum ad id valere contendunt, ut eos praescierit vel pradestinaverit vel proposuerit eligere, qui fuerant credituri."

113. *Ep.* 226.4, 6 (CSEL 57: 473, 476; *Letter* 226, 98, 99).

114. *Ep.* 226.7 (CSEL 57: 476–77; *Letter* 226, 100).

115. *Ep.* 226.8 (CSEL 57: 477; *Letter* 226, 100). Aug., *De libero arbitrio* 3.23.66–68 (CCL 29: 314–15).

116. *Ep.* 226.8 (CSEL 57: 478; *Letter* 226, 100).

117. *Ep.* 226.9 (CSEL 57: 478; *Letter* 226, 101).

118. *Ep.* 226.9 (CSEL 57: 479; *Letter* 226, 101): "tuae sanctae prudentiae est dispicere, quid facto opus sit, ut talium et tantorum superetur vel temperetur intentio. Cui ego iam parum prodesse existimo te reddere rationem, nisi et addatur auctoritas, quam transgredi infatigabiliter contentiosa corda non possint."

an authoritative response, that is, a conciliar decree. It is this *auctoritas* these opponents cannot *transgredi.*

Hilary also requests that Augustine send a copy of his *Retractationes* when it is complete, in order to be able to know which books Augustine no longer approves.[119] In addition, Hilary sought a copy of *De gratia et libero arbitrio,* which he believes will be useful.[120] Hilary adds that he is not writing because he doubts Augustine's writings, but because he felt a duty, out of love for Christ and Augustine, to inform Augustine of the situation.[121]

Observations

It does not appear that Hilary and Prosper were well acquainted with each other at this point. Hilary was not aware that Prosper had already written a letter and received a response from Augustine—a relevant detail that would not have gone unnoted had they engaged in any significant discussion.[122] Hilary could have known about Prosper's previous contact with Augustine had he read Prosper's letter before attaching it to his own, which he did not. From whatever Hilary knew of Prosper, which appears secondhand, perhaps through Leontius, he was impressed by Prosper's zeal for Augustine. Hilary included Prosper's letter in order to convey the seriousness of the situation in Provence: that the resistance to Augustine's teachings on grace was adamant and pervasive, extending beyond his own social circle and contacts.

The differences in Hilary's and Prosper's account of the reactions to Augustine's views on grace can be best attributed to the fact that they moved in different circles and presented their individual views of the situation. Prosper spoke of two distinct groups that opposed Augustine's views in Marseilles, while Hilary presented one general

119. *Ep.* 226.10 (CSEL 57: 479; *Letter* 226, 101). The discrepancy between some of Augustine's earlier and present views were exploited by Hilary's opponents.

120. *Ep.* 226.10 (CSEL 57: 479; *Letter* 226, 101).

121. *Ep.* 226. 10 (CSEL 57: 480; *Letter* 226, 101).

122. *Ep.* 226.10 (CSEL 57: 480; *Letter* 226, 102): "He [Prosper] should be judged worthy of your knowledge." *Ep.* 225.1 (CSEL 57: 454–55; *Letter* 225, 87): "I [Prosper] am, if you recall, known to you by my thoughts and words. For I sent you a letter and received one back from you."

group that he witnessed or knew of in Marseilles and other places in Gaul. It does not appear that Prosper and Hilary were necessarily referring to the same group—Prosper's second group and Hilary's group—as previously thought.[123] Hilary specifically referred to an opposition consisting of high-ranking clerics, while Prosper included ascetics and those who attained the highest clerical rank.[124] Prosper had been exposed to at least one meritorious ascetic in Marseilles: Cassian.[125] Hilary's description of his group included their opponents' use of Augustine's earlier works to their advantage. Such an effective and problematic critique would hardly have gone unnoted by Prosper. Hilary also included the attack on the doctrine of perseverance, which was not detailed in Prosper's letter.

There were different groups and levels of opposition to Augustine in Marseilles and other places in Gaul. Prosper and Hilary moved in their own particular social circles, as reflected in their different perspectives on the reactions to Augustine's doctrine of grace. However, it is not the case that Prosper and Hilary moved in mutually exclusive circles, but that their circles overlapped, as did the social circles of their opponents. Thus, Prosper and Hilary observed some things in common.

Common to both observations was that *De correptione et gratia* provoked further negative reactions among *doctores Gallicani*, that they opposed Augustine's doctrine of predestination because it was novel, and that this doctrine undermined the role of preaching and free will. These *doctores* argued that human beings have the free choice to believe and thus to be saved. In the process of salvation, it is the movement of the human will that precedes grace, *initium fidei*. God predestines, but not in the way that Augustine asserts. God's predestination is based on the foreknowledge of future belief or unbelief.

123. Chéné ("Le semipélagianisme," 324–30) and Ogliari (*Gratia et Certamen*, esp. 99–102) identify Prosper's second group with Hilary's opponents.

124. Hilary, *Ep.* 226.9 (CSEL 57: 478; *Letter* 226, 101): "sunt ex parte tales personae, ut his consuetudine ecclesiastica laicos summam reverentiam necesse sit exhibere." Prosper, *Ep.* 225.7 (CSEL 57: 465; *Letter* 225, 92): "Quia multum nos et vitae meritis antecellunt et aliqui eorum adepto nuper summi sacerdotii honore supereminent."

125. *Ep. ad Rufinum* 3–4 (PL 51: 79–80; *Letter to Rufinus*, 23–24).

What Prosper and Hilary understood equally was their inability to combat the opponents any further. In addition, they both accepted the authority of Augustine and his doctrine without question. Both sought further clarification from Augustine, but Hilary, perhaps more aware of the challenges ahead, suggested conciliar action on the part of Augustine. The identification of Prosper as the overzealous defender of Augustine, at least here, seems more appropriately applied to Hilary.

How accurately Prosper and Hilary portrayed the situation is questionable. Were the opponents of Augustine's doctrine of grace so upset that they did not bother with a written response? Certainly, Prosper and Hilary exaggerated the threat and character of the opposition, but it is clear that Augustine's doctrine of predestination was opposed by some, but not at a level that warranted a written response from them, at least for now.

De correptione et gratia may have convinced the monks of Hadrumetum, but for the *doctores Gallicani* the work confirmed, in no uncertain terms, the objections to Augustine's teaching on grace they already held. This was a different context, Augustine's authority was not beyond question, Cyprian meant little to such men, and they were not simple-minded monks. Their responses, reflecting their intellectual and sophisticated background, posed serious challenges to Hilary and Prosper, which they were unable to meet on their own.

Carmen de ingratis

Prosper was certain that the opponents of Augustine's doctrine of predestination were in error, even if they presented questions and issues that he was unable to resolve. While awaiting the response from Augustine to their letters, Prosper wrote a polemical poem to counter the detractors of Augustine's doctrine of predestination, *De ingratis.*[126]

The poem consists of 1,002 lines, with an introduction, and re-

126. The critical edition of the text and facing translation in *Carmen de ingratis: A Translation with an Introduction and a Commentary.* Citations of the poem will indicate both the pages of the Latin text and the facing English translation.

iterates the contents of his letters to Rufinus and Augustine.[127] The only thing new in this poem is the tone. Prosper had described his opponents as closely related to the Pelagian heresy in his letter to Augustine, but now the identification with the heresy of Pelagianism is unequivocal:

> ... *novi partus oriuntur in ipso securae matris gremio, quae crescere natis visa sibi; discors horret consurgere germen, degeneres pavitans inimico ex semine foetus....*[128]

There appears to be a progression in Prosper's view of his opponents from being in error (*Epistula ad Rufinum,* 426), to closely resembling Pelagianism (*Epistula ad Augustinum,* 427), and now to being an offspring from the seed of Pelagianism. Prosper has come to the estimation that these men were heretics, and his harsh language in the poem reflects this newly found belief. The purpose was not to convince them of their errors, but to condemn them.

What caused this change in perception is unclear. It does not appear that it was caused by any changes in the position of the opponents of Augustine's doctrine of predestination—Prosper reiterates the same beliefs he described in his previous letters. Perhaps it was because Prosper came to a better understanding of his opponents, but if it was the case that he now viewed them as an offspring of Pelagianism, why did Prosper not wait for the authoritative response from Augustine? Whatever the reason may have been, Prosper is intentionally provoking an open conflict with those who have been up to this point content merely to discuss their opposition without resorting to writing. It is as though Prosper is seeking a response from these men in hopes that it would escalate to an open conflict. Prosper, it appears, wanted a controversy. Prosper wrote to Augustine describing his opponents in such a way that would compel the bishop to respond directly to the situation, and Prosper's *De ingratis* was a

127. For the outline and style of the poem, see Huegelmeyer, "Introduction," in *Carmen de Ingratis,* 12–40. The judgment that the poem reiterates the two previous letters is commonly shared; see Weaver, *Divine Grace,* 50; Ogliari, *Gratia et Certamen,* 91–92 n. 4; and Huegelmeyer, "Introduction," 11.

128. *Carmen de ingratis* 1.4 (ed. Huegelmeyer, 50–51). Cf. *Ep.* 225.4, 7 (CSEL 57: 460, 465; *Letter* 225, 90, 93).

direct attack against these “ungrateful” men, whom he accused of heresy—a charge that Prosper thought would provoke these men into direct literary action. Prosper had orchestrated this plan to open a new front in the battle against Pelagianism. All there was left was for the two parties to engage each other in, what was in Prosper’s mind, the struggle over the Church’s view on grace.

In addition to the *De ingratis,* Prosper wrote two short epigrams, the *Epigrammata.*[129] The incendiary treatment of the opponents of Augustine, and their link to Pelagius and Julian of Eclanum, suggests that these very short epigrams were written around the same time as the *De ingratis.*[130]

Augustine’s Reply to Prosper and Hilary

Prosper’s and Hilary’s request for a response could not have come at a more inopportune time in Augustine’s life. Augustine was engaged not only with the daily tasks of a bishop, but also in writing *De haeresibus* and *Contra secundam Iuliani responsionem imperfectum opus* and keeping up with his many correspondents.[131] Augustine was not a little annoyed by their request on a matter that he felt he had already sufficiently addressed in his past writings.[132] Such a request only added to Augustine’s frustration expressed in a newly discovered letter:

129. Prosper, *Epigramma in obtrectatorem Augustini* (PL 51: 149A–50A) and *Epigramma in eumdem aut alium quempiam Augustini obtrectatorem* (PL 51: 149C–152A). The two epigrams total twenty-six lines, fourteen and twelve, respectively. Cf. D. Lassandro, “Note sugli epigrammi de Prospero d’Aquitania,” *Vetera Christianorum* 8 (1971): 211–22.

130. *Epigramma in obtrectatorem Augustini* (PL 51: 150A): “Si pastorem ovium laedere vis, lupus es.” *Epigramma in eudem* (PL 51: 149C–151A): “Contra Augustinum narratur serpere quidam Scriptor. . . . Aut hunc fruge sua aequorei pavere Britanni [Pelagius], Aut hunc Campano [Julian] gramine corda tument. Quae concepta fovet promat, quae parturit edat.”

131. Aug., *De haeresibus* (CCL 46: 286–345; *Heresies,* in *Arianism and Other Heresies,* trans. Roland Teske, WSA I/18 [Hyde Park, N.Y.: New City Press, 1995], 30–77). *Contra secundam Iuliani responsionem imperfectum opus* (CSEL 85/1, books 1–3; PL 45: 1337–1608, books 4–6; *Unfinished Work in Answer to Julian,* in *Answer to the Pelagians,* vol. 3, trans. Roland Teske, WSA I/25 [Hyde Park, N.Y.: New City Press, 1999]).

132. *De praedestinatione sanctorum* 1.2 (PL 44: 961; *The Predestination of the Saints,* in *Answer to the Pelagians,* vol. 4, 149): “I am pleased so much that I cannot express it

But I find it annoying that the things that people from one side or another unexpectedly call upon us to dictate interfere with the projects that we have under way and that neither cease nor can be put off.[133]

Nonetheless, Augustine yielded to their requests with a treatise divided into two books, *De praedestinatione sanctorum* and *De dono perseverantiae.*[134]

Augustine was more than conscious of the threat of heresy, especially Pelagianism. Augustine was preoccupied with Julian and with writing a book about heresy at the time. However, in Augustine's estimation, these men, whom Prosper and Hilary referred to as opponents, were "brothers." And they were not Pelagian because they affirmed what was essentially anti-Pelagian:

These brothers of ours over whom your pious love is concerned have, however, come to believe with the Church of Christ that the human race is born subject to the sin of the first man and that no one is set free from this evil except by the righteousness of the second man. They also come to admit that the wills of human beings are anticipated by the grace of God and agree that no one is by himself sufficient for either the beginning or carrying out any good work. The retention of these convictions to which they have come, therefore, separates them very much from the error of the Pelagians.[135]

It was the last three truths—that no one is set free from this evil except by the righteousness of the second man; that the wills of human beings are anticipated by the grace of God; and that no one is by himself sufficient for either the beginning or carrying out any good work—that are problematic because, although these brothers had expressed these statements, they interpreted the statements contrary to Augustine's.

---

that you desire that I write still more on this topic after so many books or letters of mine on this subject. And yet I do not dare to say that I am pleased as much as I ought to be. Hence, see, I write to you again, though I am not now dealing with you, I am still dealing through you with an issue with which I believed I had sufficiently dealt with."

133. *Ep.* 23A* .4 (CSEL 88: 168–69; *Letter* 23A*, in Letters 211–70, 1*–29*, vol. 4, 322). Quotation in Brown, *Augustine of Hippo,* 468.

134. *De praed. sanct.* (PL 44: 959–92; *Predestination,* 149–87); *Perseverantiae* (PL 45: 993–1034; *Perseverance,* 191–240).

135. *De praed. sanct.* 1.2 (PL 44: 961; *Predestination,* 149–50).

The statement "that no one is set free from this evil except by the righteousness of the second man" is a rephrasing from Prosper's "no one can be saved by his own works, but only rebirth through the grace of God. All human beings without exception have, nonetheless, been offered the reconciliation which is present in the mystery of the blood of Christ."[136] According to Prosper, although they profess that one cannot be set free except through grace, they hold that this freedom is offered to all, so that "whoever chooses to come to the faith and to baptism can be saved."[137]

The second statement, "They also come to admit that the wills of human beings are anticipated by the grace of God," is drawn from Prosper's letter, but Prosper immediately added that these opponents of Augustine interpreted this grace of God to pertain to the grace of creation. This *initialis gratia,* which establishes free choice and rationality in human nature, anticipates the human will.[138]

The third statement, "that no one is by himself sufficient for either the beginning or carrying out any good work," is drawn from Hilary's letter, but Hilary pointed out that they interpreted good works to be the result of the gift of the Holy Spirit by which one can do good works.[139] However, the gift of the Holy Spirit, and thus good works, is given to those who will to believe, which is entirely a human will.

Augustine certainly knew the "brothers" interpreted these statements in a conflicting manner. The question of why Augustine presented them as "brothers" and positively endorsed their anti-Pelagian statements on grace, even though Augustine knew they did not share his interpretations of these statements, has led one recent scholar to suggest that the situation had changed in and around Marseilles. According to Ogliari, the problem with attributing these statements to these brothers can be resolved if these brothers had actually changed their minds on these statements, interpreting them as Augustine did, at some point between the time Prosper and Hi-

136. *Ep.* 225.3 (CSEL 57: 457; *Letter* 225, 88).
137. *Ep.* 225.3 (CSEL 57: 457; *Letter* 225, 88–89).
138. *Ep.* 225.4 (CSEL 57: 460; *Letter* 225, 90).
139. *Ep.* 226.3 (CSEL 57: 472; *Letter* 226, 97).

lary had written to Augustine (*Epp.* 225 and 226) and Augustine's response.[140] This was not the case. Augustine attacked their incorrect interpretations of the correct statements as expressed in the letters of Hilary and Prosper, and, in fact, these brothers will remain remarkably consistent in their views on grace and their opposition to Augustine's doctrine of predestination.

The problem can be best resolved in the context of Augustine's conviction about Christian progress. Augustine's reaction to the situation of these brothers across the sea reflects Augustine's view that Christian understanding is a journey, a progress toward a greater understanding of Christian truth. The *Confessiones* detail Augustine's own spiritual journey, and the *Retractationes* were written in chronological order for the reader to witness the progress and evolution of his understanding of Christian truth.[141] The error of these brothers stemmed from their not having read Augustine's books carefully enough to have progressed along with him in the understanding of predestination, or not having read his books to begin with.[142] Augustine acknowledges that these brothers have progressed in the truth, but not enough. They have "come" *(pervenerunt)* to the most basic truths of Original Sin and Christ's redemption. They also *per-*

140. Ogliari (*Gratia et Certamen,* 154 n. 296), against the weight of scholarly opinion, believes that the "lengthy letters" which Augustine referred to in *De praed. sanct.* 3.7 (PL 44: 964; *Predestination,* 153: "I had already completed two books of that work before I had received your more lengthy letters.") indicate additional letters from Hilary and Prosper to Augustine after *Epp.* 225 and 226. Ogliari argues that the different structure of Augustine's response in comparison to *Epp.* 225 and 226 reflects the new description of the situation presented by the "lengthy letters." In addition, Ogliari argues, "In our view this could also explain why Augustine praises some of the affirmations of the Massilians concerning the human will and its relationship to prevenient grace, whereas in the context of the *Epp.* 225 and 226 such affirmations actually have a meaning contrary to Augustine's teaching" (*Gratia et Certamen,* 154 n. 296). However, Augustine's response, in fact, follows the general structure and concerns of Hilary, primarily, and Prosper's to a limited degree. Furthermore, both Hilary (*Ep.* 226.9) and Prosper (*Ep.* 225.1) referred to previous letters in *Epp.* 225 and 226. Thus, the "lengthy letters" to which Augustine referred can be none other than *Epp.* 225 and 226.

141. Brown (*Augustine of Hippo,* 433): "[regarding the *Retractationes*] Augustine wanted to see his works as a whole, that might be read, in future, by men who had reached the same certainty as himself, by mature Catholic Christians. Such men must appreciate the long journey which Augustine had taken to reach his present views. This is why, instead of being arranged by subjects, the books are deliberately criticized in chronological order."

142. *De praed. sanct.* 4.8 (PL 44: 965–66; *Predestination,* 154–55).

venerunt to the truth of prevenient grace—that grace anticipates the wills of human beings. In addition, they *pervenerunt* to realize that a person alone is not sufficient to begin or carry out any good work. According to Augustine, these truths to which they *pervenerunt* "separate them very much from the error of the Pelagians."[143] Augustine was aware of the brothers' nuances of these statements, but nonetheless the brothers have come to the right convictions. Now what is needed is for them to come to the right understanding of these convictions through prayer: "If they continue in these convictions and pray to him who gives understanding, God will also reveal this to them, if on some point their thoughts differ concerning predestination."[144] Augustine, however, will help these brothers come to a correct understanding of these convictions. Augustine's goal is to make them aware that their nuances are Pelagian so that they will correct themselves and be able to progress to the truth of predestination and perseverance. It was a strategy of teaching, not condemning outright, that appealed to their intellectual and spiritual capacity to grow in knowledge and truth.

De praedestinatione sanctorum

Augustine begins by establishing the correct understanding of the conviction about prevenient grace. This is fundamental, for from the correct understanding of prevenient grace comes the correct understanding of predestination and perseverance. These brothers hold that the beginning of faith comes from human beings and is not a gift of God, but that the increase in faith is a gift from God.[145] It is this fundamental error that prevents them from the correct understanding of predestination and perseverance. This first book addresses this error.

The beginning of faith is a gift of God, which is a truth drawn from Scripture.[146] Augustine acknowledges that he had been in error earlier in his life concerning this understanding, but had come to the truth. Against the view that human nature possesses free choice

143. *De praed. sanct.* 1.2 (PL 44: 961; *Predestination,* 149–50).
144. *De praed. sanct.* 1.2 (PL 44: 961; *Predestination,* 150).
145. *De praed. sanct.* 2.3, 21.43 (PL 44: 961, 992; *Predestination,* 150, 185).
146. *De praed. sanct.* 2.3–6 (PL 44: 961–64; *Predestination,* 150–52).

from an initial grace or the grace of creation, Augustine makes a distinction between the possibility of having faith, which is part of human nature, and actually having faith, which is not a part of human nature but belongs to grace.[147] God's mercy prepares the will for faith; the will that is not prepared for faith is due to God's judgment; and human works have no place in God's mercy.[148] As to why God does not teach everyone so that they come to faith, Augustine makes the claim that God, "in a certain way," teaches everyone because God teaches everyone who comes to Christ, but then concedes Romans 9: 22–23.[149] The reason why some believe when they hear the gospel preached and others do not is that those who have been given the gift of faith hear God externally and internally, while those who have not been given the gift of faith hear the gospel only externally. For why some are given this gift and others not, Augustine claims Romans 9: 20 and 11: 33.[150]

Having established that faith is a gift of God, Augustine addresses foreknowledge and predestination. Augustine first clarifies a statement he made in *Epistula* 101 on foreknowledge, which he does not consider erroneous, but rather imprecise.[151] Predestination is the preparation for grace, and grace is predestination's actual bestowal.[152] "Predestination cannot exist without foreknowledge, but foreknowledge can exist without predestination."[153] Thus, predestination is only for the good (salvation), and not for damnation. It is strictly a single predestination.

As for the argument that salvation is based on God's foreknowledge of future merits, Augustine cites the example of the gratuitous

147. *De praed. sanct.* 5.9–11 (PL 44: 967–69; *Predestination,* 156–58). Cf. *Ep.* 225.4 (CSEL 57: 461; *Letter* 225, 90–91).

148. *De praed. sanct.* 6.11–8.14 (PL 44: 968–71; *Predestination,* 158–60).

149. *De praed. sanct.* 8.14 (PL 44: 971; *Predestination,* 161). Augustine's restricted sense of "everyone" to mean everyone who comes to God is consistent with his interpretation of "all" in 1 Tim. 2: 4, which he also cites in this passage.

150. *De praed. sanct.* 8.15 (PL 44: 972; *Predestination,* 162).

151. *De praed. sanct.* 9.17–18 (PL 44: 973–74; *Predestination,* 163–64). Cf. Aug. *Ep.* 102.2.14 (CSEL 34: 556; *Letter* 102, 27).

152. *De praed. sanct.* 10.19 (PL 44: 974; *Predestination,* 165): "Quod praedestinatio est gratiae praeparatio, gratia vero iam ipsa donatio."

153. *De praed. sanct.* 8.17–18 (PL 44: 975; *Predestination,* 165): "Quae sine praescientia [praedestinatio] non potest esse: potest autem esse sine praedestinatione praescientia."

predestination of infants and of Christ. In the case of infants, because of Original Sin, all are evil, and when these infants die, they "either pass by the merit of rebirth [baptism] from evil to good or pass by the merit of their origin from evil to evil."[154] Augustine claims that this view is catholic and that even some heretics agree with it, which is why, to his "wonder and amazement," such talented men as these brothers believe that judgment of these infants is based on the merits they would have had if they lived longer in the body—foreknowledge of future merits. Such an idea deserves contempt.[155] Furthermore, the belief that infants who die have been granted or denied baptism is based on God's foreknowledge of how they would live their lives denies Original Sin. In such a scenario, infants who are not baptized are punished, not because of Original Sin, but because of the penance they would not have done had they had lived longer. Such a view of foreknowledge denies Original Sin, which, Augustine points out, is Pelagian.[156]

Augustine cites the authority of Cyprian in support of his views, whom he qualifies as "highly praised by many and nearly all who are fond of ecclesiastical writing."[157] Augustine also cites Wisdom 4: 11, "He was carried off so that evil would not change his mind," which he interprets as referring to the evil in this life, and not pertaining to God's foreknowledge of what was in the future.[158] Against the claim that the Book of Wisdom is not canonical, Augustine asserts that this book has been read in the Church with veneration and regarded as authoritative by all Christians.[159] Augustine reminds them that even the Pelagians do not dare to question the canonicity of the book, and that he could not even "dream" that anyone would assert that the dead are judged on the basis of future actions had they lived.[160]

The truth of predestination and the error of these brothers' view of foreknowledge are illustrated in the example of the predestination of

154. *De praed. sanct.* 12.24 (PL 44: 978; *Predestination,* 169).

155. *De praed. sanct.* 12.24 (PL 44: 978; *Predestination,* 169).

156. *De praed. sanct.* 13.25 (PL 44: 978–79; *Predestination,* 169–70).

157. *De praed. sanct.* 14.26 (PL 44: 979; *Predestination,* 170).

158. *De praed. sanct.* 14.26 (PL 44: 979–80; *Predestination,* 170–71).

159. *De praed. sanct.* 14.27–28 (PL 44: 980–81; *Predestination,* 171–72). Cf. *Ep.* 226.4 (CSEL 57: 473; *Letter* 226, 98).

160. *De praed. sanct.* 14.29 (PL 44: 981; *Predestination,* 173).

Jesus Christ. Augustine asks rhetorically how it could be that Christ's human nature merited to be the Word, coeternal with the Father into the unity of his person, and to be the only begotten Son of God.[161] Jesus was predestined so that he was going to be the son of David according to the flesh and the Son of God in power.[162] Just as preceding merits were not the cause of Christ's birth, preceding merits, then, cannot be the cause for the rebirths of his members. Christ's birth of the Spirit and the Virgin was not a recompense, but simply given. In the same way rebirth through the Spirit and water is a gift and not a recompense for some merit. Since faith brings one to rebirth, but since one does not bring anything to merit this rebirth, faith is predestined. God makes one believe in Christ, producing in human beings the beginning of faith and its perfection in Jesus (Heb. 12: 2).[163]

Thus, God calls the predestined children in order to make them members of God's predestined only Son. This is a *certa vocatio* distinct from the general calling of God that can be refused (Luke 14: 16–20). The *certa vocatio* is for those called according to God's plan "whom he foreknew and predestined to be conformed to the image of his Son" (Rom. 8: 28–29), which is a calling "not on the basis of works, but because of the one who calls" (Rom. 9: 12–13). Whoever belongs among those called will absolutely not perish.[164] The apostles bear witness to this calling, as does the Letter to the Ephesians.[165]

Ephesians condemns the Pelagian view that predestination is based on the foreknowledge that they would be holy and spotless through the choice of free will.[166] Although these brothers may share this belief that Ephesians condemns the Pelagian view, their view that God foreknew only the faith by which one begins to believe and on that basis is chosen and predestined is also in error. God's calling precedes faith, for God chooses not because one has believed, but in order that one might believe.[167]

161. *De praed. sanct.* 15.30 (PL 44: 981–82; *Predestination,* 173).
162. *De praed. sanct.* 15.31 (PL 44: 982; *Predestination,* 174).
163. *De praed. sanct.* 15.31 (PL 44: 983; *Predestination,* 175).
164. *De praed. sanct.* 16.32–33 (PL 44: 983–85; *Predestination,* 175–77).
165. *De praed. sanct.* 17.34–18.35 (PL 44: 985–87; *Predestination,* 177–79).
166. *De praed. sanct.* 18.36 (PL 44: 987; *Predestination,* 179).
167. *De praed. sanct.* 19.38 (PL 44: 988; *Predestination,* 181).

Augustine ends the book with further proofs that the beginning of faith is a gift of God by citing numerous scriptural passages (Eph. 1: 13–15; Gal. 6: 7; 1 Thess. 2: 13; Col. 4: 2–4; 1 Cor. 16: 8–9; Jn. 6: 66; Mt. 13: 11; 2 Cor. 2: 12–16; Acts 16: 14), and concludes that the idea that the beginning of faith belongs to human initiative is absurd.[168]

De dono perseverantiae

Having established the beginning of faith as a gift of God, Augustine turns his attention to establishing perseverance as a gift of God. Perseverance is defined as the gift by which one perseveres up to the end of one's life. Therefore, it is uncertain whether anyone had been given this gift as long as they are still living. It is only at the moment of death that it can be known if one has been given this gift: if one dies a believer, the gift of perseverance was given; if one dies an unbeliever, however long or short one may have believed, but fell away before death, the gift was not given.[169]

Augustine begins with the proof of the gift of perseverance from the Lord's Prayer as explained by Cyprian, in his book *De dominica oratione*.[170] The brothers who state that they "do not want this perseverance to be preached in the sense that it can neither be merited nor lost by rebellion" do not pay enough attention to what they are saying.[171] The gift of perseverance can be merited by prayer, for God has granted the gift of perseverance when one asks for it, but once given it cannot be lost by rebellion.[172] It is the work of God, the predestination of the saints, which causes believers to remain in Christ and not depart from God.[173]

As for why this grace is not given according to human merits or why it is not given to all, Augustine responds that since all deserve

168. *De praed. sanct.* 19.39–41 (PL 44: 989–90; *Predestination*, 182–83).

169. *De don. pers.* 1.1 (PL 45: 993–94; *Perseverance*, 191).

170. *De don. pers.* 1.3–5.9 (PL 45: 996–99; *Perseverance*, 192–96, 198). Cf. Cyprian, *De dominica oratione* 12, 16, 17, 18, 22, 26 (CCL 3A: 96, 99–101, 104, 106–7).

171. *De don. pers.* 6.10 (PL 45: 999; *Perseverance*, 196). Cf. *Ep.* 226.4 (CSEL 57: 473; *Letter* 226, 98).

172. *De don. pers.* 6.10 (PL 45: 999; *Perseverance*, 197): "Hoc ergo Dei donum suppliciter emereri potest: sed cum datum fuerit, amitti contumaciter non potest."

173. *De don. pers.* 7.14–15 (PL 45: 1001–2; *Perseverance*, 199).

to be condemned in Adam, one should acknowledge God's mercy in setting so many free, and God's justice in punishing those who deserve judgment. Why some have good faith but have not been given the gift of perseverance up to the end is because God deemed that they should mingle among those who have been given the gift so that those who have been given the gift may not be proud and confident, but fearful and humble.[174] The temptations and snares of this world confuse the mind and spirit such that it is not in the power of human beings to attain to the good and persevere up to the end, "for our hearts and our thoughts are not in our power," but in the power of God.[175] Those who do not persevere to the end were not called according to the plan (Rom. 8: 28); they were not chosen in Christ before the creation of the world (Eph. 1: 4); and they were not predestined according to the plan (Eph. 1: 11).[176] Yet this judgment of God is just, although inscrutable.[177] To claim that God punishes the future sins of a dead person, which God foreknew would take place had a person lived, is absurd and shameful.[178] God predestines those who will be saved and punishes those who have not been predestined without regard to future merits.[179]

However, Augustine acknowledges that he had hesitated in pronouncing punishment of little ones in his earlier work *De libero arbitrio,* which these brothers have cited against him.[180] Augustine explains that he commented on this issue in his *Retractationes,* where he stated that he could not resolve it or was unable to fully address it at the time, but had since come to a definite conclusion.[181] Those infants who were baptized before their deaths enter salvation, while

174. *De don. pers.* 8.19 (PL 45: 1003; *Perseverance,* 201).

175. *De don. pers.* 8.19–20 (PL 45: 1003–4; *Perseverance,* 201–2). Augustine quoting Ambrose, *De fuga saeculi* 1.1 (CSEL 32/2: 163).

176. *De don. pers.* 9.21 (PL 45: 1004–5; *Perseverance,* 203).

177. *De don. pers.* 11.25 (PL 45: 1007; *Perseverance,* 206).

178. *De don. pers.* 9.22, 10.24 (PL 45: 1005, 1006–7; *Perseverance,* 203, 205).

179. *De don. pers.* 11.25 (PL 45: 1007; *Perseverance,* 206).

180. *De don. pers.* 11.26 (PL 45: 1008 ; *Perseverance,* 207). Cf. *Ep.* 226.8 (CSEL 57: 477; *Letter* 226, 100); *De libero arbitrio* 3.23.66–68 (CCL 29: 314–15; *The Problem of Free Choice,* 208–10).

181. *De don. pers.* 11.27 (PL 45: 1008; *Perseverance,* 207). Cf. *Retractationes* 1.9.2 (CCL 57:23; *Retractations,* 42).

those not baptized enter into eternal death.[182] Furthermore, baptism of these infants depends on the will of God, not the will of their parents or future merits of these infants had they lived longer. Infants die without baptism because God does not will the baptism to take place.[183] Infants who have been baptized and who live into adulthood are not assured of eternal life. Some of these will persevere to the end, and others will fall before they die, in which case they will enter eternal punishment. Only those who have been given perseverance will, even if they fall at a point in life, return to God before they die.[184] The grace of God, then, for the beginning of faith and persevering up to the end is not given according to merits, but given according to the most hidden, most just, most wise, and most beneficent will of God.[185]

Contrary to the claims that predestination is an obstacle to the usefulness of preaching, Augustine argues that preaching and predestination are both found in Scripture, and are thus not contradictory.[186] Nor should the preaching of predestination impede the preaching of perseverance and its exhortations to obedience. That is, one must, as Cyprian did, continue to preach the gospel and exhort people to faith, pious conduct, and perseverance up to the end, even though perseverance is a gift.[187]

Augustine next addresses an objection raised by these brothers, which occasions his lengthiest response. Their objection is this:

> No one can be roused by the stings of rebuke if it is said in the assembly of the church in the hearing of many: The definitive judgment of the will of God regarding predestination is such that some of you came to the faith from unbelief after receiving the will to obey or that you remain in the faith

182. *De don. pers.* 12.30 (PL 45: 1010–11; *Perseverance,* 210).

183. *De don. pers.* 12.31 (PL 45: 1011–12; *Perseverance,* 211): "What shall I say when a little one at times expires before it can be helped by the ministry of someone baptizing it? For often, though the parents are making haste and the ministers are ready to give baptism to the little one, baptism is, nonetheless, not given because God does not will it who did not keep the little one in this life a little longer in order that it might be given."

184. *De don. pers.* 13.32 (PL 45: 1012; *Perseverance,* 211–12).

185. *De don. pers.* 13.33 (PL 45: 1012; *Perseverance,* 212).

186. *De don. pers.* 14.34 (PL 45: 1013–14; *Perseverance,* 213).

187. *De don. pers.* 14.36–37 (PL 45: 1015–16; *Perseverance,* 215). Cf. Cyprian, *Ad Quirinum (testimoniorum libri tres)* 3.4 (CSEL 3/1: 116).

after receiving perseverance, but the rest of you who dally in the delight of sins have not yet risen up because the help of merciful grace has not yet raised you up. If any of you have, nonetheless, not yet been called, but he has predestined you by his grace to be chosen, you will receive the same grace by which you are going to will this and be chosen. And if any of you are now obedient, but are predestined to be rejected, the power to obey will be withdrawn, and you will stop obeying.[188]

Augustine understands their objection to be primarily about the difficulty of the doctrine to "many," which should be passed over in silence. Augustine counters that this should not keep one from being silent and prevent one from proclaiming the truth of predestination and perseverance.[189] Perseverance is a gift, and just as wisdom is a gift and is exhorted, so perseverance is to be exhorted.[190] Furthermore, since predestination is not only found in Scripture, but has also been taught by Cyprian and Ambrose, this doctrine must be preached.[191] Augustine points out that he had taught this doctrine even before his dealings with Pelagius, and his recent book *De correptione et gratia* contains nothing new.[192]

However, he conceded that these truths should not be preached to the slow or uneducated. It would be more appropriate, in preaching to the general believers of the church, to simply state, "The definite decision of the will of God comes to this: Having received the will to obey, you have come from unbelief to the faith, and having received perseverance, you continue in the faith."[193] In addition, the preacher to the people should add words of hope and encouragement, emphasizing the positive side of predestination.[194] Those who are slow of

188. *De don. pers.* 15.38 (PL 45: 1016; *Perseverance,* 216–17). Quoted from *Ep.* 226.5 (CSEL 57: 474; *Letter* 226, 98); however, Augustine does not quote Hilary's description of the objections verbatim. It is a paraphrase, but Augustine added "in the assembly of the church in the hearing of many."

189. *De don. pers.* 15.38–16.41 (PL 45: 1017–18; *Perseverance,* 217–19).

190. *De don. pers.* 16.41–44 (PL 45: 1018–21; *Perseverance,* 219–22).

191. *De don. pers.* 19.47–20.51 (PL 45: 1022–25; *Perseverance,* 223–27). Cf. Cyprian, *Ad Quirinum (testimoniorum libri tres)* 3.4 (CSEL 3/1: 116); Ambrose, *De fuga saeculi* 1.1–2 (CSEL 32/2: 163).

192. *De don. pers.* 20.52–21.55 (PL 45: 1025–28; *Perseverance,* 227–30).

193. *De don. pers.* 22.57–58 (PL 45: 1028–29; *Perseverance,* 230–31).

194. *De don. pers.* 22.62 (PL 45: 1030–31; *Perseverance,* 233). Augustine knew his

heart and weak, who cannot understand the Scriptures and their explanations, should pay attention to the prayers of the Church, which is a gift of God, by which she was born, grew, and increased.[195]

Augustine admonishes Hilary and Prosper to join with him in praying for their enemies, but especially these brothers, that they may understand and confess that grace is gratuitous and not given according to preceding merits.[196] Augustine concludes this treatise by citing the example of the predestination of Christ briefly, before he requests prayer and careful reading of his words so that those who do not understand him may come to it by further reading and God's interior instruction to them. He ends by humbly acknowledging that future teachers of the Church may deign to correct his writings.[197]

Observations

Although written in response to specific concerns raised by the letters of Hilary and Prosper, Augustine's treatise is his most comprehensive and cogent expression of his doctrine of predestination and perseverance. Augustine's response was not exactly what Hilary and Prosper had in mind. Augustine did not regard their opponents as Pelagian, much less see the need for conciliar action. They were not completely innocent, however. These brothers were not Pelagian, but some of their views were similar to those of the Pelagians. Yet Augustine took care to address the brothers in a tone and manner that reflected his appreciation of their context.

Augustine recognized the limits of his authority across the sea among the sophisticated and highly placed brothers of Provence.

---

teaching was difficult to grasp and was better left for those who were spiritually mature. Mathisen concluded that the Gauls considered Augustine's teaching on predestination to be a topic for experts ("For Specialists Only: The Reception of Augustine and His Teachings in Fifth-Century Gaul," in *Presbyter Factus Sum,* Collectanea Augustiniana 2 [New York: Peter Lang, 1993], 35). As evidenced here it was these "experts" that Augustine had in mind when he wrote the treatise. That these experts considered Augustine's teachings "for specialists only" was exactly Augustine's intent.

195. *De don. pers.* 23.63–64 (PL 45: 1031–32; *Perseverance,* 233–35). Augustine was again referring to the liturgical "Prayers of the Faithful"; see above n. 23. This particular liturgical practice will become the defining element in Prosper's final understanding of grace; see chapter 6.

196. *De don. pers.* 24.66 (PL 45: 1033; *Perseverance,* 236).

197. *De don. pers.* 24.68 (PL 45: 1034; *Perseverance,* 237).

These were not simple African monks. Augustine appealed to the universal authority of Scripture, the Church, and the Fathers. Realizing that Cyprian's special status among Africans was not paralleled in Gaul, Augustine took care to qualify Cyprian as "highly praised by many and nearly all who are fond of ecclesiastical writing."[198] Augustine also added Ambrose, a Father whose figure and authority these brothers could fully appreciate. Augustine also appealed to the fact that the Church prayed in accordance with Augustine's doctrine of predestination, but most of all, it was an appeal to Scripture.

Augustine acknowledged that he had been in error in his past and had shared the views of these brothers, but had since progressed to this truth claiming, "I worked hard in defense of the free choice of the human will, but the grace of God conquered."[199] And this was Augustine's hope for these brothers. Nearing the end of his life, exhausted and overburdened with work, he had written as persuasively as he could to correct these brothers, but knew it would be the grace of God that would have to conquer them as it did him. For those who understand him, Augustine exhorts, "let them thank God, and those who do not understand pray that God may be their interior teacher, from whom come knowledge and understanding."[200]

Augustine envisioned that his views on grace would continue to be questioned and even objected to and—in a moment of profound introspection, acknowledging the mystery of God's grace—was open to the possibility of being in error and in need of correction. Augustine knew his limitations. He did not have exclusive insight into the mystery of grace, and could imagine future teachers of the Church correcting his statements, if they should deem his works relevant.[201] The Church would correct his statements, but it was done at the hands of Prosper, something Augustine probably never envisioned.

198. *De praed. sanct.* 14.26 (PL 44: 979; *Predestination,* 170).

199. *De praed. sanct.* 4.8 (PL 44: 966; *Predestination,* 155): "Laboratum est quidem pro libro arbitrio voluntatis humanae; sed vicit Dei gratia."

200. *De don. pers.* 24.68 (PL 45: 1034; *Perseverance,* 237).

201. *De don. pers.* 24.68 (PL 45: 1034; *Perseverance,* 237): "Qui vero errare me existimant, etiam atque etiam diligenter quae sunt dicta considerent, ne fortassis ipsi errent. Ego autem cum per eos qui meos labores legunt, non solum doctior, verum etiam emendatior fio, propitium mihi Deum agnosco: et hoc per Ecclesiae doctores maxime exspecto; si et in ipsorum manus venit, dignanturque nosse quod scribo."

~5

Servus Dei II (430–440)

Augustine and the Roman Church

ALTHOUGH AUGUSTINE responded to Prosper's and Hilary's doctrinal questions with *De praedestinatione sanctorum* and *De dono perseverantiae,* these works were not exactly what they had in mind. Augustine did not regard the opponents of Hilary and Prosper as Pelagian, much less see the need for conciliar action. Augustine referred to Hilary's and Prosper's opponents as brothers in the faith who had yet to progress to the truth of predestination. They needed correction, which Augustine provided, and prayer, which Augustine admonished Hilary and Prosper to make for these brothers. Not only did Augustine disagree with Hilary and Prosper about the dangers posed by such men, but he also implied that their prayers, in addition to his treatise, were sufficient for the situation. The treatise was a spectacular failure. The work did not persuade the brothers in the least; rather, it inspired even further and more serious disagreements.

In the wake of Augustine's death in 430, Prosper was left with the daunting task of defending Augustine's doctrine of predestination against these brothers, but also against others beyond Marseilles. In the course of this period, 430–440, the debate became even more polemical, with each side caricaturing the views of the other, as well as branding one another with the charge of heresy.

In his last two works of this period, Prosper took his initial, but dramatic, steps away from Augustine's teachings, before spending the next five years reflecting on and reevaluating his understanding of catholicity and Augustine's teachings. After these five years of literary inactivity, Prosper emerged still maintaining his fidelity to the Church, but increasingly looked to Rome as its center of authority. Prosper reevaluated his understanding of Augustine's authority and teaching on grace in light of this emerging recognition of the authority of the Roman Church and its teachings.

Pro Augustino responsiones ad exerpta Genuensium

Augustine's involvement in the controversy ended with the *De praedestinatione sanctorum* and *De dono perseverantiae.* He may very well have resolved that the issue was not so important as to warrant further involvement—and there were other more pressing concerns, as well as his failing health. Whatever the case, Augustine died shortly afterward. After the death of Augustine, two priests, Camillus and Theodore, wrote to Prosper seeking clarification on some passages from Augustine's *De praedestinatione sanctorum* and *De dono perseverantiae.* Prosper responded to their request with *Pro Augustino responsiones ad exerpta Genuensium.*[1]

Apparently, by this time, Prosper had come to be regarded as the leader of the Augustinian faction in Marseilles. Why these priests appealed to Prosper and not Hilary or Leontius is uncertain. Leontius and especially Hilary were much more intimately connected with Augustine than Prosper. Perhaps Prosper's *Epistula ad Rufinum* and *De ingratis* or his vocal support of Augustine in Marseilles drew more attention to him than to his associates. In his response, Prosper was quick to point out that he would reflect the collective views of the Augustinian faction in Marseilles, presumably Hilary's and Leontius's.[2] Their request is also the first indication of the resistance

1. *Pro Augustino responsiones ad exerpta Genuensium* (PL 51: 187–202; *Answers to the Extracts of the Genoese,* 49–69).

2. *Resp. ad Gen.,* Praef. (PL 51: 188; *Answers to Genoese,* 49): "I shall briefly expound

to Augustine's doctrine of predestination beyond the monastic milieu and geography of Provence.

Prosper responded with little tact and much condescension. It was an unwarranted and unprovoked attack—these priests had the courtesy to ask for clarification rather than simply draw their own conclusions. They were not attacking Augustine's doctrine per se, but Prosper took their curiosity as nothing less than an attack on a person who was so clearly catholic in Prosper's estimation. Prosper's response was obnoxious, even by Prosper's standards. Although Prosper acknowledges their higher status as priests when he rhetorically asks, "You wish to know how I understand them [passages of *De praedestinatione sanctorum* and *De dono perseverantiae*] and what I think of them—as though I had more light to grasp the meaning of those texts than you!" Prosper immediately added that they should have studied Augustine's works themselves, and if they had difficulty they should have appealed to God who gives "the Spirit of wisdom and understanding." Nonetheless, Prosper will condescend to their request, "with the help of the Lord, who gives wisdom to little ones (Ps. 18:8)."[3] It is unclear, and perhaps intentionally ambiguous, to whom the "little ones" referred to, but the condescending tone of the letter suggests Prosper had the priests in mind.

The priests requested a response to ten passages excerpted from Augustine's recent works, seven from *De praedestinatione sanctorum* and three from *De dono perseverantiae.* Prosper answered these excerpts by faithfully reiterating the arguments made in *De praedestinatione sanctorum* and *De dono perseverantiae.*

The first three excerpts are related to Augustine's correction of his previously held views in which he had asserted that God chose to save those whom God foreknew would believe; that faith is not a gift of God; and the insufficient manner in which he explained the distinction between those called according to God's decree and those simply called, but not elected.[4] Prosper answered that Augustine's

what I think of these passages in agreement with those our brethren here outstanding in virtue and learning."

3. *Resp. ad Gen.*, Praef. (PL 51: 187–88; *Answers to Genoese*, 49).

4. *Resp. ad Gen.* 1–3 (PL 51: 187–89; *Answers to Genoese*, 49–50). Cf. *De praed. sanct.*

earlier statements were made before he became a bishop, but that he had since perfected his learning by constant and steady progress through long years of study.[5] According to Prosper, these priests, despite studying Augustine's teachings, have not progressed with Augustine in the truth.[6] Moreover, by maintaining what Augustine had earlier believed, which favored the Pelagian view, the priests were, by implication, Pelagian.

Excerpts four to six and eight are related to the issue of God's gift of faith to some and not to others. Prosper answers that God prepares in the elect the will to believe, which is based on God's mercy, and God's justice is the reason why God does not prepare the will to believe in others.[7] Faith's beginning and perfection are gifts of God, which, consistent with Scripture, are given to some and not to others. To deny the former is to hold the Pelagian position, to deny the latter is to contradict Scripture.[8] The reason why faith is not given to all should not disturb the faithful since it is perfectly just for God to punish everyone because of Adam's sin. It is a great grace of God that so many are saved. As for the reason why some are saved but not others, it is best to acknowledge the mystery of God's incomprehensible judgments and unfathomable ways (Rom. 11:33). To believe otherwise is to claim that the mystery of God's mind and ways can be known, and to deny Original Sin.[9] Furthermore, anyone who denies that predestination is the foreknowledge and the preparation of the gifts by which God saves infallibly all those who are saved, but

3.7 (PL 44: 964–65; *Predestination*, 152–54). Prosper's quotation of the third excerpt is incomplete. In the original passage Augustine added: "But I neither thought that I should ask myself whether the merit of faith is also a gift of God, nor did I say it was" (*De praed. sanct.* 3.7 [PL 44: 965; *Predestination*, 154]). Note that P. de Letter's attribution of Excerpts 1–3 to *De. Praed sanct.* 1.3 should read 3.7 (*Prosper of Aquitaine: Defense of St. Augustine*, 50 nn. 6–8).

5. *Resp. ad Gen.* Responsio ad haec tria (PL 51: 187–88; *Answers to Genoese*, 53).

6. *Resp. ad Gen.* Responsio ad haec tria (PL 51: 187–88; *Answers to Genoese*, 53). Prosper referring to *De praed. sanct.* 4.8 (PL 44: 965; *Predestination*, 154).

7. *Resp. ad Gen.* 4 (PL 51: 191–93; *Answers to Genoese*, 53–56). Cf. *De praed. sanct.* 5.10 (PL 44: 968; *Predestination*, 158).

8. *Resp. ad Gen.* 5 (PL 51: 193–94; *Answers to Genoese*, 56–58). Cf. *De praed. sanct.* 8.16 (PL 44: 972; *Predestination*, 162–63).

9. *Resp. ad Gen.* 6 (PL 51: 194–95; *Answers to Genoese*, 58–59). Cf. *De praed. sanct.* 8.16 (PL 44: 972–73; *Predestination*, 163).

also claims that predestination is only a recompense for faith, which God foreknew the person will have, has not received the faith or has lost it and follows the error of the Pelagians.[10]

Excerpt seven refers to the claim that the power to commit sins is located in human wickedness, but that the power to control the effects of sin is in God. Prosper responds that even those with little instruction in doctrine know that God makes use even of evil intentions in accordance with God's designs and decrees.[11]

Excerpt nine is drawn from Augustine's quote of those who parodied the effects of the preaching of Augustine's doctrine of predestination on the congregation. Prosper reminds the priests that the excerpt belongs to the objectors of Augustine, and that it does not accurately reflect Augustine's instructions on how to teach predestination so as to make it bearable to the slow and weak in faith. Prosper clarifies this point by adding that the preaching of predestination is necessary, but should be done in the manner prescribed by Augustine. Anyone who opposes the preaching of this doctrine *apertissimus est Pelagianae elationis adiutor.*[12]

Prosper does not list the contents of excerpt ten because he thought that it should have been joined to excerpt eight, the answer for which is sufficient for both. Prosper concludes that nothing is obscure for those who hold on to the truth of predestination and grace, which is the origin of all good works and perseverance.[13]

Prosper's response to the Genoese priests demonstrates his absolute endorsement of and fidelity to Augustine's doctrine of predestination. Augustine's *De praedestinatione sanctorum* and *De dono perseverantiae* provided Prosper with clear and convincing explanations and proofs for the doctrine of predestination. However, Prosper failed to follow the tone and spirit of Augustine's work. Augustine's

10. *Resp. ad Gen.* 8 (PL 51: 196–98; *Answers to Genoese,* 61–65). Cf. *De don. pers.* 14.35 (PL 45: 1014; *Perseverance,* 213–14).

11. *Resp. ad Gen.* 7 (PL 51: 195–96; *Answers to Genoese,* 59–61). Cf. *De praed. sanct.* 16.33 (PL 44: 984; *Predestination,* 176).

12. *Resp. ad Gen.* 9 (PL 51: 198–200; *Answers to Genoese,* 65–68). Cf. *De don. pers.* 15.38 (PL 45: 1016; *Perseverance,* 216–17).

13. *Resp. ad Gen.* 9 (PL 51: 200–202; *Answers to Genoese,* 68–69). Cf. *De praed. sanct.* 1.2 (PL 44: 961; *Predestination,* 150).

work was meant to explain and teach in hopes that these brothers would progress to the truth. Although Prosper had acquired an appreciation of Augustine's view of progress toward Christian truth, his intention was more to chastise and condemn the priests, and not so much to instruct and persuade them.[14]

For Prosper, Augustine's doctrine of predestination was catholic and sensible, and anyone who opposed any aspect of his doctrine *apertissimus est Pelagianae elationis adiutor.* On the issue of grace, one is either with Augustine or with the Pelagians.

There are no further exchanges or references to this work, and it appears that the situation came to an end with Prosper's response. Prosper and Hilary then turned their attention to the situation at home, where the resistance to Augustine's doctrine of grace only grew as a result of *De praedestinatione sanctorum* and *De dono perseverantiae.* Although their opponents had yet to produce a literary response, Prosper and Hilary sensed the need for a papal decision on this contentious matter. The Augustinian faction was overwhelmingly outranked and outnumbered and, like so many dissatisfied Gauls, Prosper and Hilary sought the only recourse available.[15] Prosper and Hilary set out for Rome to present their case before Pope Celestine. While they were warmly received, Celestine's response to their situation was lukewarm.

Celestine's *Apostolici verba*

Contents

In response to Prosper's and Hilary's appeal, in May 431, Celestine wrote a letter to the bishops of Gaul, commonly known as the *Apostolici verba,* addressing six of them by name.[16] The order of the

14. Prosper's appreciation of Augustine's view of progress is reflected in *Resp. ad Gen.* Responsio ad haec tria (PL 51: 187–88; *Answers to Genoese,* 49): "Though they took pains to study the whole of his teaching, they refused to follow him in his progress in the truth." Cf. *De praed. sanct.* 4.8 (PL 44: 965–66; *Predestination,* 154–55): "They have not taken care to make progress with me as they read my books."

15. Mathisen, *Ecclesiastical Factionalism,* 48, 131.

16. Celestine, *Epistola 21, ad episcopos Galliarum* [*Apostolici verba*] 1 (PL 50: 528).

six were as follows: Venerius, Marinus, Leontius, Auxonius, Arcadius, and Fillucius.[17] Venerius was the bishop of Marseilles, and Leontius bishop of Fréjus, whose territory included Lérins.[18] The rest cannot be positively identified.[19]

Celestine begins by reiterating the charge made by Hilary and Prosper that presbyters were being allowed to raise undisciplined questions in public, preaching things contrary to the truth.[20] Celestine then rebukes the bishops for being negligent in their duty to preach, their silence when these presbyters speak out, and their failure to exercise their authority over these presbyters.[21] If what Hilary and Prosper claim is the case, Celestine admonishes, *desinat . . . incessere novitas vetustatem, destinat ecclesiarum quietem inquietudo turbare.*[22]

Celestine ends the letter with a defense of Augustine against the presbyters who have no reason to oppose Augustine.[23]

We have always kept Augustine of saintly memory in our communion for the power of his life and merits, nor has even the rumor of a sinister suspicion touched him: We remember him to be of great learning, who has always been held by our predecessors before us among the best teachers.

17. Celestine, *Ep.* 21.1 (PL 50: 528–30).

18. Élie Griffe (*La Gaule chrétienne à l'époque romaine,* vol. 3 [Paris: Letouzey et Ané, 1965], 367), Palanque ("Les Évêchés Provençaux à l'époque Romaine," 135), and Jacquin ("La question de la prédestination," 288) identified Leontius as the bishop of Fréjus. Mathisen (*Ecclesiastical Factionalism,* 132 n. 66) speculates Leontius was the bishop of Trois-Châteaux.

19. Mathisen (*Ecclesiastical Factionalism,* 132) suggests the possibility that Auxonius was bishop of Aps/Viviers and Arcadius the bishop of Orange.

20. Celestine, *Ep.* 21.2 (PL 50: 528): "Filii nostri praesentes Prosper et Hilarius, quorum circa Deum nostrum sollicitudo laudanda est, tantum nescio quibus presbyteris illic licere qui dissensioni Ecclesiarum studeant, sunt apud nos prosecuti, ut indisciplinatas quaestiones vocantes in medium, pertinaciter eos dicant praedicare adversantia veritati."

21. Celestine, *Ep.* 21.2 (PL 50: 529): "Quid illic spei est, ubi, magistris tacentibus, ii loquuntur qui, si ita est, eorum discipuli no fuerunt? . . . Sciant se, si tamen censentur presbyteri, dignitate vobis esse subiectos. . . . Nam quid in ecclesiis vos agitis, si illi summam teneant praedicandi? Nisi forte illud obsistat, quod non auctoritate, non adhuc ratione colligitur, ut aliqui e fratrum numero, nuper de laicorum consortio in collegium nostrum fortassis admissi, nesciant quid sibi debeant vindicare."

22. Celestine, *Ep.* 21.2 (PL 50: 529).

23. Celestine, *Ep.* 21.3 (PL 50: 530): "Unde resistatur talibus, quos male crescere videmus?"

Therefore, all have a good perception of him, as he was loved and honored everywhere by all.[24]

Observations

It may be helpful here to provide the context of Celestine's response. The activities of the bishops of Gaul had been a concern of Celestine's before Prosper's and Hilary's arrival. In 428, Celestine rebuked the bishops in Narbonne and Vienne for the practice of officiating in church wearing monastic garb.[25] In the early fifth century, a tract of Gallic origin was published entitled *De septem ordinibus ecclesiae,* which stressed the rights of presbyters, including the privilege to preach in church.[26] Celestine rebuked this practice and, if Venerius wrote this tract, perhaps that was why Celestine singled out Venerius for special attention, in addition to the fact that Venerius was the bishop of the city that was at the epicenter of the controversy.[27] When Prosper and Hilary appealed for papal intervention, Celestine used the opportunity not only to rebuke a Gallic ecclesiastical practice, but also to display his authority over the fiercely independent Gallic bishops.

Celestine was in a difficult situation, however. It is safe to assume that Prosper and Hilary portrayed the situation in the most dramatic terms and in their favor—that the opponents of Augustine were defaming the memory of the bishop of Hippo, that the views of these opponents were Pelagian, and that action needed to be taken against them. Yet Celestine was aware, as were his predecessors, of the lim-

24. Celestine, *Ep.* 21.3 (PL 50:529–30): "Augustinum sanctae recordationis virum pro vita sua atque meritis in nostra communione semper habuimus, nec umquam hunc sinistrae suspicionis saltem rumor aspersit: quem tantae scientiae olim fuisse meminimus, ut inter magistros optimos etiam ante a meis semper decessoribus haberetur. Bene ergo de eo omnes in communi senserunt, utpote qui ubique cunctis et amori fuerit et honori."

25. Celestine, *Ep.* 4.2 (PL 50: 431): "Discernendi a plebe vel caeteris sumus doctrina, non veste; conversatione, non habitu; mentis puritate, non cultu."

26. Ps. Jerome, *Ep.* 12, *De septem ordinibus ecclesiae* (PL 30: 148–62). See Mathisen, *Ecclesiastical Factionialism,* 134–35.

27. Mathisen (*Ecclesiastical Factionalism,* 132–33) suggests the possibility, based on the evidence of some manuscripts, that Venerius composed the work for Rusticus, which would help explain why Venerius was listed first among of the bishops. Venerius was very unlikely the most senior bishop, and the special metropolitan status accorded to Proculus was to end with Proculus's death.

its to papal authority in Gaul. Celestine could ill afford to isolate the powerful bishops of Gaul. To further complicate matters, John Cassian, one of the leaders of the opposition, was on the best of terms in Rome. Cassian had lived in Rome, was perhaps ordained there, and was a friend of Archdeacon Leo, who commissioned him to write the Roman Church's response to Nestorianism.[28] A condemnation was out of the question.

Since Prosper and Hilary presented the issue as one between Pelagians and Augustine, Celestine naturally sided with Augustine. However, Celestine cautiously qualified his admonition, *desinat ... incessare novitas vestustem,* with *si ita res est.*[29] It was not an admonition to all the *doctores Gallicani,* but only those, if it is true, who allow profane novelties, that is, Pelagianism, to spread. It was not the *doctores Gallicani* who were accused of being pro-Pelagian, but some of those under their authority. The real issue, the conflict between Augustine's doctrine of predestination and the *doctores Gallicani,* was not addressed by Celestine. Celestine would only go as far as rebuking the pro-Pelagians who were attacking Augustine, but not to the point of affirming his doctrine of predestination or of rebuking the *doctores Gallicani* for opposing Augustine.

Celestine's letter provided Prosper and Hilary with a general endorsement of Augustine and a rebuke against the pro-Pelagians, if that were the case. They had gone to Rome with the belief that Augustine's doctrine of predestination would be affirmed catholic and the *doctores Gallicani* as Pelagian, yet the pontiff confirmed neither belief. They left Rome having exhausted their one and only chance for support in their battle against an enemy more powerful and numerous. There was plenty of time for Prosper and Hilary to contemplate the events at Rome, among other things, on their long voyage back home.[30]

28. Chadwick, *John Cassian,* 131. Cassian, *De incarnatione Christi contra Nestorium haereticum* (CSEL 17: 235–391).

29. Celestine, *Ep.* 21.3 (PL 50: 529).

30. It is likely that Prosper and Hilary traveled by ship. A similar voyage was taken years before by Rutilius Namatianus from Rome to Gaul, detailed in his *De reditu suo* (ed. Rudolf Helm [Heidelberg: C. Winters Universitätsbuchhandlung, 1933]; *Return to Gaul,* in *Minor Latin Poets,* trans. J. Wight Duff and Arnold Duff [Cambridge, Mass.: Harvard University Press, 1954], 764–829).

Prosper and Hilary returned to Marseilles armed with a letter from the pope that they both knew would do little to bolster their claims against their opponents. In fact, Celestine's letter did not quiet the opposition in Marseilles, and did not deter Cassian from attacking Augustine's doctrine of grace in his *Conlatio* 13. Hilary ceases to be actively involved in the conflict after the trip—he is never heard from or referred to again by Prosper or their opponents. The situation for the Augustinian faction looked rather bleak and may have caused Hilary and others to reevaluate their cause— Leontius too is never heard from nor referred to again. Prosper, however, remained convinced in the rightness of their cause and continued to defend Augustine.

Cassian's *Conlatio* 13

There has been a great deal of speculation on the relationship of Cassian's *Conlatio* 13 to Augustine's *De correptione et gratia.*[31] Stewart has concluded that although Augustine's responses to the monks of Hadrumetum were available in Gaul by the time Cassian composed *Conlatio* 13, Cassian did not write a direct rebuttal of Augustine's latest works so much as he wrote a "general response to aspects of Augustine's thought—already known in Gaul." Stewart's claim is based on the observation that *Conlatio* 13 "fits so well into the overall scheme of the *Conferences.*"[32] Adalbert de Vogüé has also noted the complex, but logical interrelationship among the individual *conlationes.*[33] Moreover, as Stewart notes, *Conlatio* 13 "develops themes introduced initially in book 12 of the *Institutes.*"[34] Stewart's and de Vogüé's views seems most plausible. *Conlatio* 13 may not have specifically targeted Augustine's *De correptione et gratia,* but that it attacked Augustine's teaching on grace is clear.[35]

31. For the various views, see Olgiari, *Certamen et Gratia,* 133–34 nn. 196–97.

32. Stewart, *Cassian the Monk,* 20.

33. Adalbert de Vogüé, "Understanding Cassian: A Survey of the Conferences," *CSQ* 19 (1984): 101–21.

34. Stewart, *Cassian the Monk,* 78. See also D. J. Macqueen, "John Cassian on Grace and Free Will," *RTAM* 44 (1977): 5–28.

35. Casiday (*Tradition and Theology,* 117) suggests that *Conlatio* 13 was directed not

The title of *Conlatio* 13, *De protectione Dei*, is a bit misleading, for the subject of this *conlatio* is the relationship between the human and divine will in the economy of salvation. Like the rest of *Conlationes*, *Conlatio* 13 was written in the form of a dialogue between distinguished abbots of the East; as such the form was not conducive to a strictly systematic presentation.

Two Models of Salvation

Cassian presents a myriad of answers to the difficult and complex question on the relationship of free will and grace in the economy of salvation. The different and conflicting answers resist any attempt at a single interpretation of Cassian's view on grace and free will. Instead, it appears that Cassian is presenting his arguments along two distinct lines of thought. There appear to be two models of salvation, but they are intermixed in the dialogue and difficult to distinguish. The two models represent Cassian's twin concerns, the integrity of free will and the gratuity of grace; however, it is clear that Cassian's overriding concern is his insistence on the freedom of the will.

The first model, which I term the cooperative model, is initially stated at the beginning:

> From this it is clear that the origin not only of good acts but even of good thoughts is in God. He both inspires in us the beginnings of a holy will and grants the ability and the opportunity to bring fulfillment the things that we rightly desire. . . . It is He who begins what is good and carries out and fulfills it in us.[36]

---

against Augustine's writings per se, but against the "outbursts of ill-considered or otherwise amateurish theological blathering" coming from Augustine's supporters in Marseilles. However, the Augustinian members, at this stage in the conflict, faithfully adhered to the teachings of Augustine.

36. *Conlatio* 13.3.5 (CSEL 13: 364; *Conferences*, 468): "quibus manifeste colligitur non solum actuum verum etiam congitationum bonarum ex deo esse principium, qui nobis et initia sanctae voluntatis inspirat et virtutem atque oportunitatem eorum quae recte cupimus tribuit peragendi . . . qui et incipit quae bona sunt et exsequitur et consummat in nobis."

To which Cassian immediately adds, "But it is up to us to conform humbly to the grace of God that daily draws us on."[37] Thus, in this first proposition, it is God who initiates throughout the process, but the human will, presumably, has the power to conform to or resist God's grace.

In the twelfth chapter, he further clarifies this model by explaining the power of the human free will. Every human soul has the *virtutum semina,* which have been placed there by the kindness of the Creator, but the seeds need to be germinated by the help of God to be able to increase in perfection.[38] Cassian then cites a passage from the *Shepherd of Hermas,* which speaks of two angels attached to every human being, one good and one bad, as proof that it is up to the human being, to a certain extent, to choose which to follow.[39] Thus, there always remains a free will in the person that can either neglect or cooperate with the grace of God.[40] This first model is then summarized at the end of the *conlatio* when Cassian states:

> Everything is granted us by the Divinity when we are not always resisting and constantly unwilling. . . . Therefore it is understood by all the Catholic fathers, who have taught perfection of heart not by idle disputation but in fact and in deed, that each person be inflamed to desire everything which is good, but in such a way that the choice of a free will faces each alternative fully. Likewise, the second aspect of divine grace is that the aforesaid practice of virtue bears results, but in such a way that the possibility of choice not be extinguished. The third aspect is that is pertains to the gifts of God that one persevere in a virtue that has been acquired, but not in such a way that a submissive freedom be taken captive.[41]

According to the cooperative model, the grace of God initiates and inspires the free will toward the good, but the free will

37. *Conlatio* 13.3.6 (CSEL 13: 364; *Conferences,* 469): "nostrum vero est, ut cotidie adtrahentem nos gratiam dei humiliter subsequamur."

38. *Conlatio* 13.12.7 (CSEL 13: 380; *Conferences,* 479–80).

39. *Conlatio* 13.12.7 (CSEL 13: 381; *Conferences,* 480): "in hominis vero optione consistere, ut eligat quem sequatur." Cf. *Shepherd of Hermas* Mandate 6.2, ed. and trans. J. B. Lightfoot in *The Apostolic Fathers* (London: MacMillian and Co., repr. 1893), 428–29.

40. *Conlatio* 13.12.8 (CSEL 13: 380–81; *Conferences,* 480): "Et idicirco manet in homine liberum semper arbitrium, quod gratiam dei possit vel neglegere vel amare."

41. *Conlatio* 13.18.3–4 (CSEL 13: 395; *Conferences,* 490).

can choose to follow or resist the actions of grace at each stage in the process of perfection. Thus, grace and free will are compatible as long as grace is understood as resistible. Cassian sees the truth of this model illustrated in Paul's statement in 1 Corinthians 15: 10: "His grace in me was not in vain, but I have labored more abundantly than all of them—yet not I, but the grace of God with me." "I have labored" indicates the efforts of Paul's own will; "Yet not I, but the grace of God" indicates the power of God; and "with me" shows that God and Paul have worked together.[42]

The second model, which I term the alternative model, is presented extensively in chapter nine. The alternative model asserts that the human or divine will initiates the process of salvation. Cassian notes that Scripture contains instances where God at times begins the process of salvation and at other times it is by the human will.

> Hence human reason does not easily discern how the Lord gives to those who ask, is found by those who seek, and opens to those who knock, and on the other hand how he is found by those who do not seek, appears openly among these who were not asking for him, and stretches out his hands the whole day to a people who do not believe in him.[43]

What follows are seven sets of scriptural passages, each set containing passages that support the divine initiative (grace) and passages that supports the human initiative (free will). For each set, Cassian asks who can understand these passages together.[44] Cassian draws the conclusion that the grace of God and the freedom of the will are both affirmed. However, Cassian believes that it is grace that begins and completes a good will most of the time. Sometimes, however, because of the goodness of human nature, the beginnings of the good will come from a person, although God must guide its perfection.[45]

42. *Conlatio* 13.13.4–5 (CSEL 13: 384; *Conferences,* 482).

43. *Conlatio* 13.9.1 (CSEL 13: 372; *Conferences,* 474).

44. *Conlatio* 13.9.2 (CSEL 13: 372–73; *Conferences,* 474–75). Cf. Is. 1: 19 and Rom. 9: 16; Rom. 2: 6 and Phil. 2: 13, Eph. 2: 8–9; James 4: 8 and John 4: 44; Prov. 4: 26 (LXX) and Ps. 5: 9, 16.5; Ezek. 18: 31 and Ezek. 1: 19–20; Jer. 4: 14 and Ps. 50: 12, 9; Hos. 10: 12 (LXX) and Ps. 93: 10, 145: 8, 12: 4.

45. *Conlatio* 13.9.5 (CSEL 13: 374; *Conferences,* 475): "ut autem evidentius clareat

According to this alternative model, a person is either inspired by God for the beginning and the completion of the good will, or a person alone begins the good will and is then assisted by grace, which does not occur as much as in the former case. Cassian further adds that in some cases God is the one who draws people to salvation, and in other cases the way of salvation was shown as a reward.[46]

The reason why God works in either of these two ways is because salvation is imparted by grace according to the measure of faith each person possesses or according to the measure of faith God has imparted.[47] This faith is either found in the person, presumably one's own, or given by God. Again, a list of scriptural quotations follows, which assert God responding to a person's faith or God instilling faith.[48] Cassian provides a summary of the alternative model in 13.17.1:

> He inspires some, who wish it and thirst for it, to a greater ardor, while some others, who do not even wish it, he compels against their will. Sometimes he helps to accomplish the things he sees we desire for our own good, and at other times he inspires the beginnings of that holy desire and bestows both the commencement of a good work and perseverance in it.[49]

Cassian concludes, with the Augustinians and the Pelagians in mind, "For many who hold to one of these alternatives and assert it

---

etiam per naturae bonum, quod beneficio creatoris indultum est, nonnumquam bonarum voluntatum prodire principia, quae tamen nisi a domino dirigantur ad consummationem virtutum pervenire non possunt."

46. *Conlatio* 13.15.2 (CSEL 13: 389; *Conferences*, 486): "Cornelio precibus et elemosynis iugiter insistenti velut remunerationis vice via salutis ostenditur." Note here that Cassian asserts that salvation can be a reward for prayer and almsgiving. This contradicts what Cassian asserted in 13.3.2 (CSEL 13: 363; *Conferences*, 468): "Yet human pride should never strive . . . nor should it try to make itself a sharer in the gifts of God in such a way as to think that its own efforts have brought upon it the divine generosity, boasting that its own deserving toil has been responded to with an abundant harvest."

47. *Conlatio* 13.15.2 (CSEL 13: 389; *Conferences*, 486): "et ita multiformis illa sapientia dei salutem hominum multiplici atque inscrutabili pietate dispensat ac secundum capacitatem uniuscuiusque gratiam suae largitatis inpertit, ut ipsas quoque curationes non secundum uniformem maiestatis suae potentiam, sed secundum mensuram fidei, in qua unumquemque repperit vel sicut unicuique ipse partitus est."

48. *Conlatio* 13.15.3–5 (CSEL 13: 389–90; *Conferences*, 486–87).

49. *Conlatio* 13.17.1 (CSEL 13: 393; *Conferences*, 488–89): "quorundam quidem volentium ac sitientium cursum ad maiorem incitare flagrantiam, quosdam vero etiam nolentes inuitosque conpellere, et nunc quidem ut inpleantur ea quae utiliter a nobis desiderata

more freely than is right have fallen into different self-contradictory errors."[50] Instead, though they seem mutually opposed to one another, these two different ways of salvation must be affirmed and accepted because of the *ecclesiasticae fidei regula.*[51]

Separately these two models are coherent, but together they appear contradictory. According to the cooperative model, grace can be resisted or it can cooperate with free will. However, according to the alternative model, grace can be irresistible. Perhaps another way to view these two models is to consider the context of these writings. The alternative model was primarily aimed at providing a solution to the Pelagian conflict—that neither the Pelagians nor the Augustinians were correct in arguing one over the absolute neglect of the other. The cooperative model was directed toward a more practical end. This model addresses his monks, calling them to an active pursuit of perfection that involves both their wills and the grace of God together. Cassian's warning toward the end of *Conlatio* 13 seems appropriate to his monks, which refers to the cooperative model: "If something cleverly gleaned from human argumentation and reasoning seems contrary to this understanding, it should be avoided rather than called forth to the destruction of the faith."[52]

Contradictions aside, Cassian's manifold understanding of grace and free will introduces a completely new vision of grace and free will that goes beyond the strictly narrow bifurcated debate. It is an innovative view that Prosper was quick to attack.

Cassian and Augustine

Conlatio 13 was not only a rebuttal, but also a carefully crafted attack on Augustine's teaching on grace. Besides presenting a different view of grace, there are three specific places where Augustine is

---

perspexerit adiuvare, nunc vero etiam ipsius sancti desiderii inspirare principia et vel initium boni operas vel perseverantiam condonare."

50. *Conlatio* 13.11.1 (CSEL 13: 376; *Conferences,* 476): "multi enim singula haec credentes ac iusto amplius adserentes variis sibique contraries sunt erroribus involuti."

51. *Conlatio* 13.11.4 (CSEL 13: 377; *Conferences,* 477–78).

52. *Conlatio* 13.18.5 (CSEL 13: 396; *Conferences,* 490): "si quid sane versutius humana argumentatione ac ratione collectum huic sensui videtur obsistere, vitandum magis est quam ad destructionem fidei proucandum."

challenged, though indirectly. In chapter seven, Cassian presents his own interpretation of 1 Timothy 2: 4 against Augustine's. After quoting from three passages (Mt. 18: 14; 2 Kings 14: 14; Ezech. 33: 11), which proclaim God's desire that no one perish, Cassian asks how it is possible to believe that God does not wish all to be saved universally, but only a few instead of all. The grace of God calls everyone to come to him (Mt. 23: 37), without exception, because God desires "all to be saved and to come to the knowledge of the truth."[53] Cassian then concludes that if God does not call everyone universally, but only a few, "it follows that not all are burdened by Original Sin and by present sin."[54] For Cassian, to deny the universal will of God and affirm a limited call of salvation is to deny Original Sin and actual sins.

It appears unclear, at first, how Cassian has come to this conclusion or the meaning of it, but Cassian assumes that all human beings have been tainted by Original Sin and actual sins, and since all are in need of salvation because of this, God calls everyone to be saved. Cassian also implies that God's *propositum, voluntas,* and *vocatio,* which are synonymous for Cassian, do not entail a force or action, but a sentiment. God desires all, but forces none to be saved. God's will can be followed or rejected. Thus, if God calls only a few to be saved, then not everyone has Original Sin or actual sins, but only those few who are called. Since everyone has Original Sin and actual sins, therefore, God calls everyone.

The second critique is in 13.11.1, where Cassian referred to the Pelagians and Augustine, when he stated that those who hold only one view, either the human or divine initiative in the producing of a

53. *Conlatio* 13.7.2–3 (CSEL 13: 369–70; *Conferences,* 472). According to Boniface Ramsey ("John Cassian: Student of Augustine," 6), Cassian alluded twice to Augustine's views in chapter seven. The first is the universalistic interpretation of 1 Tim. 2: 4 in contrast to Augustine's limited definition of "all." The second allusion, which Ramsey claims is more specific, is to Augustine's belief in the damnation of unbaptized infants, which is countered with the possibility of unbaptized infants. The claim of the second allusion is unconvincing. The fate of unbaptized infants can certainly be inferred from the chapter, but it does not seem to suggest a reply to Augustine.

54. *Conlatio* 13.7.3 (CSEL 13: 370; *Conferences,* 472): "si autem non omnes universaliter, sed quosdam advocat, sequitur ut nec omnes sint onerati vel originali vel actuali peccato."

good will, have fallen into self-contradictory error.[55] Thus, Augustine is in error, and, to make matters worse, Augustine is equally in error with the Pelagians on this issue.

The third critique of Augustine comes at the conclusion of *Conlatio* 13 with an admonition to avoid rather than call forth anything drawn from human argumentation and reasoning that is contrary to this understanding. Faith does not come from understanding, but understanding comes from faith. After quoting Isiah 7: 9, "If you do not believe, you will not understand," Cassian delivers what at first appears to be an acknowledgment of the mystery of God: "For how God works all things in us on the one hand and how everything is ascribed to free will on the other cannot be fully grasped by human intelligence and reason."[56] However, it is nothing short of a sharp rebuke. The premise is that faith is required to understand, and if one does not understand how God and free will are equally true, then one does not have faith. In other words, if one does not understand grace and free will as Cassian explained, then one does not have faith. It is a subtle, but powerful, rebuke.

Cassian's tone is much more aggressive and ungracious than Augustine's. In the beginning of *De praedestinatione sanctorum,* Augustine acknowledged that the opponents, whom Hilary and Prosper wrote about—including Cassian—were brothers in the faith and held the right convictions, which "separates them very much from the error of the Pelagians."[57] What was needed was for these brothers to come to the right understanding of these convictions through prayer: "If they continue in these convictions and pray to him who gives understanding, God will also reveal this to them, if on some point their thoughts differ concerning predestination."[58] The point of writing his treatise was not so much to rebuke these brothers as it was for them to be able to progress to the truth of predestination and perseverance. Augustine ended his treatise humbly acknowledging that his view of God's grace was open to being wrong and

55. *Conlatio* 13.11.1 (CSEL 13: 376; *Conferences,* 476).
56. *Conlatio* 13.18.5 (CSEL 13: 396; *Conferences,* 491).
57. *De praed. sanct.* 1.2 (PL 44: 961; *Predestination,* 149–50).
58. *De praed. sanct.* 1.2 (PL 44: 961; *Predestination,* 150).

in need of correction. Augustine knew his limitations. He did not have exclusive insight into the mystery of grace, and could imagine future teachers of the Church correcting him, if they should deem his works relevant.[59] No such sentiment is found in Cassian. Cassian was unflinchingly confident his views were consistent with Scripture and the teachings of the Church.

For Cassian, human nature, though fallen, still possesses the *virtutum semina,* which has been placed there by the kindness of the Creator.[60] This natural goodness is the implicit reason why some are able to produce the beginnings of a good will and initiate salvation.[61] And the human will is able to freely choose good or bad, to either neglect or love the grace of God, but always working together with the grace of God.[62]

For Augustine, the Fall had more pronounced effects. All human beings became evil as a result of Adam's sin, and live under the dominion of sin and the judgment of condemnation.[63] Humans have the free choice to do good or evil, but in doing evil one is devoid of righteousness and enslaved to sin.[64] For Augustine, salvation in all its aspects was due to grace, at the expense of human contributions. For Cassian, salvation was due to grace and human contributions, at the expense of a strict inner logic.

Another difference between the two was their approach to the problem of grace and free will. Augustine approached the problem by seeking to probe the depths of the mind of God, whereas Cassian

59. *De don. pers.* 24.68 (PL 45: 1034; *Perseverance,* 237): "Qui vero errare me existimant, etiam atque etiam diligenter quae sunt dicta considerent, ne fortassis ipsi errent. Ego autem cum per eos qui meos labores legunt, non solum doctior, verum etiam emendatior fio, propitium mihi Deum agnosco: et hoc per Ecclesiae doctores maxime exspecto; si et in ipsorum manus venit, dignanturque nosse quod scribo."

60. *Conlatio* 13.12.7 (CSEL 13: 380; *Conferences,* 479–80).

61. The reference to the *virtutum semina* is made in 13.12.7, but the explicit connection to its being the reason for why some are able to produce the good will is not made.

62. *Conlatio* 13.12.8 (CSEL 13: 381; *Conferences,* 480): "et idicirco manet in homine liberum semper arbitrium, quod gratiam dei possit vel neglegere vel amare."

63. *De corr. et gr.* 1.2, 6.9, 10.28 (CSEL 92: 219–20, 226, 252; *Rebuke and Grace,* 110–11, 113, 128).

64. *De corr. et gr.* 1.2 (CSEL 92: 220; *Rebuke and Grace,* 109): "Liberum itaque arbitrium et ad malum et ad bonum faciendum confitendum est nos habere, sed in malo faciendo liber est quisque iustitiae servusque peccati."

was much more interested in the way the mystery played out in the human person.[65] Put in another way, Augustine was concerned with how God worked in the process of salvation, and Cassian with how humans worked in the process.

Cassian's and Augustine's conflicting appreciations of grace and free will are based on their respective understanding of anthropology. In many ways their view of anthropology reflects the two different worlds they inhabited.[66] Cassian's life, although marked by ecclesiopolitical controversy in his time in the East, seems to have experienced "no radical revolution in heart and mind and will."[67] Cassian, a monk from a young age, was surrounded by devoted and earnest men in pursuit of perfection. In Marseilles, Cassian had established a community for the sole purpose of providing a space in which one could live out the virtuous life, attracting earnest and motivated men drawn from the Gallo-Roman aristocracy.

Augustine's life was dramatically different. As Chadwick poignantly and succinctly put it, "Augustine had come through to faith and the good life, as he felt, against his will. He had been converted though he had not willed it. He had received the gift of chastity though he had not wanted it. All was of God."[68] That one could will to be saved contradicted Augustine's past experiences and what he observed as a pastor. His was a world full of people who struggled with even the basics of Christian piety. Augustine did not deal with Cassian's "athletes of Christ," but with spectators.[69]

Cassian's view of grace and his opposition to Augustine's doctrine of grace are but one set of expressions among the opponents of Augustine in Gaul. Cassian's tactic also distinguishes him. Whereas some attacked Augustine's specific views, Cassian provided a positive formulation of grace, while opposing Augustine on Cassian's own terms. In this way, Cassian was able to avoid addressing the difficult issues of predestination and the mystery of God's gratuitous election. One of the implications from *Conlatio* 13, in not addressing Augustine on his terms, is that grace and free will can be understood

65. Stewart, *Cassian the Monk,* 80.
66. Chadwick, *John Cassian,* 126–27.
67. Chadwick, *John Cassian,* 127.
68. Chadwick, *John Cassian,* 117.
69. *De institutis* 5.17.1 (CSEL 17: 94; *Institutes,* 127).

without reference to Augustine's views. One can come to an understanding of grace without the concepts and issues raised by Augustine.

Conlatio 13 represents Cassian's contribution to the ongoing discussions sparked by Augustine's views. It is also the first direct literary critique of Augustine's doctrine of grace among the *doctores Gallicani.* Instead of reacting to Augustine per se, Cassian provided his own view of grace, which should not be mistaken as the collective expression of all those who opposed Augustine. There was no single leader or spokesman for those who opposed Augustine, as clearly witnessed in Celestine's letter. Cassian was one, although one of the better known and certainly among the most influential and powerful *doctores Gallicani,* of many who opposed, in various ways, the teachings of Augustine in Gaul.

De gratia Dei et libero arbitrio, liber contra collatorem

Prosper's arrival back to Marseilles marks the beginning of a series of responses to the growing criticism to Augustine's doctrine of predestination. The chronology of these writings is as follows: around 432, Prosper wrote *Contra collatorem* against Cassian's *Conlatio* 13, and *Epitaphium Nestorianae et Pelagianae haereseon;* in 433, Prosper completed the first edition of his *Chronicon;* in 434, Vincent published his *Commonitorium;* then shortly afterward came the appearance of the *Capitula obiectionum Gallorum* and *Capitula obiectionum Vincentianarum.* In addition, there are three other relevant works that may belong to this period: the *Hypomnesticon,* the *"Capitula sancti Augustini" in urbem Romam transmissa,* and the Pseudo-Augustinian *De praedestinatione et gratia,* none of whose dates and relationship to the works above can be determined precisely.[70]

70. Weaver (*Divine Grace,* 132) and de Letter ("Introduction," in *Prosper of Aquitaine: Defense of St. Augustine,* 6–13) suggest the same chronology for Prosper's responses. Cappuyns suggests a similar chronology for all the writings associated with this period ("Le premier," 317–21). For a different chronology, see Jacquin ("La question de la prédestination," 276–99), who places Prosper's *Contra collatorem* at the end, and Mathisen (*Ecclesiastical Factionalism,* 131), who places Prosper's response to the Gauls and the Vincentian articles before the visit to Rome.

Having returned to Marseilles, Prosper was determined to continue defending Augustine, despite the lukewarm reception of Augustine in Rome. Prosper quickly set about the task of refuting Cassian, namely his *Conlatio* 13, and others who continue to attack the memory of Augustine and, according to Prosper, the catholic faith, which Augustine expressed in his writings. Prosper, at least initially, was determined to present Celestine's pronouncement as a definitive endorsement of Augustine in his response to Cassian's *Conlatio* 13.[71] With the death of Celestine in 432, Prosper also took the occasion to enlist the support of Sixtus, the new pope, in his response to Cassian.

Contents

Prosper's response reveals his continued fidelity to Augustine, but also an appreciation of the authority of the Apostolic See. Prosper correctly interpreted Cassian's *Conlatio* 13 as a critique of Augustine's doctrine of grace.[72] However, Prosper's strategy was not so much to counter with Augustine's doctrine, as much as it was to counter with the weight of papal authority.

Prosper begins by situating the present conflict in the context of the Church's struggle against Pelagianism. Prosper claims that the opponents of Augustine are endangering the Church by claiming that the Bishop of Hippo did not defend the doctrine of grace in the right way against the Pelagians. Although they stand within the Church and are not Pelagians, their attack on Augustine's writings against the Pelagians favors the Pelagians and creates the opinion that the condemnations of the Pelagians were unjust in the minds of the uneducated. In addition, their attack on Augustine is an attack against all the pontiffs and especially those of the Apostolic See. Why, Prosper wonders, do the enemies of Augustine insist on starting a war that was finished and disturb the peace already won?[73]

71. See Prosper, *Contra collatorem* 21.2 (PL 51: 271–72; *Against Cassian,* 134–35). Mathisen (*Ecclesiastical Factionalism,* 133) alone asserts Celestine's letter was a favorable response to Prosper's and Hilary's appeal. Others conclude the letter was ambiguous. Cf. Weaver, *Divine Grace,* 121; Ogliari, *Gratia et Certamen,* 92 n. 4; and Chadwick, *John Cassian,* 132.

72. Cf. Casiday, *Tradition and Theology,* 23–29.

73. *Contra collatorem* 1 (PL 51: 215–17; *Against Cassian,* 70–72).

Prosper then deals with *Conlatio* 13, but without directly mentioning Cassian by name.[74] The theme of Prosper's attack of *Conlatio* 13 is the insistence that Cassian's model of grace—Prosper combines the two models into one—supports Pelagianism.

According to Prosper, Cassian is perfectly catholic when he claims that God is responsible for the beginning of the good will and its completion.[75] However, Prosper notes that in 13.9, Cassian, after asserting the divine initiative, introduces a contradictory proposition, which Prosper takes as Cassian's abandonment of the doctrine he had previously professed.[76] Prosper then quotes Cassian as asserting that most come to grace because of the alertness of their free wills, while others are drawn by the power of God.[77] Prosper concludes that Cassian condemns the catholics and the heretics together.[78] It is here that Prosper rhetorically asks if Pope Innocent, the Eastern bishops at Diospolis, the local councils of Milevis and Carthage, the Council of Carthage (418), Pope Zosimus, and the African bishops who wrote to Zosimus were all wrong in asserting the divine initiative over human free will.[79] Since the debates over the origin of the good will and the beginning of faith and charity have been settled, there is no longer a need to try to propose the alliance between the two doctrines.[80] Prosper, then, ends this section by going over some more of Cassian's "new art" of combining mutually exclusive scriptural statements.

74. *Contra collatorem* 2.1 (PL 51: 218; *Against Cassian,* 72): "Igitur in libro cuius praenotatio est, de Protectione Dei, vir quidam sacerdotalis, qui disputandi usu inter eos, quibuscum degit, excellit."

75. *Contra collatorem* 2.2–2.3 (PL 51: 218–20; *Against Cassian,* 73–74). Cf. *Conlatio* 13.3.5, 13.3.6, 13.6.3, 13.8.3, 13.8.4 (CSEL 13: 364, 367, 371; *Conferences,* 468, 469, 471, 474).

76. *Contra collatorem* 2.4–2.5 (PL 51: 220–21; *Against Cassian,* 74–75). Cf. *Conlatio* 13.9.1–4 (CSEL 13: 372–74; *Conferences,* 474–75).

77. *Contra collatorem* 2.4 (PL 51: 220; *Against Cassian,* 74–75). Cf. *Conlatio* 13.9.2–4 (CSEL 13: 372–73; *Conferences,* 474–75). Prosper does not quote directly from *Conlatio* 13.9.2–4, and inaccurately summarizes this part.

78. *Contra collatorem* 5.3 (PL 51: 226; *Against Cassian,* 81–82). Cf. *Conlatio* 13.9.2–4 (CSEL 13: 372–73; *Conferences,* 474–75).

79. *Contra collatorem* 5.3 (PL 51: 227–28; *Against Cassian,* 82–83). Prosper qualifies the pronouncement at Diospolis: "The Oriental bishops . . . compelled him [Pelagius] outwardly at least to appear as a Catholic and to anathematize those who say that grace is given in answer to our merits."

80. *Contra collatorem* 6 (PL 51: 229; *Against Cassian,* 84).

According to Prosper, Cassian is neither fully Pelagian nor catholic, but an inventor of an unknown, deformed third way.[81] Cassian's system is not fully Pelagian because it claims the initiative of grace, but it is not catholic because it claims the initiative of free will. And in asserting both alternatives, Cassian's new system presents the catholic position as corrupt and the Pelagian one as correct.[82] Prosper interprets Cassian's use of scriptural passages that support free will or grace as creating two classes among humans, those saved by grace and those justified by law and nature.[83]

Chapters nine to fifteen address Cassian's views on the nature of humanity. Prosper refutes Cassian's claim made in 13.12.1: "For it must not be believed that God made the human being in such a way that he could never will or be capable of the good. He has not allowed him a free will if he has only conceded that he wills what is evil and be capable of it but not of himself either will the good or be capable of it."[84] After noting the disastrous effects of the Fall on human nature, in perfect fidelity to Augustine, Prosper concludes, "Hence, it is clear that man could have an evil freedom through his own fault, but he could not be given freedom for virtue without the help of his Savior."[85] In chapters ten and eleven Prosper refutes Cassian's claims that humanity did not lose the knowledge of what is good after the Fall, nor did it lose the power to do it.[86] Prosper fails to answer the former, only insisting that what remains of natural gifts cannot make one love and do what one should do.[87] As for the latter claim, after quoting 13.12.5, "We must be on the watch lest we attribute all good works of holy persons to the Lord in such a way that we ascribe nothing but what is bad and perverse to human na-

81. *Contra collatorem* 3.1 (PL 51: 221; *Against Cassian*, 76): "Tu informe nescio quid tertium."

82. *Contra collatorem* 5.2 (PL 51: 226; *Against Cassian*, 81).

83. *Contra collatorem* 3.1 (PL 51: 222–23; *Against Cassian*, 77). Cf. *Conlatio* 13.11.1 (CSEL 13: 376; *Conferences*, 476).

84. *Contra collatorem* 9.2 (PL 51: 236; *Against Cassian*, 91). Cf. *Conlatio* 13.12.1 (CSEL 13: 378; *Conferences*, 478).

85. *Contra collatorem* 9.2–5 (PL 51: 236–39; *Against Cassian*, 91–96).

86. *Contra collatorem* 10–11 (PL 51: 239–42; *Against Cassian*, 96–100). Cf. *Conlatio* 13.12.3, 5 (CSEL 13: 378, 379–80; *Conferences*, 478, 479).

87. *Contra collatorem* 10.3 (PL 51: 241; *Against Cassian*, 98).

ture," Prosper identifies this claim to be in conformity with what Pelagius and Caelestius have stated:

> There you have in a few brief words not only two but a whole string of statements against the faith which, if you were to scrutinize them closely, you would find are not different from another series, that of the condemned heresy.[88]

Prosper then explains what Cassian meant according to Prosper's interpretation.[89] Prosper's liberal interpretation of Cassian's meaning served Prosper's purpose of connecting Cassian with the Pelagians.

Prosper argues that human nature, which has retained its substance, form, life, intelligence, reason, and the other gifts of body and soul, cannot by these powers attain to what is truly good or be able to lead to eternal life. It is not by one's strength that one succeeds in attaining to the beginning of salvation, but it is the hidden and powerful grace of God.[90] Prosper concludes his attack of Cassian's anthropology by addressing Cassian's claims that the Creator has implanted the *virtutum semina* in every soul, and that the truth of free will can be drawn from the story of the two angels in the *Shepherd of Hermas.* Prosper argues that the *virtutum semina* were lost because of the sin of Adam, and cannot be recovered unless God restores them.[91] Moreover, all that pertains to a life of godliness is not from nature, which fell in Adam, but grace, which heals nature.[92] As for the *Shepherd of Hermas,* Prosper views the text as of no value, and Cassian's conclusion drawn from the story of the two angels to be in error for two reasons.[93] Cassian's conclusion that humans always keep their free will is in error because it is not true for all of humanity, namely, infants who cannot act of their free will, and the insane,

88. *Contra collatorem* 11.2 (PL 51: 243; *Against Cassian,* 99). Cf. *Conlatio* 13.12.5 (CSEL 13: 379; *Conferences,* 479); Aug., *De praed. sanct.* 2.3; Aug., *De gest. Pel.* 14.30.

89. *Contra collatorem* 11.2 (PL 51: 243; *Against Cassian,* 99–100).

90. *Contra collatorem* 12.4 (PL 51: 246; *Against Cassian,* 103).

91. *Contra collatorem* 13.2 (PL 51: 248; *Against Cassian,* 105). Cf. *Conlatio* 13.12.7 (CSEL 13: 380; *Conferences,* 479–80).

92. *Contra collatorem* 13.5 (PL 51: 250; *Against Cassian,* 107).

93. *Contra collatorem* 13.6 (PL 51: 250–52; *Against Cassian,* 108–10); cf. *Conlatio* 13.12.7 (CSEL 13: 380–81; *Conferences,* 480); *Shepherd of Hermas* Mandate 6.2.

who are deprived of reason.[94] And even if the conclusion was meant for those able to use their free wills, it would mean that there would be no need for God to remake souls.[95]

Prosper then deals with Cassian's error of asserting that grace is given according to human merit. Prosper views Cassian's conclusion that the centurion would not have deserved praise or merit if Christ singled out in him what Christ had given him "to contain almost the whole of the Pelagian heresy."[96] And Prosper points out that Cassian condemns himself when he later states that it is an unholy opinion to declare that grace is given according to merit.[97]

In chapter eighteen, Prosper argues that Cassian's attempt "to cover up the incoherence and contradiction" of the different propositions by combining what are mutually contradictory, creates two groups of believers: those whose good works and thoughts are initiated and brought to completion by God, and those who are given grace according to merit.[98] Prosper concludes that Cassian's division of humanity renders Christ as the Savior for some and a refuge for others. God compels the former to accept the gratuitous gift of grace, and for the latter, God is the refuge who provides the reward for those who anticipated the divine call by the fervor of their free wills.[99] To preach both doctrines suggests that the Pelagians hold what Catholics hold, and when these contrary doctrines are mixed, it is the catholic faith that is destroyed.[100]

Prosper then lists the twelve propositions he had just refuted from *Conlatio* 13, with a brief summary of his refutation after each

94. *Contra collatorem* 13.6 (PL 51: 251; *Against Cassian,* 109).

95. *Contra collatorem* 13.6 (PL 51: 251; *Against Cassian,* 109). Here again is another instance of Prosper taking great liberty with Cassian's meaning: "So great, according to our author, is the soundness and power of free will that men can acquire even charity, which is the highest of all virtues, not through a favor of God but of their own doing."

96. *Contra collatorem* 16.1 (PL 51: 259; *Against Cassian,* 118). Cf. *Conlatio* 13.14.4 (CSEL 13: 385; *Conferences,* 483). Cf. Matt. 8: 10.

97. *Contra collatorem* 17 (PL 51: 261; *Against Cassian,* 121). Cf. *Conlatio* 13.16.1 (CSEL 13: 391; *Conferences,* 487).

98. *Contra collatorem* 18.1 (PL 51: 262–63; *Against Cassian,* 123).

99. *Contra collatorem* 18.2 (PL 51: 263; *Against Cassian,* 124).

100. *Contra collatorem* 18.2 (PL 51: 264; *Against Cassian,* 125).

proposition.[101] Prosper concludes his critique of *Conlatio* 13 by summarizing what Cassian teaches: that the soul and free will were unaffected by Adam's sin; neither Adam nor his descendants lost the knowledge of good; every soul possesses the *virtutum semina,* and with them humans are able to anticipate the grace of God and merit God's help to more easily attain perfection; the natural powers of humanity are undamaged and able to fight against and endure all the torments of the devil without the help of God; these natural powers are possessed by all humans, but not all are willing to make use of them; God is the helper for those who are willing, and the Savior of those unwilling; since one section of the Church is made just by grace, and the other by their own free wills, the latter have more glory than those liberated by grace; and Adam's descendants are able to do every good work as Adam was able to do before he sinned.[102]

In chapter twenty-one, having summarized the views of Cassian, Prosper draws upon the authority of the Apostolic See to combat him. Prosper asserts that Cassian's teachings are the dogmas of the teachers who, in order to corrupt the minds of Catholics, speak against the defenders of grace and those among the most outstanding doctors of the Church at the time, hoping to break down all the defenses of the Church's authority. These teachers are following in the footsteps of the Pelagians and say nothing that was not already stated by the condemned Pelagian heretics. Thus, these teachers have been defeated along with the Pelagians when the popes condemned the heresy.[103]

Prosper next provides a brief history of the defeat of the Pelagians, which, according to Prosper's version, was led primarily by the actions of the popes. Innocent had cut the heads of the Pelagians with his sword. The Palestinian bishops at Diospolis had forced Pelagius to condemn himself and his followers. Zosimus had placed the sword of Peter in the hands of the African bishops when he added his authority to the decrees of Carthage. Boniface defeated the Pelagians through his decrees and directed the emperors to issue

101. *Contra collatorem* 19 (PL 51: 265–69; *Against Cassian,* 126–31).
102. *Contra collatorem* 20 (PL 51: 269–70; *Against Cassian,* 132).
103. *Contra collatorem* 21.1 (PL 51: 270–71; *Against Cassian,* 133).

imperial decrees. Boniface also asked Augustine to write answers to the books of the Pelagians. Celestine, observing the judgment of past decrees, did not grant Caelestius a new trial, and he banished him from Italy. Celestine also took care to cleanse Britain from the heresy, and to keep it free he ordained Palladius to draw the pagan nation to the Christian fold. Celestine was involved in the cleansing of the Eastern churches by helping to condemn the Nestorian and Pelagian heresies.[104]

Prosper immediately summarizes, according to Prosper's view, Celestine's reaction to Prosper's and Hilary's report of the opposition in Gaul:

> The same Pope intimated to those who in Gaul censured the writings of Augustine of saintly memory that they could no longer speak against this doctor; he welcomed the application of some consultants [Prosper and Hilary] and praised the holy teaching of Augustine's books, in opposition to those misguided censors; he gave an official pronouncement on the authority of these writings, and declared openly how much he was displeased with the novel rashness of people so insolent as to rise against ancient doctors and disturb the preaching of the truth by their uncontrolled slander.[105]

This is followed by a direct quotation from Celestine's *Apostolici verba:*

> We have always kept Augustine of saintly memory in our communion for the power of his life and merits, nor has even the rumor of a sinister suspicion touched him: We remember him to be of great learning, who has always been held by our predecessors before us among the best teachers. Therefore, all have a good perception of him, as he was loved and honored everywhere by all.[106]

104. *Contra collatorem* 21.1–2 (PL 51: 271; *Against Cassian,* 133–34).

105. *Contra collatorem* 21.2 (PL 51: 271–72; *Against Cassian,* 134–35).

106. *Contra collatorem* 21.2 (PL 51: 272; *Against Cassian,* 135). Cf. Celestine, *Ep.* 21.3 (PL 50: 529–30): "Augustinum sanctae recordationis virum pro vita sua atque meritis in nostra communione semper habuimus, nec umquam hunc sinistrae suspicionis saltem rumor aspersit: quem tantae scientiae olim fuisse meminimus, ut inter magistros optimos etiam ante a meis semper decessoribus haberetur. Bene ergo de eo omnes in communi senserunt, utpote qui ubique cunctis et amori fuerit et honori."

Thus, Prosper wonders, how anyone could interpret such a loud and high praise from so venerable and authoritative a declaration in a sinister way, or claim what is clear and sincere to be ambiguous.[107] As to the charge that since the pope did not explicitly mention the titles of the books of Augustine, the papal approval applies only to his earlier writings, Prosper responds that even if that charge is granted, Augustine's earlier works, before and during the Pelagian conflict, are consistent with his latest works.[108] Furthermore, when the Apostolic See approves books submitted to its judgment, it also approves the other books that do not differ from the approved books.[109] Since these teachers—Prosper's opponents—do not agree with these earlier writings of Augustine and cannot find in them anything that could serve their criticisms of his later works, these teachers must be resisted not so much by disputation, as by authority.[110]

Prosper views these teachers as a *pars minima* of the Pelagian heresy that endeavors to restore itself through its new growth. Thus, Prosper hopes that God's protection, granted through Popes Innocent, Zosimus, Boniface, and Celestine, will continue in Pope Sixtus, the present pope.[111]

In the final chapter, Prosper proclaims that these teachers are the ones who started this war within the Church, but as long as they are not cut off from fraternal society, the hope of their amendment should not be given up. Prosper adds:

107. *Contra collatorem* 21.3 (PL 51: 272; *Against Cassian,* 135): "Contra istam clarissimae laudationis tubam, contra istam sacratissimi testimonii dignitatem, audet quisquam malignae interpretationis murmur emittere, et perspicuae sincerissimaeque sententiae nubem obliquae ambiguitatis obtendere?"

108. *Contra collatorem* 21.3 (PL 51: 272–73; *Against Cassian,* 135–36). Prosper cites Augustine's works on grace before 431: *De peccatorum meritis* (CSEL 60: 1–151), *Epp.* 186, 194 (CSEL 57: 45–80, 176–214), *De gratia Christi* (CSEL 42: 123–206), *De nuptiis et concupiscentia* (CSEL 42: 209–52), *De natura et gratia* (CSEL 60: 231–99), *Contra Iulianum* (PL 44: 641–874), *De gestis Pelagii* (CSEL 42: 49–122), *De perfectione iustitiae hominis* (CSEL 42: 1–48), *Contra duas epistulas Pelagianorum* (CSEL 60: 421–570).

109. *Contra collatorem* 21.3 (PL 51: 273; *Against Cassian,* 136): "Apostolica enim sedes quod a praecognitis sibi non discrepat, cum praecognitis probat."

110. *Contra collatorem* 21.3–4 (PL 51: 273; *Against Cassian,* 136).

111. *Contra collatorem* 21.4 (PL 51: 273; *Against Cassian,* 137). Pope Sixtus (432–440).

Until the Lord be pleased to settle, through the instrumentality of the princes of the Church and the lawful ministers of His justice, the trouble aroused by the pride of a few and the ignorance of some others, let us with the help of God endeavor with calm and humble patience to render love for hatred, to avoid disputes with the silly, to keep to the truth and not fight with the weapons of falsehood.[112]

Observations

Throughout the treatise Prosper remains consistent with Augustine's view of anthropology and the general relationship between grace and human free will, but he does not go any further. The discussion of predestination is uncharacteristically absent. It is the earliest work in which Prosper does not argue for predestination, after embracing Augustine, terms that were so consistently and zealously defended in his previous works.[113] However, the absence of the defense of predestination may be attributed to the method of his argument rather than an indication of change in Prosper's convictions. Moreover, Prosper's defense of predestination is implied in Prosper's assertion that Celestine's approval included Augustine's later works.[114]

Prosper's response was not aimed at convincing Cassian and those who opposed Augustine. In Prosper's mind, his opponents were the enemy in the war against heresy.[115] Prosper's tract was directed at persuading the general public in Gaul, and, most importantly, the pope, that the enemies of Augustine were the enemies of the Church. However, in defending the memory of Augustine, Prosper's zeal got the better of him. Prosper was less than truthful or fair.[116]

Prosper's critique of Cassian's contradictory statements has mer-

112. *Contra collatorem* 22 (PL 51: 274; *Against Cassian,* 137–38).

113. Chadwick, *John Cassian,* 134.

114. *Contra collatorem* 21.3 (PL 51: 272; *Against Cassian,* 135).

115. *Contra collatorem* 22 (PL 51: 274; *Against Cassian,* 137): "peremptorumque armis intestinum bellum moventes."

116. Casiday ("Rehabilitating John Cassian" and *Tradition and Theology,* esp. 17–29) provides scathing critiques of Prosper's misrepresentation of Cassian's *Conlatio* 13.

it, but Prosper's caricature of only one of Cassian's two models of grace does not do justice to the complexity and nuances of Cassian's views. Although Prosper acknowledged that Cassian and the other opponents of Augustine belonged within the Church, Prosper all but names them Pelagians.[117] Prosper's linking of Augustine's opponents with the Pelagian heresy is at best disingenuous, and the implication that one is either with the Pelagians or with Augustine and the Church is a charge that not even Augustine could agree with. And then there are the places where Prosper misquotes and misrepresents Cassian's words and intentions, the clearest example of which is Prosper's summation of Cassian's views in chapter twenty.[118]

Prosper's history of the Pelagian conflict is also deeply flawed, a revisionist account that served Prosper's purpose at the expense of facts and the complexity of the conflict.[119] And Prosper's interpretation of Celestine's *Apostolici verba* is astonishingly bold. According to Prosper, Celestine intimated to Augustine's opponents in Gaul to stop speaking against the doctor, and praised Augustine's books and officially pronounced the authority of his writings.[120] An intimation to stop speaking can be plausibly drawn, but the intimation of an official pronouncement on Augustine's writings is more than dubious. And Prosper's claim that Celestine's praise and endorsement of Augustine's earlier writings also applies to his later works, since they are consistent with each other, is a rather creative bit of logic, especially since Celestine never mentioned any books of Augustine.[121] Prosper also,

117. The most explicit references are in *Contra collatorem* 11.2, 16.1, 21.4 (PL 51: 243, 259, 265, 273; *Against Cassian,* 99–100, 118, 136): "Could a disciple of Pelagius or of Celestius say anything more clearly and more explicitly in keeping with their heresy?" "And you conclude in a few words which contain almost the whole of the Pelagian heresy." "As is well known, the Pelagian heresy is so cunning that, if it notices that after having made a show of self-amendment, some shoot of its own stem favors [its] being spread, it endeavors to restore itself fully from this small remnant."

118. *Contra collatorem* 20 (PL 51: 269–70; *Against Cassian,* 132).

119. *Contra collatorem* 21.1–2 (PL 51: 270–71; *Against Cassian,* 133–34). According to Prosper's account, the Palestinian bishops forced Pelagius to condemn himself, and Zosimus simply condemned the Pelagians, neither of which is completely faithful to the facts.

120. *Contra collatorem* 21.2 (PL 51: 271–72; *Against Cassian,* 134). Cf. Celestine, *Ep.* 21 (PL 50: 528–30).

121. *Contra collatorem* 21.3 (PL 51: 272; *Against Cassian,* 135). Cf. Celestine, *Apostolici verba* (PL 50: 528–30).

for good reason, neglects to include the fact that Augustine's earliest books are inconsistent with his later works on the issue of grace.[122]

Response in Marseilles

It is clear from Prosper's treatise that Celestine's *Apostolici verba* failed to secure any peace between the supporters and opponents of Augustine in Gaul. The death of Celestine left Prosper wondering about how Sixtus would judge this matter. In the face of this difficult situation, Prosper endeavored to appeal to public opinion and papal support. Despite the lukewarm support of Celestine, which his opponents have pointed out, Prosper was determined to put a positive spin on the letter. This was essential to his strategy. According to Prosper's argument, the opponents of Augustine in Gaul were Pelagian, and since all the popes, representing the Church, had condemned the Pelagians, and since Celestine had sided with Augustine against his opponents, the new pope and the general public are to support the side of Augustine.

Prosper's strategy failed. Neither the general public nor the new pope were persuaded by Prosper's treatise. Sixtus did not respond to the situation, much less condemn the opponents of Augustine through papal decree or the influence of the imperial authority.[123] It must also be noted that Leo was still archdeacon in Rome and would have made a papal condemnation still less likely.

Cassian did not respond to Prosper's rebuttal, probably due to his advanced age.[124] After Prosper's response to *Conlatio* 13, around 432, Cassian is not referenced again until he comes up in Gennadius's list, which places Cassian's death in the reign of Theodosius and Valentinian.[125] It is generally believed that Cassian's death occurred in the mid-430s.[126]

122. E.g., *De libero arbitrio* and *Expositio quarundam propositionum ex epistula ad Romanos.*

123. For Sixtus's favorable disposition toward Pelagianism, see Mathisen, *Ecclesiastical Factionalism,* 138 n. 99.

124. According to Stewart's (*Cassian the Monk,* 4, 24) estimation, Cassian was born in the early 360s and died in the mid-430s. Accordingly, Cassian was in his early 70s when he died.

125. Gennadius, *De viris inlustribus* 62 (TU 14/1: 82).

126. Stewart, *Cassian the Monk,* 24; Chadwick, *John Cassian,* 148.

Vincent's *Commonitorium*

Cassian ceased to be a concern for Prosper after his rebuttal, but there were others who continued to express their opposition to Augustine in writing. The response to Prosper's *Contra collatorem* came from Vincent of Lérins.[127] Vincent, a priest monk of the monastic community of Lérins, wrote the *Commonitorium* in 434, and was most likely the author of a list of objections against Augustine's doctrine of predestination, which will be discussed below.[128] Written under the pseudonym *peregrinus,* Vincent's stated purpose was to write down what he had faithfully received from the holy fathers, in order to produce a handbook or guide for determining orthodoxy and heresy.[129] However, Vincent's real purpose was to refute Prosper's *Contra collatorem.*[130]

Summary

Vincent begins by establishing the definition of catholicity as what has been believed *semper, ubique, ab omnibus.*[131] The definition of her-

127. B. J. Kidd (*A History of the Church to A.D. 461,* vol. 3 [Oxford: Clarendon Press, 1922], 154) is the only scholar who shares this view. On Vincent, see Augustine Casiday, "Grace and the Humanity of Christ According to St Vincent of Lérins," *VC* 59 (2005): 298–314; Mark Vessey, "Vincent of Lérins," *ATA,* 870; and Gennadius, *De viris inlustribus* 65 (TU 14/1: 83).

128. Vincent of Lérins, *Commonitorium* (CCL 64; *Commonitories,* trans. Rudolph E. Morris, in *Niceta of Remesiana, Sulpicius Severus, Prosper of Aquitaine,* FC 7 [New York: Fathers of the Church, 1949], 267–332).

129. Vincent, *Commonitorium* 1.1 (CCL 64: 147; *Commonitories,* 267). For an extensive discussion on the *Commonitorium* in the larger political-ecclesial context, see Mark Vessey, "Peregrinus against the Heretics," 530–65.

130. Scholars have disagreed on the extent of *Commonitorium*'s anti-Augustinian sentiment. Markus ("Legacy of Pelagius," 220) claims that Vincent "was not attacking the views of his Augustinian opponents on grace and free will, or defending his own." Mark Vessey ("*Opus Imperfectum* Augustine and His Readers, 426–435 A. D.," *VC* 52 [1998]: 284) concludes that Vincent was attacking Augustine, but refrained from stating the logical conclusion that Augustine was worthy of censure. Mathisen (*Ecclesiastical Factionalism,* 136) asserts Vincent's "real purpose was to respond to Celestine's letter of a few years before [*Apostolici verba*], and to defend the Gallic anti-predestinarian position. . . ." Ogliari (*Gratia et Certamen,* 431) views the work primarily as a handbook to determine orthodoxy and, within that framework, it should be viewed as an expression of Gallic resistance to Augustine's novel doctrine.

131. *Commonitorium* 2.5 (CCL 64: 149; *Commonitories,* 270).

esy, then, is any doctrine that is limited to a certain time, place, and group. Vincent labels these teachings as novelties, namely, the teaching of Augustine, caricatured in chapter twenty-six.[132] Although not mentioned by name, it becomes clear that Augustine's doctrine of predestination is the novelty Vincent was concerned with refuting.

Vincent lists the figures related to the Council of Ephesus (431), which condemned the profane novelty of Nestorius.[133] This judgment of Nestorius was shared by popes Celestine and Sixtus, who upheld the ancient tradition by condemning profane novelties. After quoting from Sixtus's letter to Bishop John of Antioch, "Let no further advance of novelty be permitted, because it is unbecoming to add anything to ancient tradition," Vincent quotes from Celestine's *Apostolici verba,* where he addressed the profane novelty of the practice of presbyters preaching: "Rightly we have to bear the responsibility, if by our silence we encourage error. Therefore, those who behave in this way should be rebuked! They should have no right to free speech."[134] Vincent, however, interprets the profane novelty to be Prosper's group, and so Celestine's rebuke was directed at Prosper's group, not at the opponents of Augustine, who maintain the tradition. Thus, according to Vincent's interpretation, Celestine maintained the tradition by asserting that "novelties should refrain from attacking tradition," that is, Prosper's group should refrain from attacking Church tradition.[135]

Vincent concludes that anyone who opposes the catholic and

132. *Commonitorium* 26.4, 8–9 (CCL 64: 185; *Commonitories,* 318–19): "So now do members speak to members, namely, members of the Devil's body to members of Christ's Body, perfidious men to the faithful, sacrilegious ones to the religious; in short, heretics to Catholics.... Here are the promises by which the heretics usually mislead those who are wanting in foresight. They dare to promise in their teaching that in *their* church—that is, in their own small circle—is to be found a great and special and entirely personal form of divine grace; that it is divinely administered, without any pain, zeal, or effort on their part, to all persons belonging to their group, even if they do not ask or seek or knock."

133. *Commonitorium* 29–31 (CCL 64: 189–92; *Commonitories,* 326–29).

134. *Commonitorium* 32.3–4 (CCL 64: 193; *Commonitories,* 329–31). Cf. Sixtus, *Ep.* 6.7 (PL 50: 609); Celestine, *Ep.* 21.1 (PL 50: 528; trans. Rudolf Morris in *Commonitories,* 330).

135. *Commonitorium* 32.7 (CCL 64: 193; *Commonitories,* 331): "Desinat ... incessere novitas vetustatem."

apostolic decrees insults the memory of Celestine, derides the definitions of Sixtus, disregards the statements of Cyril, and rejects the Council of Ephesus.[136] For Vincent, the catholic faith has already been established by the decrees of the Church, and any teaching that adds a new element to the established catholic faith is heresy.

Commonitorium and *Contra collatorem*

Vincent refuted Prosper's *Contra collatorem* by using the same method of argumentation. Prosper had defended Augustine's teachings by linking Augustine's opponents to the Pelagian heresy, and then claimed that the practice of the Church in condemning the heresy continued through the Church's endorsement of Augustine's opposition to the new form of Pelagianism. Prosper had situated the present conflict in the larger context of the Church's struggle against Pelagianism. For Prosper, the issue was catholicity. Augustine stood in the tradition of the Church, which was defended by Innocent, the Synod of Diospolis, Zosimus, the African councils, Boniface, and Celestine.[137] Moreover, Augustine's opposition to the new heresy was affirmed by Celestine and, Prosper hoped, by Sixtus, while his opponents were declared to have opposed the catholic faith.

Vincent takes the same argument but turns it on Prosper. Vincent attacks Augustine's teaching on grace by linking the older heresies to Augustine's teaching. The Church has continued the practice of opposing novelties in its opposition to Augustine's teachings. For Vincent too the issue was catholicity. Vincent had his own list that supported the tradition of opposing novelty, which included Celestine, Sixtus, Cyril, and the Council of Ephesus.[138] According to Vincent's interpretation of *Apostolici verba,* Celestine had continued to observe this practice by opposing the novelty of Augustine's teachings and by endorsing the Gauls.[139] And in regard to Prosper's hope of Sixtus's support, Vincent makes clear that Sixtus is continuing the tradition in opposing novelty, that is, Augustine.[140]

136. *Commonitorium* 33.1–2 (CCL 64: 194; *Commonitories,* 331).
137. *Contra collatorem* 21.1–2 (PL 51: 270–71; *Against Cassian,* 133–34).
138. *Commonitorium* 33.1–2 (CCL 64: 194; *Commonitories,* 331).
139. *Commonitorium* 32.4–7 (CCL 64: 193; *Commonitories,* 330).
140. *Commonitorium* 32.1–3 (CCL 64: 193; *Commonitories,* 330).

Vincent's method of argumentation parallels Prosper's *Contra collatorem* too closely to believe that it was merely a coincidence. Given the close links between the monastic communities of Marseilles and Lérins, and the limitations placed on Cassian by his advanced age, the *Commonitorium* should be viewed as a response to Prosper's attack on Cassian.[141]

The *Commonitorium* was not the definitive Gallic response to Prosper and Celestine, as one scholar has proposed; rather, it represents yet another response to the increasingly polarized debate, which will continue.[142] Vincent's work may have had an effect on Prosper.[143] Although Prosper did not formally respond to the *Commonitorium,* Prosper never again refers to Celestine's pronouncement nor specific Church decrees to defend Augustine. There were already counterclaims to Prosper's interpretation of Celestine's *Apostolici verba* prior to *Commonitorium,* and Vincent's argument for catholicity and interpretation of Celestine's pronouncement would only add to the difficulty of defending Augustine.[144] Yet, this point, the catholicity of Augustine, was the essential basis for his defense of Augustine.

Initial Steps Away from Augustine

In the course of this period, Prosper's strict fidelity to Augustine progressively wavers. The first instance of this movement away from Augustine is the absence of Augustine's name in a short work composed of a little more than two dozen lines entitled *Epitaphium Nestorianae et Pelagianae haereseon,* written sometime after 431 (Council of Ephesus), but before 433.[145] In condemning the two heresies, and in linking the Nestorian to the Pelagian heresy, Pros-

141. The relationship between the two monastic communities are detailed in Mathisen, *Ecclesiastical Factionalism,* 119–40.

142. Mathisen, *Ecclesiastical Factionalism,* 135.

143. Cappuyns ("Le premier représentant," 321) argued against this view: "Rien ne prouve qu'il ait eu connaissance du *Commonitorium. . . .*"

144. *Contra collatorem* 21.3–4 (PL 51: 273; *Against Cassian,* 134–36).

145. *Epitaphium Nestorianae et Pelagianae haereseon* (PL 51: 153–54). Muhlberger (*Fifth-Century Chroniclers,* 85 n. 77) places the date of the work shortly before the first edition of Prosper's *Chronicon,* 433.

per does not include any mention of Augustine. If, as asserted by Le Brun and Mangeant, Prosper had his Gallic opponents in mind, the absence of Augustine's name is significant.[146] In condemning, indirectly, his Gallic opponents, Prosper thought it unnecessary to appeal to Augustine. No conclusions on Prosper's motive for avoiding Augustine's name or on any changes in Prosper's convictions about Augustine can be drawn, but the avoidance of Augustine's name anticipates more pronounced and explicit expressions of Prosper's changing estimations of Augustine.

Epitoma Chronicon

In 433, shortly after his work against the two heresies, Prosper wrote the first edition of his *Chronicon.*[147] Prosper's chronicle will be treated at length in the following chapter, but there are entries on Augustine that provide significant insight into Prosper's view of Augustine in 433. Augustine does not figure large in Prosper's *Chronicon.* Augustine's elevation to bishop is noted under the year 395: "Augustine, the disciple of the blessed Ambrose and eminent in eloquence and learning, was made bishop at Hippo in Africa," and his role in the condemnation of the Pelagians under the year 416: "At this time the Pelagians, already condemned by Pope Innocent, were resisted by the diligence of the Africans and especially by the knowledge of Bishop Augustine."[148] The last entry is listed under the year 430:

> Aurelius Augustine, a bishop most outstanding in every respect, died 28 August. In his very last days he was responding to the books of Julian [of Eclanum] amidst the attacks of besieging Vandals and persevering gloriously in defense of Christian grace.[149]

146. J. B. Le Brun des Marettes and Luc Urbain Mangeant, *Epitaphium Nestorianae et Pelagianae haereseon* (PL 51: 153a): "Ad Massiliensium rursus invidiam inducitur haeresis Nestoriana, deplorans suum et Pelagianismi exterminium: eamque illius assignans causam qua non satis immunes essent Semipelagiani."

147. *Chronicon* (MGH, AA 9: 385–499; *Chronicle,* 62–76). Prosper's epitomizes Jerome's chronicle and continues it where Jerome ended in 378 to 455. Cf. Jerome, *Chronicon.* There were at least four versions that Prosper produced between 433 and 455; see Muhlberger, *Fifth-Century Chroniclers,* 56.

148. *Chronicon,* sub ann. 395, 416 (MGH, AA 9: 463, 468; *Chronicle,* 64, 65–66).

149. *Chronicon,* sub an. 430 (MGH, AA 9: 473; *Chronicle,* 68).

Although the mention of Augustine is necessary limited by such a short work, the absence of any mention of the conflict in Gaul is alarming. Neither Cassian nor any of the *doctores Gallicani* associated with opposing Augustine in Gaul are mentioned. Prosper was in middle of a heated battle with powerful Gauls over Augustine's teaching on grace, yet Prosper fails to include this information.

Prosper has restricted Augustine's teachings on grace to the Pelagian conflict. Prosper's primary concern, in regard to ecclesiastical affairs, is the theological and disciplinary authority of the Apostolic See in the struggle against heresy.[150] In the larger struggle, Augustine was a contributor, but not the decisive voice or authority in the fight against Pelagianism.

Prosper's appreciation of the catholic faith and especially the authority of the Apostolic See had already been evident in Prosper, but at the same time Augustine had been understood as the representative of the catholic position on grace. Now the claim of Augustine's catholicity and the importance of his involvement in the Pelagian conflict have receded, and the conflict over Augustine's catholicity in Gaul is absent.

Perhaps the absence can be explained by the brevity of the work, but such an important issue in Prosper's life at the time could not have gone unmentioned had Prosper felt more sure of his views of Augustine. Prosper's *Chronicon* reveals, at minimum, an unwillingness to claim the catholicity of Augustine's doctrine of grace against his Gallic opponents. The *Commonitorium* may be to blame for Prosper's discontinued use of his detailed catholicity argument, including Celestine's *Apostolici verba,* but the extent to which it contributed to Prosper's personal reevaluation of Augustine is unknown. What is evident in this work is a diminished appreciation of Augustine. Augustine was catholic in opposing the Pelagians, but without the inclusion of the current debate, the implication is that Augustine's catholicity in relation to his Gallic opponents and the issues involved, namely predestination, is uncertain.

150. Muhlberger, *Fifth-Century Chroniclers,* 86.

Pro Augustino responsiones ad capitula obiectionum Gallorum calumniantium and *Pro Augustino responsiones ad capitula obiectionum Vincentiarum*

The once zealous defender of Augustine took further steps away from Augustine in Prosper's last two works of this period, *Responsiones ad capitula obiectionum Gallorum calumniantium* and *Responsiones ad capitula obiectionum Vincentiarum.* These works cannot be dated more precisely than belonging to the period probably after the 433 edition of the *Chronicon,* but definitely before 435.[151] There are two significant changes evident in the two works: the presentations of predestination and the nature of the defense of Augustine. Prosper did not include predestination in his response to Cassian's *Conlatio* 13, which, as argued above, was implied; when Prosper addresses predestination in these two responses, however, he adds an element foreign to Augustine's predestination, which Augustine had actually condemned.[152] Such a view of predestination was common among the Gallic opponents. In addition, the description and defense of Augustine in *Responsiones ad capitula obiectionum Gallorum calumniantium* are significantly toned down, while *Responsiones ad capitula obiectionum Vincentiarum* does not contain any mention of Augustine at all.

Both works answer a set of objections drawn from Augustine's doctrine of grace that are not extant. The exaggerated objections are consistent with the critiques thus far expressed by the opponents of Augustine, but exaggeration to some degree by Prosper cannot be ruled out, as this was a common strategy employed by both sides. These two works were written sometime between 433 and 435, and the more pronounced shift away from Augustine in *Responsiones ad capitula obiectionum Vincentiarum* compared with *Responsiones ad capitula obiectionum Gallorum calumniantium,* suggesting a progression, favors the view that *Responsiones ad obiectionum Gallorum*

151. The *terminus ante quem* of 435 is based on Chisholm's conclusion on the date of the *Hypomnesticon,* which was affirmed by de Plinval. Since the *Hypomnesticon* was written in the same period, all three were written before 435. Cf. Chisholm, *Pseudo-Augustinian Hypomnesticon,* vol. 1, 129 n. 1. See chapter 1.

152. Cf. *Contra collatorem* 21.3 (PL 51: 272; *Against Cassian,* 135).

was written first.[153] Thus, the first work, in response to the Gauls, referred to Augustine by name and a Church council; the second work, in response to the Vincentian articles, avoids the mention of Augustine by name, but refers to the authority of the Apostolic See. Taken together, the works reveal not only a break with Augustine's doctrine of grace, but perhaps something of what Cappuyns termed a concession to his opponents.[154]

In *Responsiones ad capitula obiectionum Gallorum* Prosper refutes fifteen objections to Augustine's teachings on grace by drawing faithfully from Augustine's works.[155] It is unclear who compiled these objections, but Prosper attributes them to the Gauls. That Prosper referred to them as Gauls suggests that the objections came from beyond Marseilles. These objections may have been known to Prosper as separate objections, which he collected into one set of objections, or they may have existed as a complete set. Whoever these objectors were, Prosper displayed an uncharacteristic level of restraint in responding to them. The work was intended to convince rather than condemn. Missing in this treatise is the bitter polemical device of linking his opponents to heresy or Pelagianism; instead, Prosper refers to one who holds contrary views merely as *non est catholicus.*[156]

The fifteen objections are related to the issue of predestination, and are exaggerated expressions of Augustine's teachings. Prosper provides an answer after each objection, then lists the objections and answers them in summary form at the end of the work—the same method used against Cassian's *Conlatio* 13 in *Contra collatorem.*

Prosper's answers are, as he stated in his preface, faithful to Augustine's teachings, except in the answers to objections two and three. At the end of the answer to objection two, Prosper states, "since God's prescience was neither uncertain nor mistaken about the future actions of this man, He never elected nor predestined

153. Cappuyns, "Le premier," 321 n. 34.

154. Cappuyns, "Le premier," 322–26.

155. *Res. Gall.,* Praef. (PL 51: 156–57; *Answers to Gauls,* 139): "In nullo recedens a tramite earum definitionum quae in sancti viri disputationibus continentur."

156. *Res. Gall.* 2 (PL 51: 169–74; *Answers to Gauls,* 157–62).

him, nor did He set apart from eternal damnation him who was to be a reprobate."[157]

Prosper's statement here asserts that God's nonpredestination is based on God's foreknowledge of a person's evil ways. The same view is expressed in the answer to objection three: "Rather, the reason why they were not of the predestined is that God foreknew they would be impenitent through their own fault."[158] This is also repeated again in the conclusion to the answer: "And though they were reborn from sinfulness and made just, yet they were not predestined by God, who foreknew that they would be impenitent."[159] While these statements may imply that God's positive predestination is based on God's foreknowledge of future good actions of a person, Prosper elsewhere remains faithful to the Augustinian view of predestination to salvation: faith, works, and final perseverance are predestined gifts from God.[160]

Prosper maintains the Augustinian view of predestination to salvation, but introduces the view that God's withholding of predestination is based on foreknowledge. It is an innovation, foreign to the earlier Prosper and the later Augustine, but not to their opponents.[161] Previously in *Responsiones ad exerpta Genuensium,* Prosper wrote, "God could have saved them in His mercy had he been pleased to do so," and left the discrimination as a mystery of God.[162] Prosper now refutes the same opinion he had once held.[163]

157. *Res. Gall.* 1.2 (PL 51: 158; *Answers to Gauls,* 141): "Quod quia Dei praescientiam nec latuit, nec fefellit, sine dubio talem numquam elegit, numquam praedestinavit, et periturum numquam ab aeterna perditione discrevit."

158. *Res. Gall.* 1.3 (PL 51: 158; *Answers to Gauls,* 141): "Sed ideo praedestinati non sunt, quia tales futuri ex voluntaria praevaricatione praesciti sunt."

159. *Res. Gall.* 1.3 (PL 51: 159; *Answers to Gauls,* 142): "Atque ab hoc licet fuerint renati, fuerint justificati, ab eo tamen qui illos tales praescivit non sunt praedestinati."

160. *Res. Gall.* 1.14 (PL 51: 169–70; *Answers to Gauls,* 155): "Fides autem et charitatis opera, atque in eis usque in finem perseverantia, quia homini per Dei gratiam conferuntur, recte et ipsa, et quae eis retribuenda sunt, praedestinata dicuntur."

161. Cf. Aug., *De Praed. sanct.* 13.25 (PL 44: 978–79; *Predestination,* 169–70).

162. Prosper, *Resp. ad Gen.* 8 (PL 51: 197; *Answers to Genoese,* 63).

163. Cf. Prosper, "Letter 225," 43–44: "Our Lord Jesus Christ, they hold, has died for the whole of mankind. Not one man is excluded from the redemption which He hath wrought in His blood. . . . The sacrament of divine mercy is meant for all men. If many fail to be reborn in baptism, it is because God foreknew that they had no desire to be reborn."

The presentation of Augustine has also changed. Augustine is referred to only once in the preface, and without the characteristic zeal or full appreciation of Augustine's catholicity. Prosper merely describes Augustine as a catholic bishop of saintly memory and a writer of highest renown, who for a number of years defended and taught doctrines against the Pelagians in accordance with the apostolic tradition.[164] Augustine or his connection to and endorsement by the apostolic tradition are absent in the body of the treatise. The only reference to a council is to the Council of Carthage (418), but only with the mention of the two hundred and fourteen bishops acting against the enemies of grace.[165]

In defending Augustine's teaching, Prosper claims that anyone who ascribes to the objections is not catholic.[166] In Prosper's view, anyone who opposes Augustine's teachings is not catholic, but it was not a faithful expression of Augustine's teaching that Prosper defended, namely, answers two and three. According to Prosper's view of catholicity, then, the withholding of predestination is due to God's foreknowledge. The implication is that this is Augustine's teaching, which it was not.

It is unclear what Prosper's intention was in presenting this view under the teaching of Augustine. Given Prosper's familiarity with Augustine's teaching, it is impossible that he genuinely believed that Augustine held this position. Perhaps Prosper was reinterpreting Augustine's teaching to conform to Prosper's understanding of catholicity. In Prosper's estimation, Augustine's doctrine of predestination was not exactly the expression of the catholic view of grace. However subtle, this was a significant step away from an absolute adherence to Augustine's doctrine of predestination, which will also be expressed in the next work.

In *Responsiones ad capitula obiectionum Vincentiarum* Prosper turned his attention to a set of sixteen objections attributed to Vincent of Lérins, which claim to be the expressions of Prosper's group.[167]

164. *Res. Gall.*, Praef. (PL 51: 155–57; *Answers to Gauls,* 139).

165. *Res. Gall.* 1.8 (PL 51: 164; *Answers to Gauls,* 148–49).

166. *Res. Gall.* 2 (PL 51: 169–74; *Answers to Gauls,* 157–62).

167. Although the set of objections are not existent, scholarly opinion favors Vincent

Prosper resolved to refute these objections from the Pelagians by the authority of the Apostolic See.[168] While Prosper had linked his opponents with Pelagianism, in this work they are referred to simply as Pelagian. And Prosper's intent is not to correct these Pelagians, but to persuade his readers that Prosper's faction rightly condemns them. Prosper maintains the same view of predestination expressed in his responses to the Gauls, but there is no mention of Augustine.

The objections were by far the most exaggerated expressions of Augustine's teachings on predestination, drawing the crudest and inflammatory conclusions from his doctrine. These objections present God as the cause of sin and reprobation. Prosper answers these objections by faithfully adhering to Augustine's teachings, except in the answer to objection twelve: "By the predestination of God, sons of God become sons of the devil, the temples of the Holy Spirit temples of demons, and the members of Christ members of a harlot." As in his response to the Gauls, Prosper's answer to this objection remains faithful to Augustine's predestination to salvation, "The reverse is true: it is predestination that makes of sons of the devil sons of God, of temples of demons temples of the Holy Spirit, of members of a harlot members of Christ."[169] However, as in his response to the Gauls, in explaining the reason for damnation, Prosper asserts that they were not predestined because God foresaw that they would fall.[170]

Although the objections were drawn from Augustine's teachings and answered with Augustine's teachings, except answer twelve, Augustine is never mentioned or implied. Here even the attempt to reinterpret Augustine's teaching to conform to Prosper's understanding of the catholic faith is not made. Augustine has ceased to be relevant in Prosper's defense against his opponents. It is a further

---

as the author; see Cappuyns, "Le premier," 321; Markus, "Legacy of Pelagius," 219; and Vessey, "Vincent of Lérins," 870.

168. *Res. Vinc.*, praef. (PL 51: 178; *Answers to Vincentian Articles*, 163): "Propositis igitur singillatim sedecim capitulis, sub unoquoque eorum, sensus nostri, et fidei quam contra Pelagianos ex apostolicae auctoritate defendimus."

169. *Res. Vinc.* 12 (PL 51: 183–84; *Answers to Vincentian Articles*, 172).

170. *Res. Vinc.* 12 (PL 51: 184; *Answers to Vincentian Articles*, 172): "Et quia praesciti sunt casuri, non sunt praedestinati."

indication of Prosper's movement away from Augustine, not only in doctrine, but also in his appreciation of him.

Prosper's response to Vincent shows signs of diminishing enthusiasm in defending Augustine and in opposing his opponents. The long and bitter controversy appears to have taken its toll on Prosper. Prosper refuted Vincent rather half-heartedly as compared to his previous writings. Prosper's opponents are labeled Pelagian, but without further details. Prosper states that he will oppose them by the authority of the Apostolic See, but fails to mention any documents or decrees associated with the Apostolic See. It appears Prosper was compelled to refute these charges, but in a manner that suggests Prosper no longer wished to touch upon the controversial points. Augustine's mention is deemed unnecessary, the subtleties of his opponents' positions on grace are not debated but instead reduced to Pelagianism, and the catholic view on grace has been determined by the Apostolic See, but without reference to its endorsement of or relationship to Augustine.

Prosper has distanced himself from strict adherence to Augustine's authority and doctrine. There is even evidence that Prosper modified Augustine's doctrine of predestination, revealing a position that accepts what Augustine and Prosper had previously condemned in their opponents: God's punishment or withholding of predestination based on God's foreknowledge of future sins. As Prosper's appreciation of Augustine diminishes, what is becoming more apparent is Prosper's awareness of the authority of the Roman Church, though still not fully developed.

Relevant Works from This Period

Although the following works—the *Hypomnesticon,* the *Capitula sancti Augustini in urbem Romam transmissa,* and *De praedestinatione et gratia*—cannot be dated precisely or their authors identified with any certainty, these works probably fall within the later part of this period in Prosper's life: 430–440. These three works contribute to the complexity of the reactions to Augustine's doctrine of grace.

Hypomnesticon and *Capitula sancti Augustini in urbem Romam transmissa*

The *Hypomnesticon* was written around the same period as Prosper's *Pro Augustino responsiones ad capitula obiectionum Gallorum calumniantium* and *Pro Augustino responsiones ad capitula obiectionum Vincentiarum,* sometime between 433 and 435, probably by a member of Prosper's Augustinian faction in Marseilles.[171] The similarity between Prosper's responses and the *Hypomnesticon*'s defense of Augustine's doctrine of grace, and the fact that Prosper was not the author of the *Hypomnesticon,* suggests that its author reflects the shared and evolving views of the Augustinian faction in Marseilles. Augustine's doctrine of grace is defended, and like the two responses from Prosper, the *Hypomnesticon* asserts that God's decision to withhold predestination is based on God's foreknowledge of the sinful lives they will lead.[172] Hilary, Leontius, or some other unknown member may be behind the work, but this cannot be confirmed.

The *Capitula* was written around the time of the *Hypomnesticon* and shares its moderate Augustinianism.[173] The *Capitula* presented twenty statements selected from the works of Augustine concerning the issue of grace. Like the *Hypomnesticon* and Prosper's two responses, the *Capitula* is faithful to Augustine's anti-Pelagian arguments, and presents a different view of predestination, exactly in the same manner as Prosper's responses and the *Hypomnesticon.* In explaining why some are not predestined, the *Capitula* answered that God excludes on the basis of God's foreknowledge of future sins. God's foreknowledge does not cause the free will to sin; rather, God foreknows the sins that will be committed by the free will.[174] However, unlike the *Hypomnesticon* and Prosper's two responses, the

171. For the question of authorship, date, and arguments of the *Hypomnesticon,* see chapter 1.

172. Cf. *Hypomnesticon* 6.2, 6.5 (ed. Chisholm, 192, 198) and Prosper, *Res. Gall.* 1.2, 1.3 (PL 51: 158–59; *Answers to Gauls,* 142); *Res. Vinc.* 12 (PL 51: 184; *Answers to Vincentian Articles,* 172).

173. See chapter 1 for the date. In CCL 85A: 243–73.

174. *Capitula* 14.17 (CCL 85A: 260–61): "A numero fidelium prorsus excluditur—non quod praescientia dei liberum nostrum peccare cogat arbitrium, quamuis per ipsum liberum arbitrium nos peccaturos esse praescierit."

author then adds a paraphrase of what Augustine used in connection with his doctrine of predestination in *De praedestinatione sanctorum*.[175] The author paraphrased from a work that condemned the very idea that God's punishment is based on God's foreknowledge of future sins.[176]

Such an attempt to connect the Augustinian phrase as the concluding thought to an un-Augustinian definition of nonpredestination suggests someone other than Prosper or the author of the *Hypomnesticon* was responsible for its composition. The form of the work is also something new. It was not written in response to a particular situation, but is more of a handbook summarizing the essential elements of Augustine's doctrine of grace, according to its author. This seems to suggest that the author of the *Capitula* belonged to the Augustinian faction, like the author of the *Hypomnesticon*.

The inclusion of the *Hypomnesticon* and the *Capitula* in the history of the debate sheds further light on the Augustinian faction in Marseilles. Their presence further indicates that Prosper was not alone in defending Augustine, and that Prosper's evolving views toward Augustine's doctrine of grace were shared among his faction. It may be noted, at least to this point, that Prosper's thoughts were connected to and expressed the views of a group, and not merely that of a lone individual. One could also infer that Prosper's views, up to this point, resulted from a collective effort at understanding and interpreting Augustine's doctrine of grace. That is, behind Prosper's writings on grace, there were discussions and perhaps even debates within the group on Augustine's doctrine of grace and how best to defend him in light of the opposition.

The differences amount to the method employed in defending their views of grace. In his responses to the Gauls, Prosper referred to Augustine by name and to a Church council to defend Augus-

175. Cf. Aug. (*De praed. sanct.* 8.17–18 [PL 44: 975; *Predestination*, 165]): "Quae sine praescientia [praedestinatio] non potest esse: potest autem esse sine praedestinatione praescientia." (*Capitula* 14.17 [CCL 85A: 261]): "Inter praescientiam enim et praedestinationem hoc interest, quod non omnia quae praesciuntur praedestinantur, omnia autem quae pradestinantur praesciuntur."

176. Cf. Aug., *De praed. sanct.* 13.25 (PL 44: 978–79).

tine. In response to the Vincentian articles, Prosper avoids the mention of Augustine by name, but refers to the authority of the Apostolic See. In the *Hypomnesticon,* the author refers to Augustine by name in the title, but does not draw from authoritative documents from the Church. And the *Capitula* reduce Augustine's thoughts to a series of statements, providing its readers a useful reference text in the defense of Augustine. Taken together these writings reflect the struggle to defend Augustine's doctrine of grace while at the same time modifying their defense according to their own evolving understanding of grace, and, for Prosper, an evolving appreciation of the Roman Church.

De praedestinatione et gratia

This anonymous work attempted to reconcile the Augustinian view of predestination with that of the optimistic view of free will asserted by the opponents of Augustine's views.[177] The definition of predestination is faithful to Augustine, more so than that of the *Hypomnesticon* or Prosper's responses, and explicitly condemns the idea that punishment is based on God's foreknowledge of future sins.[178] The definition of free will, corresponding to the opponents of Augustine's doctrine of grace, asserts the ability and freedom of the will to choose to follow or to reject God's call.[179]

The identity of the author is unknown, as is the particular faction he may have belonged to—Augustinian or *doctores Gallicani.* An argument can be made for each of these factions, but also for neither of these. The acceptance of both views, reflecting the most controversial idea from each side, suggests an author who remained outside of the conflict, or who came to some radical conclusion while

177. PL 45: 1665–78. Cf. A. Zumkeller, "Die pseudoaugustinische Schrift 'De pradestinatione et gratia': Inhalt, Überlieferung, Verfasserfrage und Nachwirkung," *Augustinianum* 25 (1985): 539–63.

178. *De praedestinatione et gratia* 14.16 (PL 45: 1671): "Quod de Deo quam impie dicatur, advertit quisque qui peccatis suis inde blanditur, quod Deus eum peccatorem futurum esse praescierit."

179. *De predestinatione et gratia* 9.10 (PL 45: 1671): "Ut vocatione ipsius bonorum principia sumeremus; vocati autem atque illuminati, vias mandatorum ejus rationis ingenitae intelligentia nosceremus, et eas libero vel eligeremus vel relinqueremus arbitrio.... Liberum vero quod ab eo habemus arbitrium."

engaged in the polemical battle on one side or the other. The former seems much more likely considering that Prosper and the author of the *Hypomnesticon* modified Augustine's predestination, but not the opposition to the *initium fidei* idea. In fact, Prosper will continue to oppose his Gallic opponents' idea of the *initium fidei* to the very end of his life, as will be evident in the following chapter.

All that can be said about the anonymous author is that he represents yet another reaction to Augustine's doctrine of grace, beyond the views of the two central parties. Or, as Markus commented, "Treatises were now produced which took up a mediating position between the theology associated with the monastic milieu of Marseilles and the proponents of Augustinian views."[180]

Conclusion

These five works reveal just how complex the reaction to Augustine's doctrine of grace was in Gaul. The Augustinian faction was active and dynamic. As expected, and perfectly reasonable, the reaction to Augustine's doctrine was not limited to these two groups. One such reaction appreciated the ideas from both sides. Predestination and the *initium fidei* are not mutually exclusive, but in harmony with each other. However, though such a voice of compromise could not have been unique, it would have hardly risen above the din of the fierce battle of words that characterize the conflict between the two opposing groups.

Second Period of Reflection (435–440)

Prosper's relocation to Rome at some point and his association with Leo's pontificate are well established.[181] The date and reason for Prosper's move to Rome are less certain, but it appears that he remained in Marseilles until 440 and not, as commonly asserted, that Prosper moved to Rome around 435 because of Cassian's death.

180. Markus, "Legacy of Pelagius," 219.

181. Scholars have generally accepted the view of Gennadius, *De viris inlustribus* 71 (TU 14/1: 90): "Epistulae quoque Papae Leonis adversus Eutychen de vera Christi incarnatione ad diversos datae ab isto dictatae creduntur."

Prosper's writing gave way to reflection during these years, the fruits of which are apparent in the next period of his life in Rome.

The majority of scholars have followed Cappuyns's view, which argued that as a result of Cassian's death, around 435, the storm of controversy settled down and Prosper retired from the scene to Rome.[182] Cappuyns based this judgment on Hauck's conclusion that the years 434 to 435 in Prosper's *Chronicon* indicates a new part, with Gaul giving way to Rome in terms of interest and information.[183] Hauck's conclusion has been refuted by Markus, who has found no evidence of any discernable difference in interest or information between the parts before and after the break in 433.[184]

Markus, however, did not address Cappuyns's claim that the reason for Prosper's move to Rome was the peace in Provence caused by Cassian's death. One scholar has gone so far as to suggest that Cassian's death had a "profound, even liberating effect on Prosper."[185] However, as argued above, Cassian was not the only opponent of Prosper's. Moreover, although there was peace of a sort that followed Cassian's death, in regards to the absence of written attacks against the teachings of Augustine in Gaul, this literary silence should not be taken as an end to the debate. One recalls that it took several years before the opposition to Augustine's teachings was expressed in writing, and Prosper and Hilary made repeated references to discussions where Augustine's teachings were criticized. It should also be noted that there may very well have been written objections against Augustine, but these were not preserved, as was the case with the objections from Vincent and the Gauls, which are known only through Prosper's response to them.

After Cassian's death, there were others who were still alive, and presumably still opposed to Augustine's teachings, unless, of course,

182. Cappuyns ("Le premier," 326): "L'orage provençal s'apaisa bientôt, sans doute, car Cassien s'éteignit vers 435, et Prosper se retira de la scene. Il fixa son séjour à Rome." Cf. Oligari, *Gratia et Certamen,* 432; Weaver, *Divine Grace,* 155; and Barclift, "Predestination and Divine Foreknowledge," 8.

183. Cappuyns, "Le premier," 326 n. 47, referring to A. Hauck, "Prosper von Aquitanien," RE 16/3 (1905): 126. Cf. Prosper, *Chronicon* (MGH, AA 9: 474; *Chronicle,* 69).

184. Markus, "Chronicle and Theology," 33.

185. Barclift, "Predestination and Divine Foreknowledge," 8.

they all suddenly changed their views of Augustine's teachings or stopped discussing it all together; or that the elderly Cassian, dying in his early seventies, had outlived all those referred to in Prosper's and Hilary's letters to Augustine, Celestine's *Apostolici verba,* Prosper's *De ingratis, Contra collatorem, Responsiones ad capitula obiectionum Gallorum, Responsiones ad capitula obiectionum Vincentiarum,* and the *Hypomnesticon.* Such assumptions are untenable.

It is more than plausible to assume at least some, if not a significant amount, of the people referred to by Prosper, Hilary, and Celestine continued to stand in opposition to Prosper. The argument for peace in the wake of Cassian's death as the cause for Prosper's departure for Rome cannot be maintained.

Prosper, it appears, remained in Marseilles after Cassian's death for several years, but he refused to engage his opponents, at least in writing. For five years Prosper wrote nothing. It is difficult to assess what happened during these years. However, Prosper's initial change of fidelity and appreciation of Augustine in his last works of this period, and the dramatic changes after this period, suggest that these years of silence in between were a time of reflection and reevaluation of convictions he had once held and defended with zealous enthusiasm. Such a period of literary inactivity was not unique to Prosper. After *De providentia Dei,* in 416, Prosper stopped writing for nearly a decade. As argued in chapter four, Prosper emerged from the period of study and reflection transformed as a committed Christian—a *servus Dei.* Prosper had a broad idea of what catholicity meant at that time and naively assumed Augustine's authority and doctrine of predestination were perfectly catholic. This period of silence was similar.

In these years of reflection, Prosper reevaluated his understanding of catholicity and Augustine. Prosper's initial and primary conviction of catholicity remained, but became more clearly equated with the Roman Church. As a result, he will no longer be able to maintain his convictions about the authority and catholicity of Augustine. Prosper will no longer defend the doctrine of predestination or even mention the word *praedestinatio.* By the beginning of the next period in his life, 440–455, Prosper restricts his devotion and efforts primarily to the Roman Church. In his letter to Augustine in 427, Prosper had proudly proclaimed himself to be among the *perfectae gratiae intrepidi amatores.*[186] By the end of this period, Prosper could still claim this, but this perfect grace was not Augustine's. Prosper had yet to fully accept the primacy of the Roman Church, which will be established toward the end of his life, but Prosper understood, by 440, that he could no longer defend Augustine and his doctrine of predestination.

Prosper departed from the polemical battlefield for five years, and these years afforded Prosper time to rest and reflect on the struggle that he helped to initiate and carry on, which also threatened to continue with no end in sight. Prosper will emerge into the public spotlight under dramatically different circumstances. No longer leading the charge against his opponents in Gaul, Prosper would find himself under the peaceful theological sky of Rome in the service of the Roman Church.

186. Prosper, *Ep.* 225.7 (CSEL 57: 465).

~6

Servus Ecclesiae (440–455)

The Primacy of the Roman Church

PROSPER'S RESIDENCE in Marseilles ended in 440, when he moved to Rome to serve as an advisor to the newly elected Pope Leo. Once there, Prosper quickly assimilated into the Roman Church. During this period, Prosper came to fully appreciate the role and authority of the Roman Church he had initially held in Marseilles. In Rome, Prosper was no longer a *servus Dei,* but became a *servus ecclesiae,* fully and faithfully at the service of the Roman Church. Prosper's conviction that Augustine's authority and doctrine of grace were not the measure of catholicity had come about in those years of reflection and contemplation (435–440). However, Prosper could not completely abandon his old master, but whereas he had attempted to conform the catholic faith to Augustine in the past, he now attempted to conform Augustine to the catholic faith. Nor could Prosper completely abandon his opposition to the theological factions that he had vigorously battled against in Gaul. While his views of Augustine and catholicity had changed, he remained steadfast in his opposition to his old opponents although his tone toward them had moderated.

Toward the end of his life, Prosper developed his own theology of grace, refined by the many years he had spent debating, reflecting, and writing about grace. In Prosper's last two works, the 455 edition of the *Chronicon* and the *Praeteritorum sedis apostolicae episcoporum auctoritates de gratia Dei et libero voluntatis arbitrio,* he limited his expression to what he had come to understand as catholic—the authority and teachings of the Apostolic See and the liturgical practices of the Church. Both works were written with an eye toward posterity, reflecting Prosper's desire to pass on to the future what he deemed to be of importance: the authority of the Roman Church and its definition on grace. In the end, what mattered most to Prosper was not himself—his various writings on grace or even his contributions as Leo's advisor—but the teachings and practices of the Roman Church. Prosper had, since shortly after writing *De providentia Dei,* defended the catholic faith. It took several decades for Prosper to conclude that the Roman Church defined the catholic faith.

Although Prosper's works during this period cannot be dated more precisely, the order of these works are as follows, reflecting Prosper's evolution toward a complete understanding of catholicity. The first set of works involves his attempts to define the catholic view of grace in relation to Augustine—*Expositio psalmorum a centesimo usque ad centesimum quinquagesimum, Liber sententiarum ex operibus sancti Augustini delibatarum,* and *Epigrammata ex sententiis sancti Augustini*—and to Prosper's Gallic opponents—*Epistula ad Demetriadem de vera humilitate.* Prosper concludes this attempt by presenting his own view, an alternative to both, in *De vocatione omnium gentium.* The 455 edition of the *Chronicon* and the *Praeteritorum episcoporum sedis apostolicae auctoritates de gratia Dei et libero voluntatis arbitrio* are the last works. They reflect Prosper's full and absolute adhesion to the Roman Church, and Prosper's final development on the issue of grace. In the *Auctoritates,* Prosper does not attempt to explain grace through his own understanding, as he had struggled to do for decades, but to present only the view of grace as strictly defined by the Apostolic See and Church liturgy. In the *Chronicon,* Prosper goes even further. He deliberately omitted the Church's internal struggle over Augustine's views of grace. All the time and efforts of the most important figures in the West spent on behalf of the struggle to define grace, to which Prosper personally devoted a quarter century of his life, was, in the end, not significant enough to be even mentioned in the *Chronicon.* The issue of grace was of interest to Prosper, and where it clearly manifested a concern—Pelagianism—it was noted, but the overriding concern was Prosper's ecclesiology. It is the Church, inspired by its liturgy and guided by the Apostolic See, which is at the center of Prosper's vision of the unfolding drama of history.

Meeting in Gaul

Although Prosper and his fellow residents in Marseilles were safely removed from the political and military unrest that wreaked havoc in Gaul, one particular political episode would change the course of Prosper's life. The Roman general, Aetius, who ruled over the Western Empire as *magister utriusque militiae* and patrician from 433 to 454, became embroiled in a conflict with Albinus, a powerful Italian aristocrat, in 440.[1] It is not known exactly what the circumstances of the conflict were, but only that Archdeacon Leo was sent to Gaul to resolve the conflict between the two men, which threatened the stability and security of Gaul.[2] While Leo was on this mission, Pope Sixtus died on June 24, 440, and Leo was summoned back to Rome to become the forty-third bishop of the Roman Church.[3] It was then that Leo invited Prosper to become his advisor. Valentin, after subtly suggesting that Leo met Prosper in Gaul in 440, argued:

> Il est difficile de croire que saint Léon n'ait pas été frappé de la valeur intellectuelle de saint Prosper, et c'est sous cette impression, fortifiée encore par la réputation dont jouissait en Gaul l'illustre Aquitain, qu'il se serait décidé à lui confier les fonctions de secrétaire. . . .[4]

1. For Aetius, see E. A. Freeman, *Western Europe in the Fifth Century: An Aftermath* (London: Macmillian, 1904), 305–70, and A. M. H. Jones, *The Later Roman Empire 284–602: A Social, Economic and Administrative Survey,* vol. 1 (Oxford: Oxford University Press, 1964), 176.

2. Trevor Jalland, *The Life and Times of St. Leo the Great* (New York: Macmillian, 1941), 38. B. L. Twyman ("Aetius and the Aristocracy," *Historia* 19 [1970]: 491) has surmised that Albinus was sent on an official mission from the Italian aristocracy to oppose Aetius's taxation practices in Gaul. See Prosper, *Chronicon,* sub an. 440 (MGH, AA 9: 478; *Chronicle,* 71).

3. Prosper, *Chronicon,* sub an. 440 (MGH, AA 9: 478; *Chronicle,* 71).

4. Valentin, *Saint Prosper,* 136.

Valentin's conjecture does not seem implausible. In addition, if the meeting between Leo, Aetius, and Albinus took place in Arles, as Mathisen has conjectured, Marseilles would have been the city from which Leo and his party sailed to Rome. Even if it was not Arles, given the pressing need to return to Rome as quickly as possible, travel by ship would have been the preferred mode of travel, and Marseilles, the major port city of southern Gaul, would have been the ideal city from which to sail to Rome. Moreover, Leo, in need of advisors for his new position, knew of the talents of Prosper and his residence in Marseilles from Prosper's stay in Rome in 431. Once there, Leo would have had the opportunity to contact Prosper and invite him to serve as an advisor. Given that the flawed theory of 435 as the year of Prosper's move to Rome was based on an argument that has been discredited by Markus, and no other evidence for this early move to Rome exists, the argument for 440 as the year in which Prosper became Leo's advisor and traveled to Rome appears a viable theory.[5]

Prosper would have found an invitation to serve under Leo attractive for a variety of reasons. The conflict that he had helped start and maintain had borne no fruit for Prosper and appeared to have no end in sight. Prosper's zeal and enthusiasm in defense of Augustine and for the conflict in general had waned, as evidenced in his responses to the Gauls and Vincent, by his *Chronicon,* and by his years of literary silence. Such an invitation meant starting a new life, serving a cause he was beginning to fully appreciate, and filling the prestigious position of advising the pope, which meant Prosper would be at the center of the Roman Church. And it must be noted that Prosper had glimpsed the peaceful theological sky of Rome in his trip of 431, which was in stark contrast to the bitter and contentious atmosphere of Marseilles: "Or l'atmosphère religieuse de Rome n'offrait rien de semblable à l'effervescence théologique de la Gaule méridionale. Rome n'aimait pas la controverse; son rôle était de juger les doctrines, non de les discuter."[6]

What happened to Prosper's faction in Marseilles is unknown.

5. Cf. R. A. Markus, "Chronicle and Theology," 33.

6. Cappuyns, "Le Premier," 326.

Prosper, as usual, makes no mention of any friends or associates he had in the city. In fact, Prosper never reveals anything about his time in Marseilles in his writings at Rome. All that is known about the Augustinian faction was that it was never heard from or referred to again after Prosper's departure for Rome.

Rome

There is some evidence that Prosper's first trip involved an extended stay, and it seems improbable that he and Hilary did not take the opportunity to visit the pilgrimage sites of the city.[7] Rome, despite the absence of the imperial throne, remained symbolically its "mother" and continued as the center of the Western Church. The sack by Alaric in 410, which caused hysterical reactions throughout the Empire, did little to diminish the impressive appearance and importance of the city in the long term; in fact, Alaric's respect for the sanctity of the basilicas of Peter and Paul only added to the prestige of the Roman Church.[8] Orosius observed, in 418:

> Although the memory of the event is still fresh, anyone who saw the numbers of the Romans themselves and listened to their talk would think that "nothing had happened," as they themselves admit, unless perhaps he were to notice some charred ruins still remaining.[9]

When Prosper visited Rome thirteen years after Orosius's observation, the city had all but erased the last traces of the sack.[10]

What Prosper witnessed in Rome, in addition to the city's civic

7. Markus ("Chronicle and Theology," 35) and Muhlberger (*Fifth-Century Chroniclers,* 78 n. 65) contend that Prosper's time in Rome was not limited to his meeting with Pope Celestine, but that he also used the stay to acquire ecclesiastical and political information reflected in his 433 edition of his *Chronicon.* On the pilgrimage sites during this period, see Debra J. Birch, *Pilgrimage to Rome in the Middle Ages* (Woodbridge, U.K.: Boydell Press, 1998), 89–102.

8. Paulus Orosius, *Historiarum adversum paganos libri VII* 7.39.1 (CSEL 5: 544–45; *Seven Books of History against the Pagans,* trans. Irving Woodworth Raymond [New York: Columbia University Press, 1936], 387).

9. Orosius, *Historiarum* 7.40.1 (CSEL 5: 548–49; *History,* 388).

10. Bertrand Lançon, *Rome in Late Antiquity: Everyday Life and Urban Change, AD 312–609,* trans. Antonia Nevill (Edinburgh: Edinburgh University Press, 2000), 39.

splendors—imperial palaces, forums, temples, public baths, circuses and amphitheaters, arches, columns, statues, and obelisks—were the prestige and authority of the Roman Church.[11] Peter and Paul had been martyred in the city, the former being its first bishop. The prestige and authority of the Roman Church became increasingly visible through the construction projects begun by Constantine, including the Lateran and St. Peter's basilicas, followed by the subsequent flowering of churches under the fourth- and fifth-century popes.[12] Moreover, while the West was adjusting to the new and often times traumatic circumstances brought about by the collapse of imperial authority, the Roman Church, as Brown puts it, "stood for a sense of order and for a width of horizons, stretching even beyond the frontiers of the Roman Empire, which seemed to make the bishops of Rome, as successors of Peter and Paul, the true heirs of a Roman world order."[13]

Prosper had come to Rome to appeal to the one authority that could resolve the conflict in Marseilles. What he discovered was the embodiment of catholicity: permanence, stability, tradition, and authority. The Roman Church stood in sharp contrast to the ecclesiastical culture of Provence, and "viewed from Rome, the world looked very different from the way it looked in Gaul."[14]

Prosper entered Rome the second time, traveling in the triumphant company of Leo, amid the jubilant crowds welcoming the new pope. Prosper entered not as the simple layman of little consequence appealing to the pope for assistance, but as an integral member of the papal staff. The former refugee had found a new home and a new circle of associates. In Marseilles, Prosper had suffered from his low status and that of his circle's, whose view of catholicity was contentiously and bitterly opposed. Now Prosper was intimately connected to the leader of the Western Church, and not only that, he would help express the views of the Roman Church, and even help define its view on grace.

11. A catalog and description of the civic buildings are contained in Lançon, *Rome in Late Antiquity,* 17–26.

12. Lançon, *Rome in Late Antiquity,* 27–32.

13. Brown, *Rise of Western Christendom,* 114–15.

14. Ibid., 113–14.

Leo and Prosper

Leo

According to Gennadius's account of Leo, limited only to the details of his letter to Flavianus, the title of "Great" is hardly worthy.[15] Reflecting the Gallic opposition to Rome's claim of primacy, Gennadius neglects to account for the achievements and importance of Leo. History, however, has sided with Prosper's account of Leo in the *Chronicon*.

Little is known about Leo's personal background except that he originated from Tuscany and was the son of Quintianus.[16] Leo was probably born sometime in the 390s, and may have been the acolyte named Leo mentioned by Augustine in 418, who was carrying a letter concerning Pelagianism from Pope Zosimus to Aurelius of Carthage.[17] If this is the case, Leo was in service to the Church of Rome from early in his life. Even if Leo was not the acolyte mentioned by Augustine, he served as a key member of the papal staff at least by the pontificate of Celestine, serving as the archdeacon through the pontificate of Sixtus. In sharp contrast to Prosper, Leo had understood the importance of Roman Church from early on, having served the Roman Church under at least two popes.

From the start of his pontificate (440–461) Leo continued to stress the unique authority and power of the bishop of Rome, initiated by Damasus (366–384) and increasingly advocated by his successors. It was Leo, however, who definitively expressed the primacy of Rome in word and action.[18] Leo, going beyond the notion

15. Gennadius, *De viris inlustribus* 71 (TU 14/1: 85–86; *Lives*, 397). Cf. Leo, *Ep.* 23 [*Tome*] (PL 54: 755–82; *Letter to Flavian*, in *St. Leo the Great: Letters*, trans. Edmund Hunt, FC 34 [New York: Fathers of the Church, 1957], 92–105). Besides the letter to Flavian, Gennadius only notes that Leo was bishop of Rome and died in the reign of Leo and Majorianus.

16. *Liber Pontificalis* (*Le liber pontificalis: Texte, introduction et commentaire*, vol. 1, ed. L. Duchesne [Paris: E. Thorin, 1886], 238): "Leo natione Tuscus, ex patre Quintiano." For the early life and career of Leo, see Jalland, *St. Leo the Great*, 33–42. For a study of Leo's theology of redemption, see J. Mark Armitage, *A Twofold Solidarity: Leo the Great's Theology of Redemption*, Early Christian Studies 9 (Strathfield, Australia: St Pauls, 2005).

17. Aug., *Ep.* 191.1 (CSEL 57: 163).

18. Walter Ullmann, "Leo I and the Theme of Papal Primacy," *JTS*, n. s. 11 (1960):

of apostolic succession, established the juristic link between Peter and the bishops of Rome.[19] In his very first sermons as pope, Leo defined the connection between Christ, Peter, and the bishops of Rome. Christ is the true and eternal bishop, but has conferred on Peter the episcopel dignity to govern the Church.[20] Peter continues to preside over the Roman See and continues to maintain the fellowship with Christ, and that stability has been transferred onto the heirs of Peter.[21] As Peter's heir, the bishop of Rome assumes all the rights and duties of Peter. Leo, then, as the bishop of Rome, had assumed Peter's function, authority, and privileges as the leader of the Church.[22] Not only did Leo formulate the justification for his powers as the heir of Peter, he also acted as one. Leo exercised his leadership by imposing his authority in language whose tone was unlike that of his predecessors:

His [Leo's] is the *modus loquendi* of the *gubernator:* he orders, decides, reprehends, deposes, corrects, threatens, defines, sentences, prescribes—he insists on *obedientia,* on *coercitio,* on *corrigere inobedientiam iusta correctione,* on enforcing *canonum praecepta* or *apostolica et canonica decreta* or *statuta apostolicae sedis* or the *regulae* or on the execution of the *decreta synodolia quae apostolicae sedis confirmant auctoritas*—in short, Leo's language is the language of him who possesses the *gubernacula ecclesiae universalis:* his tone is the tone of him who governs.[23]

In the West, Leo's claim to leadership met with little resistance except for the brief affair involving Hilary of Arles, who eventually submitted to Leo's judgment.[24] The Eastern reception of Leo's uni-

25–51; Karl Baus, "Inner Life of the Church between Nicaea and Chalcedon," in *The Imperial Church from Constantine to the Early Middle Ages,* trans. Anselm Biggs, *History of the Church,* vol. 2 (New York: Seabury Press, 1980), 264–69.

19. Ullmann, "Leo I," 26–29.

20. Leo, *Sermo* 5.3–4, 3.3 (CCL 138: 23–24, 12–13; *Sermons,* 31–32, 22–23, in *Sermons,* trans. Jane Patricia Freeland and Josephine Conway, FC 93 [Washington, D.C.: The Catholic University of America Press, 1995]).

21. Leo, *Sermo* 5.4 (CCL 138: 24; *Sermons,* 32).

22. Baus, "Inner Life of the Church," 265.

23. Ullmann, "Leo I," 25.

24. Baus, "Inner Life of the Church," 265–66; Mathisen, *Ecclesiastical Factionalism,* 145–72.

versal claims to primacy was another matter. Leo proclaimed in his letter to Anastasius, bishop of Thessalonica:

> The care of the universal Church was to converge in the one see of Peter, and nothing was ever to be at odds with his leadership. He, therefore, who knows that he has been set above certain others should not take it amiss that another is set over him. But he should also display the same obedience which he demands.[25]

Yet, the East, at the Council of Chalcedon, acted independently of Rome's authority and jurisdiction and did not recognize the claims of the absolute primacy of Rome.[26] Still, the recognition of Rome's teaching authority, Leo's *Tome,* was an achievement previously unknown, and never again repeated.[27]

The authority and stature of the Roman See were further strengthened by Leo's dramatic confrontations with Attila and Gaiseric. In 452, Leo, along with two leading senators, met Attila outside of Rome, and, according to Prosper's account, Attila "was so delighted with the presence of the chief bishop that he ordered the war to be halted and, having promised peace, retired beyond the Danube."[28] Whether or not Leo's presence was really responsible for averting the disaster is unimportant. The story, as recorded for posterity, was that Leo alone, with the help of God, saved Rome and its people from the destruction of Attila's army. A few years later, in 455, Leo met Gaiseric outside the undefended gates of Rome, and through his divinely inspired supplication was able to limit Gaiseric to plundering and taking captives, saving the city from burning, killing, and torture.[29]

Leo's pontificate was extraordinary and impressive, and Prosper was a close witness to all of these events, yet the exact nature of that relationship remains unclear to this day. What can be asserted with

25. Leo, *Ep.* 14 (PL 54: 676; *Letters,* 66).
26. For Leo's relationship to the East, see Jalland, *St. Leo the Great,* 205–398.
27. Baus, "Inner Life of the Church," 268–69. Leo's letter to Flavian (*Ep.* 28 [PL 54: 755–82; *Letters,* 92–106), popularly known as the *Tome to Flavian* or *Leo's Tome,* and Prosper's possible connection to the writing will be explored below.
28. Prosper, *Chronicon,* sub an. 452 (MGH, AA 9: 482; *Chronicle,* 73–74).
29. Prosper, *Chronicon,* sub an. 455 (MGH, AA 9: 484; *Chronicle,* 75–76).

a degree of certainty is that Prosper was an advisor to Leo, helped compose his letters against Eutychianism, and was strongly influenced by the pope.

Advisor to Leo

Gennadius provided only this brief statement in regards to the relationship between Leo and Prosper: *Epistulae quoque Papae Leonis adversus Eutychen de vera Christi incarnatione ad diversos datae ad isto dictatae creduntur.*[30] Much has been made on the basis of this short and tentative statement by scholars seeking to draw conclusions about Prosper's relationship to Leo and his papal documents. Recently, three scholars have put forward different views on this relationship.

In 1986, Markus, skeptical of the veracity of Gennadius's statement linking the two, criticized the attempts to confirm Prosper's role as Leo's secretary based on the similarities between the works of Prosper and Leo. Markus pointed out that the similarities are easily accounted for by the fact that Prosper had access to Leo's writings in 431 and continued to have access to them when Prosper lived in Rome.[31] Markus concluded that Prosper was attached to the Roman See, was on friendly terms and shared common interests with Leo, and had access to papal information.[32] That was about as far as Markus would go in describing Prosper's role.

N. W. James, in 1993, argued that Prosper served as an advisor to Pope Leo in the tradition of expert advisors to late antique popes and was responsible for drafting some of Leo's letters and sermons.[33] Refining the work of N. Ertle and J. Gaidioz, James makes a strong argument for Prosper's literary involvement in Leo's writings.

30. Gennadius, *De viris inlustribus* 85 (TU 14/1: 90; *Lives,* 399).

31. Markus, "Chronicle and Theology," 35. Cf. Carlo Silva-Tarouca, "Nuovi studi sulle lettere dei papi," *Gregorianum* 12 (1931): 547–98; J. Gaidioz, "Saint Prosper d'Aquitaine et le Tome à Flavien," 270–301; N. Ertl, "Diktatoren frühmittelalterlicher Papstbriefen," *Archiv für Urkundenforschung* 15 (1938): 56–132.

32. Markus, "Chronicle and Theology," 34, 36.

33. N. W. James, "Leo the Great and Prosper of Aquitaine," 554–56; see also Francesco di Capua, "Le due redazioni di una lettera di s. Leone," and "Leone Magno e Prospero di Aquitanio," in *Scritti minori,* vol. 2, ed. A Quacquarelli (Rome: Desclée, 1959), 177–83, 184–90.

However, James did not address Markus's thesis in his article and, however persuasive his arguments may be, they are undermined by Markus's contention that the similarity between the works of Leo and Prosper can be explained by Prosper's use of Leo's works.

Four years later, Philip Barclift, in line with James's thesis, took it as a point of fact that Prosper was an advisor to Leo, who helped in the editing of Leo's sermons and was commissioned to write the *Tome.*[34] Having assumed this role for Prosper, Barclift explained the cooperation between Prosper and Leo in producing the *Tome.* Barclift's argument, like James's, does not address Markus's thesis and thus suffers from being undermined by it.

Until Markus's thesis can be refuted, any attempts to find traces of Prosper's hand in the Leonine corpus based on similarities will be susceptible to undermining by Markus's thesis. However, without delving into the complex textual question of Prosper's hand in the writing of the *Tome,* Prosper's role as advisor to Leo, based on his involvement in the composition of the *Tome,* can be affirmed. Gennadius's tentative link is strengthened by Photius's remark: "certain ones spoke freely in Rome about heresy, but a certain Prosper, a man truly of God, confounded them in inscrutable publications against them while Leo guided the Roman see."[35] Mathisen asserts that it is probably the heresy of Eutychianism, but noted that arguments have been made that it was Pelagianism by Pelland and McShane, who believed Photius had Prosper's *De vocatione omnium gentium* in mind.[36] However, the *De vocatione omnium gentium* and especially its authorship may not have been known in the East. More importantly, the work is not a formal anti-Pelagian treatise, and is but one of Prosper's writings, whereas Photius referred to "publications." The writings against Eutychianism match the plural reference.[37] It is

34. Barclift, "Leo the Great's Christological Vocabulary," 221–22.

35. Photius, *Myriobiblon sive Bibliotheca* 54 (PG 103: 97; trans. Mathisen, *Ecclesiastical Factionalism,* 138 n. 100).

36. Mathisen (*Ecclesiastical Factionalism,* 138 n. 100). Cf. Pelland, *S. Prosperi,* 144, and Philip McShane, *La Romanitas et le pape Leon le Grand: L'apport culturel des institutions impériales à la formation de structures ecclésiastiques* (Montréal: Bellarmin, 1979), 370.

37. Leo's substantial writings against Eutychianism are contained among the collection of Leo's letters; see *Epistolae* (PL 54: 582–1218; *Letters*).

more likely the heresy of Eutychianism rather than Pelagianism referred to by Photius.

In addition, Demetrias's appeal to Prosper for advice assumes a high estimation of Prosper. Such an honor was granted only to three others: Pelagius, Augustine, and Jerome. Prosper had to have been a member of the papal staff, given his otherwise low status and lack of importance, to warrant the notice of Demetrias or someone from Constantinople.

The evidence suggests that Prosper was an advisor to Leo and was known to have helped compose Leo's letters against Eutychianism. Nothing more specific about Prosper's role can be stated with any certainty.

Influence

What is more certain about their relationship is the influence of Leo on Prosper.[38] This is most clearly evident in *De vocatione omnium gentium,* but it is also reflected in general in the other writings of this period. Prosper's initially broad sense of catholicity would be refined under Leo's influence. As a member of the papal staff, he was in a unique position to witness Leo's program to establish the primacy of Rome and its role in the life and faith of the Church. In the course of this period, Prosper learned what catholicity meant from Leo.

The Catholic View of Augustine and His Opponents

Prosper's first concern in Rome was the issue of Augustine. In his *Responsiones ad capitula obiectionum Gallorum* and *Responsiones ad capitula obiectionum Vincentiarum,* Prosper had taken some dramatic steps away from Augustine's doctrine of grace. In both works, Prosper introduced an element in predestination foreign to Augustine's doctrine: nonpredestination based on God's foreknowledge of a person's evil life.[39] And, having emerged from his five years of re-

38. Markus, "Chronicle and Theology," 36.

39. *Res. Gall.* 1.2, 1.3 (PL 51: 158–59; *Answers to Gauls,* 141–42); *Res. Vinc.* 12 (PL 51: 184; *Answers to Vincentian Articles,* 172). See chapter 5.

flection and study, Prosper's transformed estimation of Augustine and his catholicity are reflected in his initial works in Rome. These are the *Expositio psalmorum a centesimo usque ad centesimum quinquagesimum, Liber sententiarum ex operibus sancti Augustini delibatarum,* and *Epigrammata ex sententiis sancti Augustini*—all summaries of Augustine's works.[40]

The direct dependence among the three works suggests that they were written in succession and should be viewed as a set with one purpose in mind: to provide the correct view of Augustine's thought. In his *Expositio psalmorum,* Prosper summarized the last third of Augustine's *Ennarationes in Psalmos,* on Psalms 100 to 150.[41] The next work is the *Liber Sententiarum,* which is a natural transition from the *Expositio psalmorum.*[42] The first part of *Liber Sententiarum* is based on the first part of *Expositio psalmorum,* and the *Epigrammata* is based on the *Liber Sententiarum.*[43]

In these three works, Prosper presents the corrected, catholic teaching of Augustine. Prosper had come to the realization, the fruit of his many years of dealing with Augustine's doctrine of grace, that Augustine's teachings were not *in toto* catholic. Prosper was in a position—by virtue of his expertise with Augustine's doctrine, his developed understanding of the catholic view of grace, and his position as papal advisor—to correct and present Augustine's doctrine of grace according to the catholic faith. These are Prosper's final works formally treating Augustine's teachings, an homage to the memory of his one-time master, whom he considered too valuable a figure to expose to criticism or overly enthusiastic adherence. It would have been perfectly natural for someone seeking to summarize the thoughts of Augustine to include his expositions on the Psalms. It was Augustine's most comprehensive work and afforded its reader a vast view of his thoughts on a variety of issues.[44] How-

40. *Epigrammata* (PL 51: 498–532); *Sententiarium* (CCL 68A: 257–365); *Expositio Ps.* (CCL 68A: 1–211).

41. Aug., *Enarrationes in psalmos* (CCL 38–40; *Expositions of the Psalms).*

42. Valentin, *Saint Prosper,* 350.

43. For the dependence of *Expositio psalmorum* and the *Liber sententiarum* on each other, see P. Callens, "Index Avctorum," (CCL 68A: 385–87).

44. For a recent study of Augustine's work on the Psalms, see M. Fiedrowicz,

ever, it is unclear why Prosper would summarize only the last third of Augustine's work.

The direct inspiration behind this set of writings and his odd choice to summarize just the last third of Augustine's expositions on the Psalms was provided by Arnobius the Younger's *Commentarii in Psalmos* and *Praedestinatus.*[45] In addition, Prosper may have had in mind the *"Capitula sancti Augustini" in urbem Romam transmissa.*[46]

The *Capitula* may have been one of the reasons for Prosper to write an alternative summary of Augustine's thought. However, the presence of the *Capitula* alone cannot be the inspiration behind Prosper's summaries. The *Liber sententiarum* and the *Epigrammata* could be viewed as a reaction to the *Capitula,* but the *Capitula* fails to explain the unusual existence of the *Expositio psalmorum.* The stimulus that best fits the content and purpose of Prosper's summaries is that provided by Arnobius the Younger, who wrote a commentary on the Psalms and a work caricaturing Augustine's doctrine of predestination: *Commentarii in Psalmos* and *Praedestinatus.*[47]

It is likely that the exiled North African wrote both works in Rome between 432 and 440.[48] In his commentary on the Psalms, Arnobius asserts a view of grace consistent with that asserted by the *doctores Gallicani:* the power and freedom to choose the good, and the necessity of grace and the help of God, all of which are expressed in his commentary for the Psalms located in the last third of the Psal-

Psalmos vox totius Christi: Studien zu Augustins Enarrationes in Psalmos (Freiburg [im Breisgau]: Herder, 1997).

45. Arnobius the Younger, *Commentarii in Psalmos* (CCL 25) and *Praedestinatus qui dicitur* (CCL 25B). *Praedestinatus* is divided into three books, the first is a list of heresies, closely following Augustine's *De haeresibus* (CCL 46: 286–345) except at no. 89, Nestorianism, and no. 90, predestination. The second book describes the error of predestination, and the third book refutes it. See Kidd, *History of the Church,* vol. 3, 155–56; Schaff, *History of the Christian Church,* vol. 3: *Nicene and Post-Nicene Christianity, A. D. 311–600,* 5th ed. (New York: Scribner's Sons, 1910), 863–64; É. Amann, "*Praedestinatus,*" DTC 12/2 (1935): 2775–80; M. Abel, "Le *Praedestinatus* et le pélagianisme," *RTAM* 35 (1968): 5–25.

46. CCL 85A: 243–73. The *Capitula* was a series of statements drawn from Augustine; see chapters 1 and 5.

47. Arnobius the Younger, *Commentarii in Psalmos* (CCL 25) and *Praedestinatus* (CCL 25B).

48. Klaus-D. Daur, "Einleitung" (CCL 25: xi); F. Gori, "Prologemena" (CCL 25B: xiii). The African origin, rather than the south Gallic origin, has been established by G. Morin ("L'origine africaine d'Arnobe le Jeune," *Revue des sciences religieuses* 16 [1936]: 177–84).

ter.[49] *Praedestinatus* contains the same view of grace, but attacks Augustine's doctrine of predestination. Arnobius claimed that a sermon on predestination bearing the name of Augustine had fallen into his hands, which expressed a double predestination—predestination to good and evil.[50] Although Arnobius claimed that the sermon was falsely attributed to Augustine, the treatise was a refutation of Augustine's doctrine of predestination caricatured.[51]

The *Praedestinatus* may have been the result of Julian of Eclanum's unsuccessful attempt to be reinstated into catholic communion in 439.[52] Kidd speculated that the *Praedestinatus* was written by one of the Pelagians in hiding in Rome disappointed with the papal ruling on Julian.[53] While Kidd's view that the *Praedestinatus* was written by someone in Rome is correct, its link to Pelagianism is not. *Praedestinatus* reflects a position closer to that of the *doctores Gallicani* than that of the Pelagians.[54]

At whatever point *Praedestinatus* and the *Commentarii in Psalmos* were written, Prosper would have had access to these works at least by the time he was in Rome. It must have concerned Prosper to encounter Arnobius's commentary on the Psalms with its view of grace he had opposed so vigorously in Marseilles, and the unfair attack on Augustine in the *Praedestinatus.* And whether or not Prosper believed Arnobius's account that an Augustinian double-predestination sermon was circulating, the idea that people could be

49. See H. Kayser, *Die Schriften des sogenannten Arnobius iunior, dogmengeschichtlich und literarisch untersucht* (Gütersloh: C. Bertelsmann, 1912), 13–46; summarized in Daur, "Einleitung," xv–xvi. Cf. Arnobius, *Ps.* 117, 126, 147 (CCL 25: 184–85, 210–12, 252–53).

50. Arnobius, *Praedestinatus* 1.90 (CCL 25B: 54–55): "quam in praefatione nostra diximus de nomine Augustini episcopi esse mentiam, Pradestinatorum nomen accepit.... Dicunt: 'etiam si voluerit bonum facere qui ad malum praedestinatus est a deo, ad bonum peruenire non poterit. Nam qui ad bonum praedestinatus est, etiam si negligat, ad bonum perducetur inuitus.'"

51. Arnobius, *Praedestinatus* 3.2 (CCL 25B: 66): "Nonagesimam haeresim praedestinati fecurent, ostendentes libros falsos quos Augustini confinguant."

52. Prosper, *Chronicon,* sub an. 439 (MGH, AA 9: 477; *Chronicle,* 73–74).

53. Kidd, *History of the Church,* vol. 3, 156.

54. Ogliari (*Gratia et Certamen,* 431–32) summarizes *Praedestinatus*'s view on grace: "God's universal salvific will, a certain priority of good will over grace, the value of human effort, and the capacity of infralapsarian free will to desire and pursue the good, together with the necessity of grace in order effectively to attain salvation."

misled by Arnobius's account warranted Prosper's reaction. Moreover, the existence of the *Capitula* may have further motivated Prosper to provide the "correct" view of Augustine's thought. Arnobius's view of grace in his commentary on the Psalms and his caricature of Augustine's teaching on grace needed to be refuted. Prosper resolved to set the record straight by countering both of Arnobius's works by providing a proper understanding of grace drawn from the Psalms and an accurate summation of the catholic teaching of Augustine.[55]

That Prosper responded primarily to Arnobius's works explains Prosper's choice to limit his summary of Augustine's work on the Psalms to Psalms 100 to 150. The view of grace that Prosper had opposed in Marseilles, and that he still opposed, was concentrated toward the end of Arnobius's commentary on the Psalms: Psalms 117, 126, and 147.[56] In order to refute this theology of grace, Prosper looked to Augustine's *Enarrationes in Psalmos.* Prosper chose to limit his summary to Psalms 100 to 150, following a convenient demarcation that encompassed the three Psalms in question. After presenting the catholic view of grace, reflecting a corrected view of Augustine's expositions on these psalms, Prosper wrote the *Liber sententiarum* and the *Epigrammata* to counter the *Praedestinatus*'s view of Augustine, presenting a corrected, catholic view of Augustine's thoughts.

Prosper's choice to limit his summary of the Psalms to 100 to 150, coinciding with Arnobius's commentary on the Psalms containing his view of grace, and to write two works based on his summary of these psalms, favors the conclusion that Prosper was reacting to Arnobius's works. There is no other explanation for Prosper's otherwise incomprehensible decision to summarize only the last third of Augustine's expositions of the Psalms.

Expositio Psalmorum

Prosper condenses the lengthy work of Augustine usually to a paragraph for each Psalm. For the most part, Prosper retains the essence of Augustine's thoughts.[57] However, Prosper edited out all ref-

55. Aug., *Enarrationes in psalmos* (CCL 38–40; *Expositions of the Psalms*).
56. Arnobius, *Ps.* 117, 126, 147 (CCL 25: 184–85, 210–12, 252–53).
57. Valentin, *Saint Prosper*, 346.

erences to *praedestinatio.* There are three psalms in which Augustine used the word *praedestinatio,* and Prosper excluded the word in all three: Psalms 136, 147, and 150.

Although *praedestinatio* is limited and not essential to Augustine's expositions of Psalms 136 and 150, the same cannot be said of Psalm 147.[58] In Psalm 147 *preadestinatio* is essential to Augustine's interpretation and is used a total of twelve times, nine of which are not from scriptural quotations. Augustine connected the snow, wool, and ashes referred in Psalm 147: 16 to *praedestinatio.*[59] Prosper removes all mention of *praedestinatio* and emphasizes the hope of salvation of all through Christ, rather than Augustine's hope of salvation through predestination.[60] Whereas Augustine addressed his predestined audience, Prosper addresses people in general and goes beyond Augustine's text and includes Matthew 9: 13 at the end.[61] Augustine saw the utter need for God's predestination for salvation in this Psalm, but Prosper saw the universal salvific will of God—*vocatione gentium*—an idea that will be expressed fully in his later work, *De vocatione omnium gentium.*[62]

Prosper had summarized Augustine's work, but at the same time he modified it in regard to predestination. It was a bold move. Prosper presented a corrected version of Augustine's work, one that conformed to and reflected his understanding of catholicity, which no longer included predestination. That same appreciation of Augustine is reflected in Prosper's next works, *Liber sententiarum* and *Epigrammata.*

58. Aug., *Enarr. Ps.* 136.21 (CCL 40: 1977; *Exposition of Psalm* 136, 240): "Natus infans futurus ciuis Ierusalem, et in praedestinatione Dei iam cuius." The one mention of *praedestinatio* in Augustine's exposition of Psalm 150 does not pertain to the psalm itself but to the significance of the conclusion of each set of fifty psalms: *Enarr. Ps.* 150.3 (CCL 40: 2193; *Exposition of Psalm* 150, 511): "Praedestinatio nostra non in nobis facta est, sed in occulto apud ipsum, in eius praescienta."

59. Aug. *Enarr. Ps.* 147.23 (CCL 40: 2158–59; *Exposition of Psalm* 147, 468–70).

60. Prosper, *Expositio Ps.* 147.16 (CCL 68A: 204).

61. Prosper, *Expositio Ps.* 147.16 (CCL 68A: 204): "Non enim quisnam ante vocationem dici iustus potest, quoniam Filius hominis non uenit iustos eligere, sed peccatores et impios saluos facere." Cf. Matt. 9: 13.

62. Prosper, *Expositio Ps.* 147.16 (CCL 68A: 204): "Sed sublimius in his gratia Dei opera sentiuntur per nivium uellera vocatione gentium figurate."

Liber sententiarum and *Epigrammata*

The *Liber sententiarum* is composed of three hundred and ninety-two brief statements primarily drawn from Augustine's works.[63] The work summarizes statements from twenty-four of Augustine's works, in addition to his sermons and letters, with a great deal drawn from *De civitate Dei, Enarrationes in psalmos,* and *Tractatus in evangelium Iohannis.*[64] Each sentence deals with a specific topic, but with no discernable organization.[65] Prosper remains faithful in general to Augustine's thoughts on grace.[66] However, although he includes Augustine's expressions on foreknowledge, perseverance, and the priority of grace to good works, there is nothing on predestination.[67] And the characteristic polemical tone of his expressions on grace is also absent, replaced by "l'amour du prochain, du pardon, de la patience."[68] The *Epigrammata* is a longer exposition in meter form of the *Liber sententiarum* and enjoyed a popular reception in the Middle Ages.[69]

This was the version of Augustine, the conclusion of the many years spent defending and interpreting Augustine's doctrine of grace and the catholic faith, that Prosper arrived at and hoped to pass on to posterity. According to Prosper, Augustine's thoughts are summarized in these works, but in strict accordance to the catholic faith. It

63. Almost the entire first seventy sentences are drawn from Prosper's *Expositio psalmorum,* while the rest are drawn directly from Augustine's works. There are four sentences drawn from Basil, Eugippius, and Jerome, and eleven sentences whose sources cannot be identified (P. Callens, "Index Auctorum" [CCL 68A: 385]). On the Augustinianism of the *Liber sententiarum,* see Valentin, *Saint Prosper,* 350–63; Pelland, *S. Prosperi,* 80–81, 91, 98; de Plinval, "Prosper d'Aquitaine," 348–50; and Lorenz, "Augustinismus Prospers," esp. 226–32.

64. For the list of works, see P. Callens, "Index Auctorum" (CCL 68A: 377–87).

65. Lorenz ("Augustinismus Prospers," 219) divides the sentences into various groups.

66. *Liber sententiarum* 22, 45, 124, 126, 131, 152, 226, 293, 299, 310, 314, 318, 325, 340, 378, 383 (CCL 68A: 262, 268, 285, 286, 292, 310, 329, 331, 334, 335, 337, 339, 344, 358, 360).

67. Foreknowledge: *sent.* 293, 383 (CCL 68A: 329, 360); perseverance: *sent.* 131, 235 (CCL 68A: 286, 312); priority of grace to good works: *sent.* 22, 56, 260, 299, 310, 340 (CCL 68A: 262, 272, 317, 331, 334, 344).

68. Valentin, *Saint Prosper,* 367.

69. Ibid.; Cappuyns, "Le premier," 334–35; Paul F. Gehl, "An Augustinian Catechism in Fourteenth-Century Tuscany: Prosper's *Epigrammata,*" *Augustinian Studies* 19 (1988): 93–110 (hereafter *AS*).

could be viewed as a final homage to an old master, or as an act of betrayal.

Epistula ad Demetriadem de vera humilitate

Prosper wrote a letter to Demetrias in response to her request for something to assist her in progressing in the ascetic life. Although the precise dating of the letter cannot be established, the letter was likely written sometime in the 440s or early 450s, after Prosper's summary of Augustine's works and before *De vocatione omnium gentium.* Prosper's letter to Demetrias was not the first to offer her advice on the ascetic life. The news of the teenaged Demetrias's consecration as a virgin, being the daughter of one of the most illustrious families in the West, inspired letters from three of the best known ascetics of their day: Augustine, Jerome, and Pelagius—around the mid-410s.[70] Prosper's letter addresses a mature Demetrias, which Prosper is quick to acknowledge.[71] Further evidence of the letter's composition in the 440s or early 450s is the commission itself. Demetrias's request to Prosper suggests a high regard for Prosper, and such a high estimation had to be the result of Prosper's reputation and importance, which he gained as Leo's advisor. Otherwise, it makes little sense for Demetrias to commission a simple layman. Thus, the letter assumes Prosper's established place in Roman society as an important member of the papal staff, which occurred in the course of Leo's pontificate. The more advanced theological development evident in *De vocatione omnium gentium* suggests that the letter was written before this work.

The theme of the letter is the maintenance of true humility against the dangers of *elatio.*[72] While the work was addressed to

70. Aug., *Ep.* 150 (CSEL 44: 380–82); Pelagius, *Epistula ad Demetriadem* (PL 30: 15C–45A); Jerome, *Ep.* 130 (CSEL 56: 175–201). See Andrew S. Jacobs, "Writing Demetrias: Ascetic Logic in Ancient Christianity," *CH* 69 (2000): 719–48.

71. Prosper, *Ep. ad Demetriadem* 1 (ed. Krabbe, 138–39): "I would altogether refuse this request, not presuming to direct my poor exhortations to a soul so mature [*maturo*] and well-instructed [*erudito*]."

72. *Ep. ad Demetriadem* 1 (ed. Krabbe, 142–43): "cavenda te elationis admoneam et humilitatis tibi sinceritatem fida suggestione commendem." All citations of the letter will indicate both the pages of the Latin text and the facing English translation.

Demetrias, Prosper had his opponents in mind. This is evident from very early in the letter when Prosper writes: "The essence of this virtue [humility] lies in acknowledging God's grace, which is totally rejected unless it is totally accepted."[73] The rest of the letter is devoted to exposing the errors of those who fail to fully acknowledge God's grace. Prosper follows his usual strategy of situating his opponents' view of grace as an outgrowth of the Pelagian heresy.

The sin of pride originated with the devil and was the cause of humanity's fall.[74] Unable to bring down certain people who had mastered their passions and desires, the devil tries to bring them down by tempting them with pride.[75] The devil incited these virtuous people to place confidence in their free will and to ascribe their progress in virtue to themselves. The faithful, led by the example of the Apostolic See, resisted this novel teaching. However, the devil poured out this teaching on some men—the Pelagians—who denied Original Sin, asserted that humans are free to avoid sin, claimed baptism bestows adoption not the removal of guilt, and asserted that grace is bestowed as a result of merit.[76]

Prosper, without specifically naming them, identifies his opponents as those who hold the last part of this teaching while opposing the rest. This identification is made abundantly clear when he writes:

> When they were with us they acknowledged the wounds of original sin, but among themselves they showed that they held that the transgression of our first parents had injured only those who had imitated it; a man's own natural endowment suffered no loss because of another's sin, and he could, if he so willed, merit the abundant bestowal of grace by his own free service.[77]

73. *Ep. ad Demetriadem* 7 (ed. Krabbe, 160–61).
74. *Ep. ad Demetriadem* 8–9 (ed. Krabbe, 164–69).
75. *Ep. ad Demetriadem* 10 (ed. Krabbe, 169–75).
76. *Ep. ad Demetriadem* 10 (ed. Krabbe, 170–73).
77. *Ep. ad Demetriadem* 10 (ed. Krabbe, 172–75): "Et cum inter nostros originalis peccati vulnera faterentur, inter suos tamen hoc tenere ostenderent: quod primorum hominum praevaricatio solis imitatoribus obfuisset, naturalem autem facultatem nihil sui in alieno amisisse peccato, cui possible esset et liberum per voluntariam devotionem promereri gratiae largitatem."

"When they were with us" refers to Prosper's time in Marseilles and his description of their view of merited grace was one of their characteristic teachings. The other characteristic teaching is the *initium fidei,* which Prosper refutes a little later.[78] Those who hold such condemned teachings are heretics, whose doctrine is rightly detested by Catholics.[79] Instead, true humility is expressed when "everything which makes a man a Christian should be referred to the gift of divine grace."[80] Free will is not taken away, but is "helped," "cured," "strengthened," and "moved by the inspiration of the eternal and immutable will of God."[81]

This work reflects Prosper's changed perception of Augustine and the catholic view on the issue of grace. Prosper appealed to the catholic faith and the Apostolic See, and avoided the terms related to predestination and to the person of Augustine. The work also reveals Prosper's continued opposition to his opponents' view of grace, not because they opposed Augustine but because they opposed catholic teaching.

Conclusion

Prosper's purpose in writing his summary of Augustine's works was to present the "correct" view of Augustine against the claims of his opponents and of those who faithfully followed Augustine in toto. The works protected Augustine's memory from the charge of heresy, and also served as a deterrent for naïve followers enthralled by the bishop, as he had been, not to follow Augustine's teachings beyond what Prosper deemed the acceptable catholic limits. In presenting the catholic Augustine, Prosper was faithful to Augustine, but not to the essential element of his teaching on grace: predestination. Prosper's letter to Demetrias was his attempt to correct his opponents' view of grace with catholic teaching. For the first time,

78. *Ep. ad Demetriadem* 14 (ed. Krabbe, 186–87): "Unde mire per Ieremiam idem Dominus manifestat quod Dei gratiam nemo praeveniat merito suo, sed propter dilectionem qua Deus diligit etiam aversos ad misericordiam trahi."

79. *Ep. ad Demetriadem* 11 (ed. Krabbe, 174–75).

80. *Ep. ad Demetriadem* 13 (ed. Krabbe, 182–83).

81. *Ep. ad Demetriadem* 13, 14 (ed. Krabbe, 184–85, 188–89).

neither Augustine nor his doctrine of grace are employed in refuting the errors of his long-time opponents.

These works reflect Prosper's reevaluation of the conflict inspired by Augustine's doctrine of predestination in Gaul. In eliminating Augustine's doctrine of predestination and in opposing the *initium fidei* and asserting the priority of grace in the good will, Prosper rejects both alternative models' explanation of grace. Augustine had gone beyond the catholic limit, while his opponents fell short of it.

De vocatione omnium gentium

Around 450, now in his sixties, having devoted most of his adult life to the issue of grace, having served as an advisor to Leo for the past decade, and having acquired a certain celebrity—evidenced by Demetrias's request and Photius's reference—Prosper sought to provide his own solution to the conflict he had helped begin and maintain. In his most comprehensive work, *De vocatione omnium gentium,* Prosper addressed the central point of contention, according to Prosper, in the conflict: the understanding of God's universal salvific will expressed in 1 Timothy 2: 4. Prosper claims that the conflict will continue between the two opposing groups "so long as they make no distinction between what can be known and what remains hidden."[82] Prosper proposes to make this distinction and reveal the limit of what can be known and where the "inquiry should stop."[83] The key issue for Prosper is the proper establishment of the limits of human inquiry in pursuing the understanding of God's salvific will.

Prosper claims that his treatise reflects an objective view in a polarized conflict. He, unashamedly, writes of the conflict as if he had been a mere observer, not a pivotal figure in it. Prosper is careful to distance himself from the two camps, who are hopelessly deadlocked

82. *De vocatione* 1.1 (PL 51: 649; *Call of All Nations,* 26): "Atque ita, contrariarum disputationum nullus terminus reperitur, dum non discernitur quid manifestum, quid sit occultum."

83. *De vocatione* 1.1 (PL 51: 649; *Call of All Nations,* 26): "Ad aliquem nos limitem pervenisse, quem non debeamus excedere."

in their discussions, before he offers his own personal view, which he claims is "moderate" and will seek to "avoid all that is offensive or wrong."[84] According to Prosper's account, he is not complicit in the conflict and only seeks to resolve it on the basis of his objectivity.

This treatise reflects Prosper's personal and speculative view on the issue, which he is quick to acknowledge. It was not intended to be an expression of the catholic faith per se—he does not claim to speak on behalf of the Church—but the reflections of an individual catholic made credible by his claim to objectivity.

Prosper's presentation on the limits of what can be known and what remains hidden is divided into two books. Both books seek to illuminate the relationship between the human and divine wills. The first book focuses primarily on the human will in the relationship, and the focus shifts to the divine will in the second book.

Summary

Book one begins with a discussion on the threefold character of the human will: animal, natural, and spiritual (1.2–6). Grace remakes and repairs the human will (1.7–8). Though Scripture refers to the whole of something in some places, such expressions should not always be understood as designating a totality, but a part (1.9–11).[85] 1 Timothy 2: 4 is to be understood in its full context, as a part of the passage preceding and following it. As such, the true meaning of the passage has to do with offering up prayers for all people to be saved (1.12). Why God's grace does not save some whom the Church prays for is a mystery and remains hidden (1.13–14). What is known

84. *De vocatione* 1.1 (PL 51: 649; *Call of All Nations,* 26): "Exercens atque discutiens modulum facultatis meae in his quae cordi meo sobrie (quantum arbitor) inhaeserunt; ut si in eas regulas processerit stylus quae nihil offensionis, nihil habeant pravitatis."

85. The application of this restrictive sense, for example of "all," would logically lead to an explanation of the "all" in 1 Tim. 2: 4, but Prosper, although he addresses this text immediately following, does not apply this principle. Instead, Prosper addresses the context of 1 Tim 2: 4 and only interprets the "all" in 1 Tim. 2: 1, "I desire, therefore, first of all, that supplications, intercessions, thanksgivings be made for all men." Oddly, Prosper interprets this "all" in the literal sense (*De vocatione* 1.12 [PL 51: 664; *Call of All Nations,* 51–52]). The restrictive sense of "all" is not explicitly stated, but implied in book two where Prosper properly addresses 1 Tim 2: 4's meaning of "all."

is that salvation is not a result of human merits (1.15). The example of the salvation of infants, deathbed conversions, and what nature is without grace attests to the unmerited quality of grace given purely out of God's good pleasure (1.16–19). God wishes to redeem not only one people, but all nations. God is faithful to the promise made to Abraham that he would be the father of all nations by saving the sons of the promise, foreknown and foreordained for the kingdom, drawn from among Jews and Gentiles, according to God's election, whose motive is unknowable (1.20). The reason for God's salvific discrimination is withheld from human knowledge, but human merit is not the reason for the discrimination (1.21). In fact, everything, from the beginning of faith to final perseverance, is God's gift (1.22–24). Why God converts one according to God's pleasure while rendering what is due to the unconverted remains a mystery, but the merits of human free will is not the answer (1.25).

Book two begins with three propositions that are certain: God wills all men to be saved and come to the knowledge of the truth (1 Tim 2: 4); those who come to salvation and the knowledge of the truth do so because of the efficacious help of divine grace, not as the result of human merits; and God's judgments are unfathomable and therefore inquiring into why God wishes to save all, but that not all are saved should be avoided. What is known about God's judgments is that God is just and merciful (2.1). God desires to save all in the unrestricted sense is evident in other parts of the Scriptures (2.2). The reason for the delay of God's call to some nations is unknown, but prayers are to be made for all people, because grace is granted as a result of God hearing these prayers (2.3).[86] Although Israel received God's special care and mercy, the Gentiles also received God's mercy and care through the goodness of God's creation (2.4). Within the people of Israel, some were justified by grace, and within the Gentiles, though sparingly, grace was also given to some (2.5). Just as grace was not given in equal measure in the past, this continues to the present in the lives of believers (2.6). The inequality of the divine

86. *De vocatione* 2.3 (PL 51: 689; *Call of All Nations*, 94): "Cum tamen Deo . . . secundum ipsius praeceptum quotidie pro omnibus supplicetur: ut et si exaudit, nota sit gratia miserationis; et si non exaudit, intelligatur judicium veritatis."

gifts in a person is not the result of human merits, but God's liberality (2.7–8). God's grace is evident in both Israelites and Gentiles, for God's grace was dispensed in varying measures, the former in saving them in the Flood, and the latter in patiently waiting for their conversion (2.9–14).

God's revelation had always been imparted to all in some measure, sufficient for salvation for some and a testimony for all. The reason for the withholding of Christ's birth and full manifestation of God's grace is because God waited for the right situation: full resistance to the message and the Roman Empire. And Christ's message, initially and providentially preached throughout the Empire, will eventually reach beyond the boundaries of the Empire to all nations at the appointed time. The reason for the delay of God's grace to these nations remains a mystery (2.15–19). Infants who die are given general grace through the faith of the believing parents, but specific grace is given only to the infants who die after baptism, and the reason for this discrimination is unknown (2.20–24). God wills and has always willed to save all through God's general grace, which is sufficient help to seek God (2.25). Grace prepares the human will for consent and cooperation with grace. From the beginning of faith to its perseverance, the human will has the power to refuse God's grace (2.26–28). General grace and the special grace of election are discussed in 2.29–33. Election does not do away with good works or prayer (2.34–37).

Prosper's solution to the problem of God's universal desire to save all and the fact that not all are saved, according to what can be known, is to interpret 1 Timothy 2: 4 as the single expression of four different wills of God for four specific groups of people. Although only two wills are mentioned when Prosper points to 1 Timothy 4: 10 as the conclusive expression of the dual will of God and the key to the solution of the controversy: "the Savior of all men, especially of the faithful,"—the first part, "the Savior of all men," affirming God's general care and goodness to all, while the last part, "especially of the faithful," affirming God's special grace to a section of humanity, which leads to salvation—Prosper implies two more.[87] There are

87. *De vocatione* 2.31 (PL 51: 716; *Call of All Nations,* 144). Cf. 2.15 (PL 51: 700; *Call of All Nations,* 114): "Adhibita enim semper est universis hominibus quaedam supernae

those who have heard of the Gospel or will hear it at the appointed time, and those who belong within the group that receives God's special grace, but are distinguished by their election. Thus, there are four different wills of God: one for general humanity (2.25, 31); one for those who have heard or will hear the gospel (2.15–18); one for a segment of humanity given special grace, but without election (2.26, 29); and one for a segment of humanity given special grace and election (2.33–37).

General Grace

God's general grace has always been present in human history through the goodness of creation. All human beings have free will, but the sin of Adam caused the human will to be fickle—*mutabilis*—and is always inclined to sin, unless converted by God.[88] Those in this group have not been converted by God, but God's care and goodness are present for all to witness, and provide sufficient help for people to seek God.[89] If these people are not saved, it is due to their own fault of sinning, and justly condemned because they are guilty of malice.[90]

This general grace really does not amount to anything more than God's care and goodness, which, although it can rightly be called grace, is not efficacious for salvation. And though he stated that general grace provides sufficient help for people to seek God, Prosper does not elaborate this idea further. However, it appears that this seeking alone is not sufficient for salvation because Prosper makes it clear that general grace needs the addition of special grace for salvation.[91] Thus, the will of God toward this group can in no way result in salvation.

---

mensura doctrina quae, etsi parcioris occultiorisque gratiae fuit, sufficit tamen, sicut Dominus judicavit, quibusdam ad remedium, omnibus ad testimonium."

88. *De vocatione* 1.6, 7 (PL 51: 652, 653–54; *Call of All Nations*, 32, 33).

89. *De vocatione* 2.25 (PL 51: 711; *Call of All Nations*, 133): "Fuerunt enim ac sunt hujusmodi dona ita generali, ut ipsorum testimonio ad quaerendum verum Deum possent homines adjuvari."

90. *De vocatione* 2.19, 29 (PL 51: 706, 715 ; *Call of All Nations*, 125, 142).

91. *De vocatione* 2.19, 29 (PL 51: 706, 715 ; *Call of All Nations*, 125, 142).

Grace of Christianity

This group consists of those who have heard or will hear the Gospel at the appointed time. Christ died for all sinners and his redemption has spread throughout the world by the preaching of the Gospel.[92] According to God's providence, God first expanded the Roman Empire so that the grace of Christianity would spread among the different nations within the Empire. Now the grace of Christianity has reached nations beyond the boundaries of the Empire, the Apostolic See accomplishing what Rome could not do by force of arms.[93] There are still nations that have not received the grace of Christianity, but will eventually hear and accept the Gospel. The reasons for the delay and the appointed time for their redemption are based on God's hidden judgment.[94]

According to this will of God, God wills the salvation of all by allowing all the nations of the world to hear the message of Christianity. Prosper fails to elaborate on the effect of this will for salvation. Presumably, this will alone is not sufficient for salvation because it only provides these people with the opportunity to hear the Gospel, which alone does not lead to salvation. These then are people who have been or will be exposed to the message of Christianity.

Special Grace without Election

Of those who have had the opportunity to hear the Gospel, some have received special grace and are converted. Those who have been given this special grace are further divided into two groups, those who are elected and those who are not, but for both, the human will has been healed and restored.[95] However, for those with special grace but who are without election, their salvation is not achieved by God's will alone, but through the cooperation between God's special grace and the human will.[96] God's special grace prepares, ex-

92. *De vocatione* 2.16 (PL 51: 702–3; *Call of All Nations,* 118–20).

93. *De vocatione* 2.16 (PL 51: 704; *Call of All Nations,* 120).

94. *De vocatione* 2.17 (PL 51: 704; *Call of All Nations,* 121).

95. *De vocatione* 1.8, 2.8 (PL 51: 654–57, 741; *Call of All Nations,* 35–40, 100–102).

96. *De vocatione* 2.26 (PL 51: 711; *Call of All Nations,* 134): "Hanc quippe abundantiorem gratiam ita credimus atque experimur potentem, ut nullo modo arbitremur esse violentam, quod quidquid in salvandis hominibus agitur, ex sola Dei voluntate peragatur."

horts, moves, inspires, rouses, and illumines the human will to cooperate with God's work.[97] Nonetheless, this help can be refused, even by those who will persevere, because God did not take away the human will's *mutabilitas.*[98] It is possible for the beginners and the advanced in faith to refuse God's help and thus leave the faith. If they fall, it is due their own *mutabilitas,* if they succeed to salvation, it is due to the help of grace.[99]

God wills the salvation of these people by providing them with special help, but because they are free to refuse this help, their salvation is ultimately based on the human will's cooperation with this help. God provides the opportunity for salvation, and this salvation can be resisted by the human will. Thus, it is not irresistible grace.

Special Grace with Election

This fourth group consists of those given special grace and election, which is really predestination. Although Prosper only once uses the word *praedestinatio* in quoting from Ephesians 1: 3–6, the full Augustinian meaning of that word is expressed by *electio:* the fixed number of the elect, based on the gift and effect of God's eternal design.[100] This election to salvation is based on God's *praecognitio, praeelectio,* and *praeordinatio,* as was its effects on the free will in the producing of human merits.[101]

The freedom of the human will is not discussed, only that the efforts of human free will are not diminished by election. God wants to crown the good works of human free will.[102] However, if the good works of human free will are preordained and caused by election, such a view of free will does not entail the same freedom of the will

97. *De vocatione* 2.26 (PL 51: 711–12; *Call of All Nations,* 134–35).

98. *De vocatione* 2.28 (PL 51: 713; *Call of All Nations,* 137–38): "Qui ad obediendum sibi ipsum velle sic donat, ut etiam a perseveraturis illam mutabilitatem quae potest nolle non auferat." It is unclear what Prosper means by "even those who will persevere." Prosper seems to suggest that even those who will persevere have the power to refuse God's help, but do not, or that they do refuse God's help at certain times, but eventually accept it.

99. *De vocatione* 2.26 (PL 51: 711; *Call of All Nations,* 135): "De sua habens mutabilitate si deficit, de gratiae opitulatione si proficit."

100. *De vocatione* 2.33 (PL 51: 718; *Call of All Nations,* 147–48).

101. *De vocatione* 2.33, 36 (PL 51: 718, 721; *Call of All Nations,* 148, 152).

102. *De vocatione* 2.36 (PL 51: 721; *Call of All Nations,* 152).

enjoyed by those with only special grace, who are free to refuse or accept God's help.[103] Apparently, for those elected their wills are not prone to *mutabilitas.*

It can be properly stated that God wills the salvation of all people according to this type of grace. That is, God elects people from every nation and condition, thousands from among the aged, youth, and children.[104] Thus God wills the salvation of all types of people, and this will for their salvation is efficacious and irresistible.

Prosper's Theology of Grace

God's salvific will is expressed in different ways at different times toward different people, but it is the same grace, just given out in different measures.[105] God's grace is manifested in creation, the preaching of the Gospel, the call to salvation, and the call of the elect. Although grace is dispensed in different measures, grace is always gratuitous and cannot be merited or anticipated by the human will. The human will, although inclined to sin, is free to accept or reject God's grace in three of the manifestations of grace, but not for those elected. Why God dispenses grace in different measures remains hidden, and for their own good God does not wish humans to know the reason behind God's discrimination—why God did not provide special grace to all, or why God elected some and not others.[106] What can be known is that God is supremely just and merciful and people rightly deserve punishment if they do not respond to God's help in the form of general grace, the grace of Christianity, or special grace without election.

De vocatione omnium gentium is Prosper's mature reflections on the long-standing conflict over the issue of grace. Prosper, no longer bound to his role as the defender of Augustine, presents a doctrine of grace according to his own interpretation of Scripture. In this regard, *De vocatione omnium gentium* is similar to *De providentia Dei,*

103. Cf. *De vocatione* 2.28 (PL 51: 713; *Call of All Nations,* 137–38).

104. *De vocatione* 2.33 (PL 51: 717; *Call of All Nations,* 146).

105. *De vocatione* 2.30 (PL 51: 716; *Call of All Nations,* 143): "Ut cum in temporibus, in nationibus in familiis in parvulis, in nondum natis et geminis quaedam aut varie aut insigniter gesta noscuntur." Cf. 2.19, 22 (PL 51: 706, 709; *Call of All Nations,* 125, 130).

106. *De vocatione* 2.30 (PL 51: 716; *Call of All Nations,* 143).

also a work expressing the ideas of an individual relying primarily on Scripture. However, much had changed in Prosper's life in those years between the two writings, and although Prosper is writing as an individual and relying primarily on Scripture, the experience gained in those years had profound effects on Prosper. Prosper's theology had certainly advanced and along with it his understanding of Scripture. Prosper now viewed grace in a wholly different manner. Grace cannot be fully appreciated by one exclusive perspective, be it Augustine's, the *doctores Gallicani's*, or Leo's. Rather than limit grace to one over the other, Prosper sees the truth in each perspective. That is, each perspective was true in part, insofar as it revealed an expression of grace. The full expression of grace is found in its variety of expressions. Prosper incorporates four different perspectives, corrects them, and presents them as the expressions of one grace.

Prosper's view of God's universal salvific will expressed in God's general grace was an idea already expressed by Augustine and Leo.[107] Prosper takes this idea, not fully explored in relation to the process of salvation by either one, and explicitly makes the connection to God's salvific will, thereby providing an answer to the problem presented by 1 Timothy 2: 4. It is true that God wills the salvation of all, even though not all are saved, because God has given everyone general grace. This is Prosper's original contribution to the problem.[108]

The manifestation of grace in the grace of Christianity owes much to Leo. Leo had expressed the providential role of the Roman Empire as the vehicle for the spread of Christianity, and the role of the Apostolic See in reaching beyond the boundaries of Empire, ruling by divine religion more widely than worldly dominion.[109] This idea is repeated by Prosper, but where Leo used the idea in support of the renewal of Rome through the Apostolic See, Prosper saw in the spread of the gospel message God's universal call of all nations, an expression of God's grace.

107. Aug., *De spiritu et littera* 33.57–58 (CSEL 60: 215–17). Leo, *Serm.* 18.2, 19.2, 24.1, 35.4, 38.3, 44.1, 67.1, 82.2, 91.1 (CCL 138–138A). Citation in Letter, *Call of All Nations*, 167 nn. 60–61.

108. Letter, "Introduction," *Call of All Nations*, 15.

109. Leo, *Serm.* 82.1 (CCL 138A: 509). On Leo's *Romanitas*, see Armitage, *Twofold Solidarity*, 198–203.

The influence of Cassian is apparent in Prosper's view of special grace without election. Cassian had insisted on the freedom of the will, though fallen, to remain able to cooperate with God's will. This is largely expressed in Cassian's first model of salvation.[110] The human will is free to accept or reject God's special help. Cassian's *initium fidei,* however, is modified. The human will can refuse even the initial inspiration to believe, but to believe requires cooperation between the human free will and grace.[111] It is both the consent of the free will and God's grace, rather than Cassian's view that the consent of free will precedes and then merits grace.[112] Prosper also borrows the *virtutum semina* idea from Cassian's first model of grace for his *superne seminium.*[113] Although Prosper reduced the seeds to a single seed and switched "virtue" for "celestial," the idea is similar. Prosper had earlier opposed Cassian's use of the term, claiming that the "seeds of virtue" had been lost as a result of Adam and could not be recovered unless God restores them.[114] It is unclear if Prosper viewed the *superne seminium* as a restored seed, or in the manner described by Cassian.

Augustine's doctrine of predestination is expressed in Prosper's view of special grace, with election. The word *praedestinatio* is avoided; Prosper instead uses the term *electio.* God is the sole and absolute actor in the salvation of the elect, but Prosper focuses more attention on the practical effects of election, or the human responsibility for good actions and prayer.[115] Prosper, mindful of the controversial, speculative, and negative force associated with *praedestinatio,* replaced it with *electio* and emphasized the role of human effort in explaining it.

110. Cassian, *Conlatio* 13.18.3–4 (CSEL 13: 395; *Conferences,* 490). See chapter 5.

111. *De vocatione* 2.26 (PL 51: 711–12; *Call of All Nations,* 135).

112. *De vocatione* 2.26 (PL 51: 711; *Call of All Nations,* 135): "Ut divino in se cooperetur operi, et incipiat exercere ad meritum, quod de superno semine concepit ad studium." Cf. Cassian, *Conlatio* 13.14.4 (CSEL 13: 385; *Conferences.* 483).

113. Cassian, *Conlatio* 13.12.7 (CSEL 13: 380; *Conferences,* 479–80).

114. Prosper, *Contra collatorem* 13.2 (PL 51: 248; *Against Cassian,* 105). For Prosper's original view of the "seed of virtue," see *De prov. Dei* 6 (ed. Marcovich, 30–31) and the discussion on the work in chapter 2.

115. Chapter 33, approximately seventy lines, deals exclusively with election, but Prosper devotes chapters 34–36, approximately one hundred lines, to the practical effects of election. See *De vocatione* 2.33–36 (PL 51: 717–22; *Call of All Nations,* 145–52).

Ironically, Prosper's doctrine of grace—grace expressed in manifold measures—owes more to Cassian than to anyone else. Prosper had earlier devoted an entire treatise, *Contra collatorem,* to refuting Cassian's appreciation of the different ways in which God's grace acts to save people.[116] Prosper interpreted Cassian's statements expressing the different actions of grace as contradictory, but he now appreciates grace in a similar manner. The difference is that of perspective. Whereas Cassian's appreciation involved different measures of grace according to the measure of faith that an individual possessed, Prosper's appreciation is based on the different measures of grace and their effects on the individual's faith. In other words, God's grace is dispensed according to the particular needs of different individuals for Cassian, but for Prosper, grace is dispensed in diverse ways, effecting individuals in different ways.

Observations

Prosper had come to the personal conclusion that grace is properly appreciated when viewed in its various expressions. Prosper had moved beyond the either/or argument. No one model of grace could fully appreciate grace. Prosper took what were partial expressions of grace from Leo, Cassian, and Augustine, corrected them, and formed an understanding of grace that more broadly expressed God's grace.

Prosper was not entirely successful in resolving the problem he set out to solve. The reason behind God's different dispensations of grace is not answered. Why does God's grace act in this manner? Prosper's only response is to plead human ignorance.[117]

However, Prosper made two significant contributions to the debate on grace. Prosper's unique contribution to the debate is not so much his general grace, as argued by Letter, as it is his grace-centered witness to the variety of expressions of God's grace.[118] The second contribution is in Prosper's interpretation of 1 Timothy 2: 4. Prosper interprets the passage in its context, within the pericope of 1 Timothy

116. See chapter 5.

117. *De vocatione* 2.30 (PL 51: 716; *Call of All Nations,* 143).

118. Letter, "Introduction," 15.

2: 1–6.[119] As a result, the passage is viewed as a part of the instruction for the Church to pray for all people:

> All priests and all the faithful adhere unanimously to this norm of supplication in their devotions. There is no part of the world in which Christian peoples do not offer up these prayers. The Church, then, pleads before God everywhere, not only for the saints and those regenerated in Christ, but also for all infidels and all enemies of the Cross of Christ, for all worshippers of idols, for all who persecute Christ in His members, for the Jews whose blindness does not see the light of the gospel, for heretics and schismatics who are alien to the unity of faith and charity.[120]

This remark from Prosper echoes the "Prayers of the Faithful," which were recited in the Roman Mass in Prosper's time.[121] Prosper's pointing to the connection between the Church's prayer and doctrine is indicative of Prosper's theological development. Prosper situates his doctrine in the life of the Church. Prosper's ecclesiology informs his theology, and this connection will be expressed in more explicit terms in his next work, *Praeteritorum episcoporum sedis apostolicae auctoritates.*[122] Another feature of *De vocatione omnium gentium* that is present in his next work is his deliberate rewriting of history. In *De vocatione omnium gentium,* Prosper assigned himself the role of objective mediator in the conflict he helped inspire and main-

119. *De vocatione* 1.12 (PL 51: 663–65; *Call of All Nations,* 51–53).

120. *De vocatione* 1.12 (PL 51: 664; *Call of All Nations,* 52).

121. Duchesne speculated that the ancient "Prayers of the Faithful" had disappeared from the mass of the Roman rite, but the form had been preserved in a series of solemn prayers for Good Friday since the eighth century, and is still used to this day. V. L. Kennedy noticed the similarity between Prosper's statements and these solemn prayers, confirming Duchesne's theory. See L. Duchesne, *Christian Worship: Its Origin and Evolution,* trans. M. L. McClure, 5th ed. (New York: MacMillian, 1927), 172–73; and V. L. Kennedy, *The Saints of the Canon of the Mass,* Studi di antichità cristiana 14 (Rome: Pontificio istituto di archeologia cristiana, 1938), 31–32. Both works are referenced in Letter, *Call of All Nations,* 184 n. 178. The original prayer is also referred to by Augustine in his letter to Vitalis (*Ep.* 217.1.2 [CSEL 57: 404 ; *Letter* 217, 52–53]). Referenced in Henri Rondet, *The Grace of Christ: A Brief History of the Theology of Grace,* trans. Tad W. Guzie (Westminster, Md.: Newman Press, 1967), 153 n. 37. For a thorough account of the scholarship on this question, and an argument against the traditional view, see Daniel Van Slyke, "*Lex orandi lex credendi:* Liturgy as *Locus Theologicus* in the Fifth Century?," *Josephinum Journal of Theology* 11, no. 2 (2004): 130–51.

122. Augustine's references to the "Prayers of the Faithful" are discussed below.

tain. Prosper deliberately and unapologetically presented an anachronistic view of the conflict, and such a tactic is not only used again in the next work, but used in a much more audacious manner.

Praeteritorum episcoporum sedis apostolicae auctoritates de gratia Dei et libero voluntatis arbitrio

Prosper wrote the *Auctoritates,* sometimes known as the *Capitula,* after *De vocatione omnium gentium,* between 450 and 455.[123] According to Prosper, it is the Church, properly interpreting Scripture through the teaching of the Apostolic See and the liturgical practices of the Church, which defines catholic grace. Prosper composed the document to appear not only contemporaneous with Celestine's letter of 431 *(Ep.* 21, the *Apostolici verba),* but also as directly related to it. In doing so, Prosper rewrites the history of the conflict so that the Roman Church made a definitive pronouncement on the catholic view of grace as early as 431.

Date and Intent

Cappuyns dated the *Auctoritates* to between 435 and 442, and noted that the work's "langage conciliant et timide" pointed to a period after 435. And the absence of Leo's *Epistola ad aquileiensem episcopum,* dated 442, in the *Auctoritates* indicated that the work could not have been written after the letter because Prosper would have included Leo's letter, which contained his statements against Pelagianism.[124] If the work was written between 435 and 442, as Cappuyns argued, then the papal pronouncements on grace would have included Celestine's statements, because *Auctoritates* claims to draw from the official pronouncements of the Apostolic See. Prosper's doctrinal development toward a greater appreciation of catholicity, embodied in the Roman Church, and fully revealed in the *Auctoritates,* is also evidence that the work followed *De vocatione omnium gentium.* Thus, the *terminus post quem* is 450, the date of *De vocatione*

123. Prosper, *Auctoritates* (PL 51: 205–12; *Pronouncements,* 178–85). See chapter 1 for the discussion on the question of authorship.

124. Cappuyns, "L'origine des *Capitula* d'Orange 529," 159.

omnium gentium, and the *terminus ante quem* is 455, the date of his last work, the *Chronicon* edition of 455.

The content of the *Auctoritates* does not reflect a post-431 situation, but rather that of the *Apostolici verba.* The beginning of the *Auctoritates* details, in the present tense, the criticisms directed at Augustine and his supporters by their—implied—Gallic opponents, which is the very context of the *Apostolici verba.*[125] There is a smooth and logical transition from the ending of the *Apostolici verba* and the beginning of the *Auctoritates.* The *Apostolici verba* ends with an affirmation of Augustine's catholic standing, and it is the challenge to this affirmation that is detailed in the beginning of the *Auctoritates.*[126] The dates of the sources cited in the *Auctoritates* do not go beyond 431.

The internal evidence leads to the conclusion that the *Auctoritates* was intentionally written to appear as if it had been written as a direct and immediate response to the *Apostolici verba.* The circumstances surrounding the actual joining of the *Auctoritates* to the *Apostolici verba* are unknown.[127] Prosper may very well have joined the documents together himself, which would not be out of character. Cappuyns concluded that Dionysius found the *Auctoritates* and the *Apostolici verba* already filed together in the papal archives.[128] Whether or not this was the case or that Dionysius collected them

125. Prosper, *Auctoritates,* Praef. (PL 51: 205–6; *Pronouncements,* 178): "Quia nonnulli qui catholico nomine gloriantur, in damnatis autem hereticorum sensibus, seu pravitate, sive imperitia demorantes, piissimis disputatoris obviare praesumit; et cum Pelagium atque Coelestium anathematizare non dubitent, magistris tamen nostris, tamquam necessarium modum excesserint."

126. Celestine, *Ep.* 21.3 (PL 50: 530): "Augustinum sanctae recordationis virum pro vita sua atque meritis in nostra communione semper habuimus, nec umquam hunc sinistrae suspicionis saltem rumor aspersit: quem tantae scientiae olim fuisse meminimus, ut inter magistros optimos etiam ante a meis semper decessoribus haberetur. Bene ergo de eo omnes in communi senserunt, utpote qui ubique cunctis et amori fuerit et honori." Cf. above.

127. Celestine, *Epistola* 21 (PL 50: 528); see chapter 5. Dionysius Exiguus, *Decreta Coelestini papae* 1–2 (*Apostolici verba,* 3–13; *Auctoritates* (PL 67: 267–74). For a discussion on the question of the origin of the *Auctoritates,* see Cappuyns, "L'origine des *Capitula* d'Orange 529."

128. Cappuyns ("L'origine des *Capitula* d'Orange 529," 270): "C'est [*Auctoritates*] là, sans doute dans les archives pontificales, que Denys le Petit les retrouve, à la fin du siècle, classes avec une lettre dup ape Célestin I en faveur de Prosper d'Aquitaine."

together, by at least the time of Dionysius it was determined that the *Auctoritates* belonged in the documents related to Celestine's pontificate. Prosper's intent of making the *Auctoritates* directly related and contemporaneous to the *Apostolici verba* was successful—the addition of the *Auctoritates* to the *Apostolici verba* made it appear, for posterity, that the controversy between the Augustinians and their opponents was settled by Celestine in 431.[129]

Summary

According to Prosper, but expressed in the "official" language of an authoritative pronouncement, those addressed by Celestine's *Apostolici verba,* while claiming to be catholics and opposed to Pelagius and Caelestius, are neither, for they hold to the condemned teachings of the heretics and oppose "our doctors," whom they criticize for overstepping acceptable limits. Since the opponents of the "doctors" profess to follow only the pronouncements by the Apostolic See against the Pelagians, a summary of these pronouncements has been collected, which expresses the faith of Catholics on the issue of grace.[130] Ten articles are then listed, each containing the catholic statement on grace followed by the corresponding papal pronouncement.[131]

The first four articles assert humanity's fallen and helpless nature, drawn from two letters of Innocent.[132] Articles 5 to 7 assert the role of grace and free will in the economy of salvation—5 and 6 drawn from Zosimus, and 7 from canons 3–5 of the Council of Carthage (418).[133] Articles 8 and 9 deal with God's universal salvific will and the mean-

129. Cf. Raúl Villegas Marán ("En polémica con Julián de Eclanum. Por unan nueva lectura del *Syllabus de gratia* de Próspero de Aquitania," *Augustinianum* 43 [2003]: 81–124), who argues that the *Auctoritates* was written in 439 and was exclusively concerned with combating Pelagianism in the context of Julian of Eclanum's appeal to the pope in 439.

130. *Auctoritates,* Praef. (PL 51: 205–6; *Pronouncements,* 178).

131. Articles 8–10 are not drawn from papal pronouncements; 8 and 9 are from Roman liturgical practice, and 10 is a conclusion. The significance of this will be addressed below.

132. *Auctoritates* 1–4 (PL 51: 205–7; *Pronouncements,* 179–80). Cf. Innocent, *Epp.* 29.2, 29.3, 29.6, 30.3 (PL 20: 584, 586, 591).

133. *Auctoritates* 5–7 (PL 51: 207–9; *Pronouncements,* 180–83). Cf. Zosimus, *Epist. Tractoria* and *Concilium Carthaginense* 3–5 (CCL 149: 70–71; *Council of Carthage,* 58–59).

ing and effect of baptism, which are drawn from the Roman liturgical prayer and the baptismal rite.[134] Article 9 also serves as the summary of the articles. The last article concludes by stating that the abovementioned articles are the expressions of the catholic faith and sufficient for the profession of faith concerning the doctrine of grace.[135]

Theology of Grace

Prosper did not include all of the papal pronouncements in his list of articles, nor did he limit his sources to Apostolic decrees. Prosper's summary of the catholic view on grace is selective, but systematic, revealing what he considers to be catholic. For Prosper, the catholic doctrine of grace is expressed in what the Apostolic See proclaimed and what the Church practices in its liturgy, consistent with Scripture. Prosper begins with the most basic element, Original Sin, then moves on to the relationship between grace and free will, which is, at the end, confirmed by the practices of the Church.

As a result of Adam's sin, humans lost their innocence and the natural ability to do the good.[136] It is only through the grace of baptism that sins can be washed away and the person raised from the abyss of sin.[137] No one is good, except God alone, who gives a share of His goodness to humans.[138]

Prosper avoids any mention of God's previous knowledge or actions, except that God knew that humans could fall back to sin after baptism, and so offers daily help to persevere in the good life.[139] Prosper seems to suggest that a free human response to this daily help is necessary to overcome the dangers of human sin, but immediately clarifies in the following articles the role of human free will and good works.[140] The proper use of free will can only occur when

134. *Auctoritates* 8–9 (PL 51: 209–10; *Pronouncements,* 183–85). Cf. Prosper, *De vocatione* 1.12 (PL 51: 664; *Call of All Nations,* 52).

135. *Auctoritates* 10 (PL 51: 211–12; *Pronouncements,* 185).

136. *Auctoritates* 1 (PL 51: 205; *Pronouncements,* 179).

137. *Auctoritates* 1 (PL 51: 205–6; *Pronouncements,* 179).

138. *Auctoritates* 2 (PL 51: 206–7; *Pronouncements,* 179).

139. *Auctoritates* 3 (PL 51: 207; *Pronouncements,* 179–80).

140. *Auctoritates* 3 (PL 51: 207; *Pronouncements,* 180): "Quotidiana praestat ille remedia, quibus nisi freti, confisique nitamur, nullatenus humanos vincere poterimus errores."

it is helped by Christ.[141] Free will is not set aside, yet it is God's grace that is the more powerful agent, inspiring every good movement, and without which humans can do nothing good.[142]

As for the controversial text from 1 Timothy 2: 4, Prosper alludes to this text, but in the context of his new conviction, initially conceived in *De vocatione omnium gentium,* and now fully realized.[143] Prosper, well aware of the controversy surrounding the interpretations of this text, and wanting to resolve the debate, provides the Church's interpretation. The catholic understanding of God's universal salvific will in 1 Timothy 2: 4 is expressed by the prayer of the Church: the "Prayers of the Faithful."[144] Prosper may have had found the inspiration from Augustine's reference of the Church's prayer.[145] However, whereas Augustine used the "Prayers of the Faithful" in support of his doctrine of grace, Prosper uses the prayers as support of his doctrine of the Church. The Church prays for the salvation of all people, *ut lex supplicandi statuat legem credendi.*[146] It is the "law of supplication" that determines the "law of believing," thus the theological controversy over the interpretation of this text has been settled by the practice of the Church.

Prosper also refers to another practice of the Church, the rite of baptism, as further proof of the redeeming power of Christ.[147] The Apostolic decrees and the Church's liturgical practices represent the

141. *Auctoritates* 4 (PL 51: 207; *Pronouncements,* 180).

142. *Auctoritates* 5–6 (PL 51: 207–8; *Pronouncements,* 181).

143. *Auctoritates* 8 (PL 51: 209–10; *Pronouncements,* 183). Cf. *De vocatione* 1.12 (PL 51: 664; *Call of All Nations,* 52).

144. See above.

145. Augustine had referred to this prayer in a few places, including *De don. pers.* 23.63–64 (PL 45: 1031–32; *Perseverance,* 233–35). See chapter 4 n. 23.

146. *Auctoritates* 8 (PL 51: 209; *Pronouncements,* 183): "Obsecrationum quoque sacerdotalium sacramenta respiciamus, quae ab apostolis tradita, in toto mundo atque in omni catholica Ecclesia uniformiter celebrantur, ut legem credendi lex statuat supplicandi." This well known maxim has been misquoted as *lex orandi, lex credendi.* See Paul de Clerck, "'Lex orandi, lex credendi': The Original Sense and Historical Avatars of an Equivocal Adage," *Studia Liturgica* 24 (1994): 178–200; Van Slyke, "Lex orandi lex credendi," 130–51; and Walter Durig, "Zur Interpretation des Axioms Legem credendi lex statuat supplicandi," in *Veritati Catholicae: Festschrift für Leo Scheffczyk zum 65. Geburtstag,* ed. Anton Ziegenaus et al. (Aschaffenburg: Pattloch, 1985), 226–36.

147. *Auctoritates* 9 (PL 51: 210; *Pronouncements,* 184).

ecclesiasticae regulae.[148] Together with Scripture, these two reveal Prosper's understanding of the catholic faith on grace:

> He [God] is the author of every good desire, every good action, every good effort, every virtuous move by which from the beginning of faith we draw near to God. We are convinced that all human merit is forestalled by the grace of God, who moves us to will and to accomplish what is good. This help and this gift of God, certainly, do not take away free will but rather set it free, and change it from darkness to light, from evil to righteousness, from sickness to health, from ignorance to wisdom. God's goodness for all men is so great that He wishes His own gifts to become our merits and will give eternal rewards for what are His own bounties. He, in fact, effects it in us that we come to will and to do what He wants; He does not allow that His gifts, granted us for use and not for disregard, should remain idle in us, so that we in turn should be co-operators with the grace of God.[149]

Prosper's theology of grace can be reduced to the belief in the priority of and the absolute need for God's grace to accomplish anything good, and that free will is set free in order that it may cooperate with God's grace. The issues related to God's discrimination—predestination, election, foreknowledge, and the like—are not included in Prosper's definition of grace. Prosper sees no need to explore or even reiterate these "more profound" and "more difficult" questions.[150] What is essential for the proper understanding of the catholic view on grace is what is contained in this document.[151] Thus, according to Prosper, the catholic view of grace need only express the priority of and absolute need for God's grace to do good, and the cooperation of the redeemed free will with God's grace.

Ecclesiology

The doctrine of grace presented in the *Auctoritates* reflects the influences of Augustine, Leo, and Prosper's developed sense of ecclesiol-

148. *Auctoritates* 9 (PL 51: 210; *Pronouncements,* 184).

149. *Auctoritates* 9 (PL 51: 210; *Pronouncements,* 184–85).

150. *Auctoritates* 10 (PL 51: 211; *Pronouncements,* 185): "Profundiores vero difficilioresque partes incurrentium quaestionum, quas latius pertractarunt qui haereticis restiterunt, sicut non audemus contemnere, ita non necesse habemus astruere."

151. *Auctoritates* 10 (PL 51: 212; *Pronouncements,* 185).

ogy. The need for and effect of grace on the human free will is Augustinian. The authority and role of the Apostolic See for establishing the faith of the Church came from Leo. However, it is Prosper's ecclesiological convictions that are at the heart of *Auctoritates.* Prosper is neither a disciple of Augustine nor of Leo, but *a servus ecclesiae.* The only element of Augustine's doctrine of grace in conformity to the Church is the positive formulation of free will and its need for grace. Leo's assertion of the Apostolic See's role and authority are affirmed, but Prosper joins the role and authority of the Apostolic See with the liturgical practices of the Church. These together rule over the Church.

Prosper's ecclesiology determines Prosper's theology of grace. In its composition and intent, the *Auctoritates* bears witness to Prosper's overriding ecclesiological concerns.

Prosper's understanding of grace evolved as he increasingly came to understand the Church to be the Roman Church. Prosper had always sought to reflect the Church's views in his writings on grace, and it was only toward the end of his life that he concluded the Church was the Roman Church. The laws of the Church—apostolic decrees and Church practices—and Scripture are the only and sufficient expressions for catholic faith on the issue of grace.

Prosper on Prosper and His Opponents

In his revisionist history, Prosper omitted the main body of his works, along with the many years of struggle he had in producing these writings. There were, however, some things he was unwilling to sacrifice, even for the sake of the Church. In writing a document that he hoped to pass on as Celestine's decree, Prosper took care to present himself positively to posterity, and to present his opponents with the stain of heretical association.

Prosper was careful not to name Augustine, but he was audacious enough to include himself, by way of implication, among the "most pious disputers" and "our masters."[152] Even if one were not well versed in the Augustinian controversy, reading just the *Apostolici verba,* which contained Prosper's role in the controversy, and the *Aucto-*

152. *Auctoritates,* Praef. (PL 51: 205; *Pronouncements,* 178): "Piissimis diputatoribus . . . magistris tamen nostris."

ritates, would have implied Prosper's inclusion among this esteemed group.[153] According to Celestine's judgment, and therefore with the weight of Apostolic authority, Prosper was judged a "most pious disputer" and one of the Church's "masters." This was, of course, not Celestine's judgment, but Prosper's shameless self-appropriation.

Besides his adherence to the catholic faith, there is one other quality that remains consistent with Prosper, and that is his enmity toward his opponents. Prosper is quick to forget social associations, neglects to mention friends or family, and breaks off old allegiances, but he never forgets his opponents. It is likely that all of his old enemies by the mid-fifth century had died—they certainly were no longer engaged in actively opposing Prosper—but that did not diminish in any way his resolve to oppose even their memory. Prosper was finally in a position of authority, and he took advantage of it in the *Auctoritates,* passing on to posterity his view of his opponents. According to Prosper's estimation, and thus the judgment of the Apostolic See, his opponents are not heretics or *Pelagianae reliquiae pravitatis,* but they are prideful, and presumptuous, and retain the opinions of heretics because they are depraved or ignorant.[154]

Conclusion

The *Auctoritates* was meant to be the catholic settlement of the conflict between the supporters of Augustine and their Gallic opponents. The implication is that the conflict that continued after the *Apostolici verba* and the *Auctoritates* was unnecessary because the Church had already resolved the issue by declaring the official catholic view of grace. In effect, Prosper acknowledges the futility and error of those many years in trying to defend his own view of grace, influenced for a time by Augustine.

The *Auctoritates* is Prosper's *Retractationes,* but, in keeping with Prosper's personality, the admission of mistakes is not explicit, but only inferred. Looking back on those years of struggle, misguided by his naïve zeal for Augustine and the lack of understanding of catho-

153. Cf. Celestine, *Ep.* 21.2 (PL 50: 528).

154. *Auctoritates,* Praef. (PL 51: 205; *Pronouncements,* 178): "Quia nonnulli qui catholico nomine gloriantur, in damnatis autem haereticorum sensibus, seu pravitate, sive imperitia demorantes, piissimis disputatoribus obviare praesumunt."

licity, Prosper concluded that the Roman Church defines catholic grace, and that personal speculations do not. Prosper was content with the parts that were illuminated by the Roman Church and his insatiable curiosity and fascination with the more hidden aspects of grace were finally satisfied.

Chronicon Edition of 455

This final edition of his *Chronicon* covers the years 451 to 455, a particularly dramatic period for the West. The message of the *Chronicon* is a theological one. Though the world may suffer material destruction at the hands of sinful men and spiritual threats from heretics, God's power intervenes to protect Christian lives and faith through holy men. And there is no greater instrument of God's power on earth than Leo, whom Prosper casts in the most saintly light.

The *Chronicon* as a whole is Prosper's view of salvation history, containing what Prosper viewed was essential to that story. What is included and excluded in the *Chronicon* reflects Prosper's final theological views, including the doctrine of grace.

Summary

The years of Prosper's last edition of the *Chronicon* are filled with extraordinary events for the Empire. In the years 451 to 455, three wars were fought, two emperors murdered, an ecumenical council held, and Rome threatened with invasion twice—the latter one resulting in the sack of the city. All of these events are connected to the role of Leo, whose actions led to peace. The two primary concerns for Prosper in the *Auctoritates*—the Apostolic See and Church liturgy—are continued in the *Chronicon.*

According to Prosper's account, Leo, through the help of God, was solely responsible for the protection of Rome while the secular powers stood by helplessly. It was Leo's presence alone, with the help of God, that dissuaded Attila from attacking Rome.[155] In 455,

155. *Chronicon,* sub an. 452 (MGH, AA 9: 482; *Chronicle,* 74): "Nam tota legatione dignanter accepta ita summi sacerdotis praesentiam rex gavisus est, ut et bello abstinere praeciperet et ultra Danuvium promissa pace discederet."

though Rome's material wealth was emptied and many captives taken by Gaiseric, Leo's supplication, through the power of God, mollified Gaiseric to the extent that Rome was spared from fire, death, and torture.[156] And at the Council of Chalcedon, Leo's definition of faith *(Tome)* was confirmed universally.[157]

The importance of the Apostolic See and the Roman liturgy are evident in the last entry—both of which are fundamental to Prosper's ecclesiology. Prosper notes that Easter was celebrated that year on April 24, but Leo protested that it should have been celebrated on April 17, according to the proper calculations.[158] According to Prosper, Leo tolerated the Eastern date for the sake of peace and unity, but did not approve of their opinion, while working to establish the proper date of Easter for the entire Church.[159]

The appearance of a liturgical matter in a chronicle reflects the importance that Prosper placed on Church liturgy, which also served to highlight Leo's role as teacher of the Church, East and West. The twin concerns of Prosper, continued from the *Auctoritates,* are evident in the *Chronicon.* Despite the almost hagiographical depiction of Leo, Prosper is careful not to present Leo as an individual acting by his own personal judgment and charisma.[160] When Leo dissuad-

156. *Chronicon,* sub an. 455 (MGH, AA 9: 484; *Chronicle,* 75): "Occurrente sibi extra portas sancto Leone episcopo, cuius supplicatio ita eum deo agente lenivit, ut, cum omnia potestati ipsius essent tradita, ab igni tamen et caede atque suppliciis abstineretur."

157. *Chronicon,* sub an. 453 (MGH, AA 9: 482; *Chronicle,* 74): "Omnes autem, qui se ab eis retraxerunt, in communionem recepti, confirmata universaliter fide, quae de incarnatione verbi secundum euangelicam et apostolicam doctrinam per sanctum papam Leonem praedicabatur."

158. *Chronicon,* sub an. 455 (MGH, AA 9: 484; *Chronicle,* 76): "Eodem anno pascha dominicum die VIII kal. Maias celebratum est pertinaci intentione Alexandrini episcopi, cui omnes Orientales consentiendum putarunt, cum sanctus papa Leo XV kal. Mai. potius observandum protestaretur, in quo nec in ratione plenilunii nec in primi mensis limite fuisset erratum."

159. *Chronicon,* sub an. 455 (MGH, AA 9: 484; *Chronicle,* 76): "Extant eiusdam papae epistolae ad clementissimum principem Marcianum datae, quibus ratio veritatis sollicite evidenterque patefacta est et quibus ecclesia catholica instrui potest, quod haec persuasio studio unitatis et pacis tolerata sit potius quam probata. . . ."

160. Muhlberger identifies Prosper's method of portraying Leo in his *Chronicon* as a precusor to the hagiographies of the next two generations (*Fifth Century Chroniclers,* 131–35). See also Mark Humphries, "Chronicle and Chronology: Prosper of Aquitaine, His Methods and the Development of Early Medieval Chronography," *Early Medieval Europe* 5 (1996): 155–75.

ed Attila and mollified Gaiseric, Prosper attributed the success to God's help.[161] The faith proclaimed by Leo, and confirmed at Chalcedon, was drawn in accordance to the *evangelica et apostolica doctrina.*[162] And Leo's dating of Easter is based on the correct calculation of the full moon and the demarcation of the first month, not Leo's personal judgment.[163]

Prosper's praise of Leo is consistent with his ultimate regard for the Apostolic See. In his continuation, Prosper avoids even the hint of impropriety, scandal, misjudgment, or anything else that detracts from the dignity and authority of the office.[164] Leo, though given special attention for his actions, is not praised because of his personal holiness, but because he is the pope par excellence, who protected Rome and promoted the peace within the Church.

Theology

Prosper was approximately sixty-seven years old (388–455) when he wrote the last edition of the *Chronicon.* He may very well have been aware that this was to be among his last works, if not his last, as it came to stand. Not surprisingly, Prosper noted for posterity the extraordinary events of the previous five years, in which Leo played a leading part. What is surprising is what Prosper left out of the *Chronicon.* That is, the *Chronicon* is Prosper's view of salvation history up to his time, and contained what was significant to that story. Yet an entire episode in the history of the Church, one in which he stood in the very center, is passed over in silence.

In adding onto the previous edition of the *Chronicon* of 451, Prosper did not significantly alter what he had previously written.[165]

161. *Chronicon,* sub ann. 452, 455 (MGH, AA 9: 482, 484; *Chronicle,* 74, 75).

162. *Chronicon,* sub an. 453 (MGH, AA 9: 482; *Chronicle,* 74): "Synodos Calchedonensis peracta Eutyche Dioscoroque damnatis. omnes autem, qui se ab eis retraxerunt, in communionem recepti, confirmata universaliter fide, quae de incarnatione verbi secundum euangelicam et apostolicam doctrinam per sanctum papam Leonem praedicabatur."

163. *Chronicon,* sub an. 455 (MGH, AA 9: 484; *Chronicle,* 76): "Potius observandum protestaretur, in quo nec in ratione plenilunii nec in primi mensis limite fuisset erratum."

164. See Muhlberger, *Fifth Century Chroniclers,* 71.

165. Muhlberger (*Fifth Century Chroniclers,* 58–60) concluded that there were four editions of the *Chronicon*—433, 445, 451, and 455—and that no significant alterations

Prosper's alteration of the *Chronicon* edition of 451, which amounts to a few change of words, is evidence that Prosper did not merely append the continuation to his previous edition but took care to go over what he had previously written.

What is essential is the Roman Church, which plays the central role in salvation history. Through its leadership, the Apostolic See, the Church is protected from both physical and spiritual assaults. The story of the Church's spiritual struggle is limited to the Pelagian, Nestorian, Manichaean, and Eutychian heresies, and the proper date of Easter.[166] In other words, these were the struggles of the Church that were essential to the story, worthy of inclusion in salvation history. These, then, were the theological conflicts that were worthy and necessary to leave to posterity. By implication, the Augustinian controversy was not essential to salvation history.

In the larger picture of salvation history, the conflict over Augustine's doctrine of grace within the Church was deemed unnecessary. Prosper had gone beyond the *Auctoritates*'s view of the conflict, in which Prosper attempted to resolve anachronistically. Here, Prosper fails to even hint at the conflict.

Reflecting Prosper's full adhesion to the Roman Church and its faith, the *Chronicon*'s theological message is centered on the Church. What the Church has declared on matters of faith is authoritative. On the issue of grace, the Church declared the Pelagians in error and rightly condemned them; that is all that needs to be included in salvation history.

Conclusion

In Prosper's final estimation, Augustine was worthy of being included in salvation history. However, Prosper is careful to praise Augustine as a bishop who represented the Church. Augustine's life

---

were made to the previous editions when Prosper reissued them in the editions of 445, 451, and 455.

166. The Pelagian heresy is mentioned under the years 413, 416, 429, 430, and 439; the Nestorian heresy under 428 and 431; the Manichean under 443; the Eutychian heresy under 448 and 453; and the date of Easter discussed under 455. *Chronicon,* sub ann. 413, 416, 428, 429, 430, 431, 439, 443, 448, 453, 455 (MGH, AA 9: 467, 468, 472, 473, 476, 479, 480–81, 482 484–85; *Chronicle,* 65, 68, 70–71, 71, 72, 72–73, 74, 76).

was chronicled—his elevation to bishop, his involvement in the struggle against the Pelagians, and his death—but nothing of his relation to the conflict he inspired in southern Gaul are detailed, and the praise of Prosper's one-time master conformed to that of the Roman Church's official view, as contained in the *Apostolici verba.*[167] Augustine was included primarily because of his eloquence as a bishop, and for his role in the opposition to the Pelagian conflict, which he is not even given full credit for leading.[168]

Although the Augustinian conflict is not mentioned, and with it his opportunity to vilify his opponents, Prosper managed to cast one last aspersion to their memory. Cassian, Vincent, and all his other opponents remain his enemies. Their existence and contributions to the Church are completely passed over in silence, unworthy to be included in the events of their own day, in which they played significant roles regardless of their involvement in the Augustinian controversy.

Prosper also neglected to include himself in the *Chronicon.* This, however, should not be seen as a display of humility. The *Chronicon* contained Prosper's view of salvation history, reflecting his own judgments. Moreover, the *Chronicon* was not written anonymously, and Prosper must have known that by continuing Jerome's chronicle, his name would be remembered and associated with Jerome's as long as Jerome would be remembered.

167. *Chronicon,* sub ann. 395, 416, 430 (MGH, AA 9: 463, 468, 473; *Chronicle,* 64, 66, 68). The *Chronicon*'s description of Augustine is consistent with Celestine's judgment. Cf. Celestine, *Ep.* 21.3 (PL 50: 529–30): "Augustinum sanctae recordationis virum pro vita sua atque meritis in nostra communione semper habuimus, nec umquam hunc sinistrae suspicionis saltem rumor aspersit: quem tantae scientiae olim fuisse meminimus, ut inter magistros optimos etiam ante a meis semper decessoribus haberetur. Bene ergo de eo omnes in communi senserunt, utpote qui ubique cunctis et amori fuerit et honori." *Chronicon,* sub ann. 395, 430 (MGH, AA 9: 463, 473): "Augustinus beati Ambrosii discipulus multa facundia doctrinaque excellens Hippone in Africa episcopus ordinatur." "Aurelius Augustinus episcopus per omnia excellentissimus moritur."

168. According to Prosper's version of events, it was the popes who led the opposition against the Pelagians, although Augustine is given credit for leading the African front against the Pelagians. Cf. *Chronicon,* sub an. 416 (MGH, AA 9: 468; *Chronicle,* 65–66): "At this time the Pelagians, already condemned by Pope Innocent, were resisted by the diligence of the Africans and especially by the knowledge of Bishop Augustine."

Death

Prosper died shortly after 455, the year of the last edition of the *Chronicon*. It is because of the special attention Prosper paid to Leo that Prosper's death can be dated to this time. Had Prosper lived significantly past 455, another edition of the *Chronicon* would have been written to detail the further activities of Leo, who was pope until 461. Scholars have put forward various dates for Prosper's death—456, 463, 465, and 466—based on documentary evidence, but none of these can be conclusively established.[169]

In 457, Victorius of Aquitaine mentioned Prosper as a *vir sanctus et venerabilis* in the prologue to his Easter cycle.[170] Some have taken this remark to indicate that Prosper had died in 456, but the description is devoid of the common designation for someone who has died—*sanctus memor.*[171] Nor can Prosper's existence be inferred from the absence of this designation, because Victorius does not use the designation in referring to Eusebius of Caeserea.[172] Moreover, Victorius's prologue, which contains the reference, is inauthentic.[173] Therefore, the remark from Victorius's prologue cannot be considered proof for either the existence or death of Prosper in 456.

Others have argued for the date of 463, citing Count Marcellinus's listing of Prosper's information under the year 463 in his sixth-century chronicle.[174] However, Marcellinus's source was Gennadius's *Lives,* which does not contain Prosper's date of death, and

169. For a summary on the scholarly opinions on Prosper's date of death, see Oswald Holder-Egger, "Untersuchen über einige annalistische Quellen zur Geschichte des fünften und sechsten Jarhhunderts," *Neues Archiv der Gesellschaft für ältere deutsche Geshichtskunde,* vol. 1 (Hanover: Hahn'sche Buchhandlung, 1876): 58–59, and Valentin, *Saint Prosper,* 139–40.

170. Victorius of Aquitaine, *Cursus paschalis annorum* DXXXII (MGH, AA 9: 681).

171. Valentin (*Saint Prosper,* 139): "Quand il s'agit des morts, les historiens ajoutent presque toujours le substantif "mémoire", (homme de sainte mémiore. . .), que ce Victorius n'emploie pas dans le passage allégué." Cf. Philip Labbe, *De scriptoribus ecclesiasticis,* vol. 2 (Paris, 1660), 249.

172. Victorius, *Cursus* (MGH, AA 9: 681): "Beati scilicet Eusebi Caesariensis . . . viri in primus eruditissimi atque doctissimi."

173. Valentin (*Saint Prosper,* 139) following Holder-Egger ("Untersuchen," 59): "der Prolog ist aber gefälscht."

174. Valentin, *Saint Prosper,* 139; Holder-Egger, "Untersuchen," 58.

Marcellinus's entry for Prosper does not indicate that it was the year of Prosper's death.[175] Moreover, Marcellinus's chronicle is often inaccurate—for example, Theodoret of Cyrus is listed under the year 466, but he died ten years earlier.[176] Muhlberger does not find Marcellinus's mention of Prosper as an indication of the year of his death, and suggests that Marcellinus may have used Prosper to fill in a year, which would have otherwise remained blank.[177] Valentin as well, following Holder-Egger, does not view the mention of Prosper for that year to warrant a date of death.[178]

Others have proposed the date of 466, based on Flaminus's *Vita S. Prosperi episcopi Rejensis.*[179] Prosper was not the bishop of Reggio and, as Noris disparagingly remarked, the work is a fable.[180]

Mommsen was content to say only that Prosper was alive in 455, and Valentin followed his opinion, admitting the timidity of his conclusion.[181] Therefore, what is certain is that Prosper was still alive in 455. Based on the theory that Prosper would have written another edition of his *Chronicon* to further detail the pontificate of Leo, if Prosper lived significantly beyond 455, it is safe to assume that Prosper died within a few years of 455.

175. Marcellinus Comes, *Chronicon*, sub. an. 463, in *Chronica Minora* 2 (MGH, AA 11: 88). Cf. Gennadius, *De viris inlustribus* 85 (TU 14/1: 90).

176. Marcellinus, *Chronicon*, sub. an. 466 (MGH, AA 11: 89).

177. Muhlberger, *The Fifth Century Chroniclers*, 54.

178. Valentin, *Saint Prosper*, 140; Oswald Holder-Egger, "Untersuchen," 58–59.

179. Jos. Ant. Flaminius, *Vita S. Prosperi episcopi Rejensius, in Surius, Historiae seu vitae sanctorum*, vol. 3 (Turin: Ex typographia Pontificia et Archiepiscopali eq. P. Marietti, 1875), 816. Cf. Antoine Rivet de la Grange, *Histoire littéraire de la France*, vol. 2 (Paris: Osmont, 1733), 377, and Felix Papencordt, *Geschichte der vandalischen Herrschaft in Afrika* (Berlin: Duncker and Humblot, 1837), 356.

180. The 1539 Lyons edition by Gryphius referred to Prosper as bishop of Reggio, but was refuted by G. Morin ("Saint Prosper de Reggio," *RB* 12 [1895]: 241–57); see chapter 1 for the discussion on the editions of Prosper's works. H. Noris, *Historia Pelagiana* (Padova: Petri Mariae Frambotti, 1673), 275. Quotation in Holder-Egger, "Untersuchen," 59, and Valentin, *Saint Prosper*, 140.

181. Mommsen, "Introduction" (MGH, AA 9: 344); Valentin (*Saint Prosper*, 140): "La conclusion de cette courte dissertation est un timide 'peut-être.' Saint Prosper vivait encore en 455, c'est tout ce que la science est en mesure d'affirmer."

Conclusion

PROSPER LIVED during a time of cultural, political, and ecclesiastical transitions. The barbarian invasions signaled the beginnings of a new period in the West, and the two defining features of the medieval Church, monasticism and the papacy, grew out of the movements of this period: asceticism and the growth of papal authority. Prosper's life was affected by all of these changes. He had suffered exile as a result of barbarian invasions to his native land, became embroiled in a controversy with ascetics, and served as an advisor to a pope who helped define the power of the papacy. In the course of his adulthood, one issue came to dominate his life: grace.

From 426 to 455 Prosper devoted his life to the defense of the catholic doctrine of grace. Prosper's defense of the catholic teaching on grace witnessed a series of developments as he became increasingly convinced of the primacy of the Roman Church. The major stages in his development are as follows: from naive, uninformed Christian, to catholic Christian, to an increasingly Roman-centered Christian, and, finally, to a faithful Roman Christian.

De providentia Dei, written in 416, reflects the work of an individual Christian relying on his classical education and knowledge of Scripture. The work lacks an appreciation of the role and teachings of the Church for the life of faith. The newly exiled Aquitanian then ceased writing for a decade. During this period, Prosper became aware of the importance of the catholic Church, broadly defined. At the same time, Prosper became an enthusiastic follower of Augustine's doctrine of grace. Prosper assumed that Augustine's doctrine of grace was the expression of the Church's view on grace. The appearance of Augustine's writings to the monks of Hadrumetum in Marseilles provoked a negative reaction among the *doctores Gallicani.* Prosper was so convinced of Augustine's orthodoxy that he defended what was, in his mind, the catholic view on grace against its opponents. The conflict quickly escalated and Prosper along with other Augustinians resolved to oppose the *doctores Gallicani.* During this time, Prosper faithfully reiterated Augustine's teachings. He identified himself and those who shared his belief in Augustine's catholicity as "intrepid lovers of perfect grace."[1] With the firm conviction that Augustine's doctrine of grace was the expression of "perfect grace," Prosper vigorously attacked Augustine's opponents for following the teachings of the Pelagians. The bitter polemic raged on both sides until the late 430s.

In his last writings while in Marseilles, Prosper began to modify Augustine's doctrine of predestination. These writings showed signs of waning enthusiasm for the extremes of Augustine's doctrine of grace as Prosper's view of catholicity began to appreciate the importance of the Roman Church. A second period of literary inactivity and reflection followed. Prosper's understanding of the catholic Church and its teachings then underwent significant development. Prosper concluded that Augustine's doctrine of grace was not the catholic teaching on grace, which he identified with the Roman Church. In 440, Prosper joined Leo, the newly elected pope, as his theological advisor.

Prosper's understanding of the Church reached its conclusion while in Rome. One of Prosper's first tasks was to conform Augustine's doctrine of grace to acceptable catholic limits. At this point, Prosper's understanding of grace was limited to what it was not. Augustine's doctrine of predestination was not catholic, but neither were the *doctore Gallicani's* views. The former issue was resolved by eliminating the doctrine of predestination in Prosper's summary of Augustine's teachings. The *Expositio psalmorum* and the *Liber sententiarum* were Prosper's efforts at presenting the correct or catholic interpretation of Augustine's teachings on grace.

1. Prosper, *Ep.* 225.7 (CSEL 57: 464; *Letter* 225, 92): "nec facile quisquam praeter paucos perfectae gratiae intrepidos amatores tanto superiorum disputationibus ausus est contra ire." For the context of the passage, see chapter 4.

Prosper's *De vocatione omnium gentium* (450) reflects the height of his personal theological reflections. It is the work of a mature theologian struggling to explain the biblical text at the center of the Augustinian controversy: 1 Timothy 2: 4. Prosper's view on grace appropriates the strengths of others, even that of his opponent, Cassian. This was a personal work, not meant as a definitive view on grace, but as the view of a catholic Christian who attempted to bring some objective view to the contentious issue.

Prosper's interpretation of 1 Timothy 2: 4 in *De vocatione omnium gentium,* which is interpreted in its original pericope of prayer and conforms to the liturgical prayer of the Church, is found again in *Praeteritorum episcoporum sedis apostolicae auctoritates de gratia Dei et libero voluntatis arbitrio.* In his final formal theological treatise, Prosper attached a series of papal pronouncements on grace along with liturgical-based arguments in support of grace. Its content reflects what the Roman Church has taught, through its popes, and what the Roman Church practices in regard to the issue of grace. Prosper intended the work to be read as directly related to Celestine's *Apostolici verba* (431), making it appear as if the Roman Church had definitively determined the catholic view on grace before much of the polemical battles took place. Prosper knew that such a work undermined all his years in struggling to defend and define grace, even his *De vocatione omnium gentium.* This act, along with the absence of the whole conflict in his *Chronicon,* attests to his complete fidelity to the Roman Church—*a servus ecclesiae.* Prosper finally arrived at the conviction that the Roman Church determined the catholic doctrine of grace through papal decrees and expressed by liturgical practices. The Roman Church alone defines catholic doctrine. The acknowledgment of this fact is a part of his understanding of the larger role of the Roman Church. The central theme of Prosper's *Chronicon* is the centrality of the Roman Church. It is the Roman Church around which all things revolve—the secular and the religious.

Though the Roman Church had not resolved all the issues on grace, Prosper was content to leave the mysterious elements of grace as mystery, secure in the knowledge that the definition of grace proposed by the Roman Church was a sufficient statement on catholic grace. Prosper had come to the full realization that the "perfect grace" for which he had long labored to understand and defend was defined and expressed by the Roman Church.

Prosper's Legacy

The generation after Prosper judged him a saint and erudite theologian, but Prosper's fame or infamy remains inextricably tied to Augustine, which is exactly what he sought to avoid.[2] Despite Prosper's efforts at providing the Roman Church with the catholic understanding of Augustine's doctrine of grace and establishing the Roman Church's view on grace, the Augustinian controversy continued after his death. Augustine's doctrine of grace was either defended or rejected as catholic doctrine and the *Auctoritates* did not keep others from exploring the mysteries of grace.

Lucidus and Faustus in the 470s clashed over Augustine's doctrine of predestination. Lucidus drew from the writings of Augustine independent of Prosper's edited "catholic" version. Faustus vehemently opposed Lucidus and in the process formulated a doctrine of grace, *De gratia,* which disregarded the limits of the *Auctoritates.* Faustus's treatise then caused a disturbance between some Scythian monks and Possessor in Constantinople over the catholicity of Augustine's doctrine of grace in the 520s.[3]

The Augustinian controversy came to something of a resolution at the Second Council of Orange in 529.[4] The doctrine of grace formulated in the decrees of Orange reflects a moderate Augustinianism and is the result of a cooperative effort with the pope. This understanding of grace was very much in line with Prosper's.[5] The Second Council of Orange, however, did not mark the end of the Au-

2. Gelasius [494] ("Concilium Romanum I" [PL 59:160]): "Prosperi viri religiossimi." Gennadius (*De viris inlustribus* 85 [TU 14/1: 90]): "Prosper, homo Aquitanicae regionis, sermone scholasticus et adsertionibus nervosus."

3. See Rondet, *Grace of Christ,* 154–58, and Mathisen, *Ecclesiastical Factionalism,* 244–68. Faustus of Reiz, *De gratia Dei et libero arbitrio libri duo* (CCL: 101–101B).

4. *Concilium Arausicorum* (CCL 148A: 55–76).

5. Rondet, *Grace of Christ,* 158–64. For a more in-depth study on the Council of Orange, see Weaver, *Divine Grace,* 199–234.

gustinian controversy. Augustine's doctrine of grace continued to be a source of controversy in the Middle Ages. During the Carolingian renaissance, Augustine became a topic of interest, and Gottschalk and Hincmar were involved in a bitter dispute concerning predestination. In the fourteenth century, Gregory of Rimini and Gabriel Biel continued the debate over Augustine's doctrine of grace, and Thomas Bradwardine, John Wyclif, and John Hus were inspired by their own independent reading of Augustine's doctrine of grace.[6] Finally, the Reformation can be viewed as a stage of the Augustinian controversy, but with much more profound consequences.

Prosper provided the Roman Church with the catholic interpretation of Augustine's doctrine of grace, that is, the way in which the Church is to understand Augustine's doctrine of grace, and formulated a catholic doctrine of grace according to the pronouncements of the Roman Church. Prosper's fears were realized by the Protestant reformers in their insistence on reading Augustine independent of Prosper's interpretation and by formulating a doctrine of grace without regard to the authority and role of the Roman Church.

The Protestants followed the earlier Prosper—the devout Augustinian—while the Catholics followed the later Prosper—the devout servant of the Roman Church—at Trent.

If Prosper was a failure in safeguarding the Church from individualistic, independent readings of Augustine's doctrine of grace, he was successful in regards to his opponents. The *doctores Gallicani* have remained under the cloud of suspicion cast by the efforts of Prosper. The advent and persistence of the term semi-Pelagian attests to that success.[7] While Cassian and the *doctores Gallicani* have received much due reevaluation and the suspicion of heretical leanings has been all but erased, such reevaluations have come at the expense of Prosper. Much of the critiques are well deserved, but the portrait of Prosper that emerges when viewed solely in the context of his polemical battles fails to appreciate the larger story of his life: the lifelong struggle to understand and defend the catholic teaching on grace.

6. Rondet, *Grace of Christ*, 176–84, 261–72.

7. Casiday has devoted an appendix containing some examples of Prosper's success in this regard (*Tradition and Theology*, 264–65).

Bibliography

Prosper: Authentic and Spurious Works

Editions

Divi Prosperi Aquitanici, Episcopi Regiensis, Opera, accurate vetustiorum exemplarium collatione per viros eruditos recognita. Sebastian Gryphius. Lyons, 1539.

Sancti Prosperi Aquitani . . . Opera. Ed. J. B. Le Brun des Marettes and L. U. Mangeant. Paris, 1711.

Authentic Works

Pro Augustino responsiones ad capitula obiectionum Gallorum calumniantium. PL 51: 155–74.

Answers to the Objections of the Gauls. In *Defense of St. Augustine,* 139–62. Trans. P. de Letter. ACW 32. Westminster, Md.: Newman Press, 1963.

Pro Augustino responsiones ad capitula obiectionum Vincentiarum. PL 51: 177–86.

Answers to the Vincentian Articles. In *Defense of St. Augustine,* 70–138. Trans. P. de Letter. ACW 32. Westminster, Md.: Newman Press, 1963.

Pro Augustino responsiones ad exerpta Genuensium. PL 51: 187–202.

Answers to the Extracts of the Genoese. In *Defense of St. Augustine,* 49–69. Trans. P. de Letter. ACW 32. Westminster, Md.: Newman Press, 1963.

Carmen de Ingratis. [Critical edition and facing translation in] *Carmen de ingratis: A Translation with an Introduction and a Commentary.* Trans. Charles Huegelmeyer. PS 95. Washington, D.C.: The Catholic University of America Press, 1962.

Epigrammata ex sententiis sancti Augustini. PL 51: 498–532.

Epigrammata in obtrectatorem Augustini. PL 51:149–52.

Epistula ad Augustinum (*Ep.* 225). [among Augustine's letter] CSEL 57: 454–68.

Letter 225. In *Letters 211–270, 1*–29**, vol. 4, 87–94. Trans. Roland Teske. WSA II/4. Hyde Park, N.Y.: New City Press, 2005.

Epistula ad Demetriadem de vera humilitate. [Critical edition of the text and facing translation in] *Epistula ad Demetriadem de vera humilitate: A Critical Text and Translation with Introduction and Commentary.* Trans. M. Kathryn Clare Krabbe. PS 97. Washington, D.C.: The Catholic University of America Press, 1965.

Epistula ad Rufinum de gratia et libero arbitrio. PL 51: 77–90.

Letter to Rufinus. In *Defense of St. Augustine,* 21–37. Trans. P. de Letter. ACW 32. Westminster: Newman Press,1963.

Epitaphium Nestorianae et Pelagianae haereseon. PL 51: 153–54.

Epitoma chronicon. In *Chronica minora* 1. MGH, AA 9: 385–485. [Prosper's chronicle from years 379 to 455 translated in] *From Roman to Merovingian Gaul: A Reader.* Trans. Alexander Callander Murray. Orchard Park, N.Y.: Broadview Press, 2000.

Expositio psalmorum a centesimo usque ad centesimum quinquagesimum. CCL 68A: 1–211.

De gratia Dei et libero arbitrio liber contra collatorem. PL 51: 213–76.

On Grace and Free Will, against Cassian the Lecturer. In *Defense of St. Augustine,* 70–138. Trans. P. De. Letter. ACW 32. Westminster, Md.: Newman Press, 1963.

Liber sententiarum ex operibus sancti Augustini delibatarum. CCL 68A: 257–365.

Praeteritorum episcoporum sedis apostolicae auctoritates de gratia Dei et libero voluntatis arbitrio. PL 51: 205–12, 67: 270–74.

Official Pronouncements of the Apostolic See on Divine Grace and Free Will. In *Defense of St. Augustine,* 178–85. Trans. P. de Letter. ACW 32. Westminster, Md.: Newman Press, 1963.

De providentia Dei. [Critical edition of the text and facing translation in] *Prosper of Aquitaine, De providentia Dei: Text, Translation and Commentary.* Miroslav Marcovich. Supplements to Vigiliae Christianae 10. New York: E. J. Brill, 1989.

The Carmen de providentia Dei Attributed to Prosper of Aquitaine: A Re-

vised Text with an Introduction, Translation, and Notes. Ed. Michael P. McHugh. PS 98. Washington, D.C.: The Catholic University of America Press, 1964.

A Poem on Divine Providence. In *Divine Providence and Human Suffering,* 64–91. Ed. and Trans. James Walsh and P. G. Walsh. Message of the Fathers of the Church 17. Wilmington, Del.: Michael Glazier, 1985.

De vocatione omnium gentium. PL 51: 647–722.

The Call of All Nations. Trans. P. de Letter. ACW 14. Westminster: Newman Press, 1952.

Spurious Works

Capitula sancti Augustini in urbem Romam transmissa. CCL 85A: 243–73.

Commonitorium quomodo sit agendum cum Manicheis qui confitentur pravitatem nefandi erroris. PL 42: 1153–56; CSEL 25/2: 979–82.

Confessio. PL 51: 607–10.

Fragmentum de duobus testibus. PLS III: 150; *Chronica Minora* I, MGH, AA 9: 493.

Hypomnesticon contra Pelagianos et Caelestianos. [Critical edition in] *The Pseudo-Augustinian Hypomnesticon against the Pelagians and Celestians,* vol. 2. Fribourg, Switzerland: Fribourg University Press, 1980.

Poema coniugis ad uxorem. PL 51: 611–16, 61: 737–42; CSEL 30: 344–48.

De promissionibus et praeditionibus Dei. PL 51: 733–854; CCL 60: 1–189.

"Prosperi" anathematismata seu Capitula S. Augustini. PL 65: 23–26.

De vita contemplativa libri tres. PL 59: 415–20.

Julianus Pomerius. *The Contemplative Life.* Trans. Mary Josephine Suelzer. ACW 4. Westminster: Newman Bookshop, 1947.

Other Sources

Ambrose. *De fuga saeculi.* CSEL 32/2.

Arnobius the Younger. *Commentarii in Psalmos.* CCL 25.

———. *Praedestinatus qui dicitur.* CCL 25B.

Athanasius. *Vita Martini.* PG 26: 837–976.

———. *The Life of Anthony and the Letter to Marcellinus.* Trans. Robert C. Gregg. New York: Paulist Press, 1980.

Augustine. *De anima et eius origine.* CSEL 60.

———. *The Nature and Origin of the Soul. In Answer to Pelagians,* vol. 1. Trans. Roland Teske. WSA I/23. Hyde Park, N.Y.: New City Press, 1997.

———. *De civitate Dei.* CCL 47–48.

———. *The City of God against the Pagans.* Trans. R. W. Dyson. Cambridge: Cambridge University Press, 1998.

———. *Confessiones.* CCL 27.

———. *The Confessions.* Trans. Maria Boulding. WSA I/1. Hyde Park, N.Y.: New City Press, 1997.

———. *Contra duas epistulas Pelagianorum.* CSEL 60: 421–570.

———. *Contra Iulianum.* PL 44: 641–874.

———. *Answer to Julian.* In *Answer to the Pelagians,* vol. 2. Trans. Roland Teske. WSA I/24. Hyde Park, N.Y.: New City Press, 1998.

———. *Contra secundam Iuliani responsionem imperfectum opus.* CSEL 85/1, books 1–3; PL 45: 1337–1608, books 4–6.

———. *Unfinished Work in Answer to Julian.* In *Answer to the Pelagians,* vol. 3. Trans. Roland Teske. WSA I/25. Hyde Park, N.Y.: New City Press, 1999.

———. *De correptione et gratia.* CSEL 92: 219–80.

———. *Rebuke and Grace.* In *Answer to the Pelagians,* vol. 4. Trans. Roland Teske. WSA I/26. Hyde Park, N.Y.: New City Press, 1999.

———. *De doctrina Christiana.* CCL 32.

———. *Teaching Christianity.* Trans. Edmund Hill. WSA I/11. Hyde Park, N.Y.: New City Press, 1996.

———. *De dono perseverantiae.* PL 45: 993–1034.

———. *The Gift of Perseverance.* In *Answer to the Pelagians,* vol. 4. Trans. Roland Teske. WSA I/26. Hyde Park, N.Y.: New City Press, 1999.

———. *Enchiridion ad Laurentium, seu de fide, spe et caritate.* CCL 46: 49–114.

———. *The Enchiridion on Faith, Hope, and Charity.* In *On Christian Belief,* 273–343. Trans. Bruce Harbert. WSA I/8. Hyde Park, N.Y.: New City Press, 2005.

———. *Enarrationes in psalmos.* CCL 38–40.

———. *Expositions of the Psalms.* Trans. Maria Boulding. WSA III/15–20. Hyde Park, N.Y.: New City Press, 2000–2004.

———. *Epistulae.* CSEL 34, 44, 57, 58, 88.

———. *Letters,* vol. 1–4. Trans. Roland Teske. WSA II/1–4. Hyde Park, N.Y.: New City Press, 2001, 2003, 2004, 2005.

———. *Expositio quarundam propositionum ex epistula ad Romanos.*

———. [Critical text and facing translation in] *Propositions from the Epistle to the Romans.* In *Augustine on Romans: Propositions from the Epistle to the Romans, Unfinished Commentary on the Epistle to the Romans,* 2–49. Ed. and trans. Paula Fredrick Landes. Society of Biblical Literature: Texts and Translations, vol. 23, series 6. Chico, Cal.: Scholars Press, 1982.

———. *De gestis Pelagii.* CSEL 42: 49–122.

———. *On the Deeds of Pelagius.* In *Answer to the Pelagians,* vol. 1. Trans. Roland Teske. WSA I/23. Hyde Park, N.Y.: New City Press, 1997.

———. *De gratia et libero arbitrio.* PL 44: 881–912.

———. *Grace and Free Choice.* In *Answer to the Pelagians,* vol. 4. Trans. Roland Teske. WSA I/26. Hyde Park, N.Y.: New City Press, 1999.

———. *De gratia Christi et de peccato originali.* CSEL 42: 123–206.

———. *De haeresibus.* CCL 46: 286–345.

———. *Heresies.* In *Arianism and Other Heresies.* Trans. Roland Teske. WSA I/18. Hyde Park, N.Y.: New City Press, 1995.

———. *De libero arbitrio.* CCL 29: 209–321.

———. *The Problem of Free Choice.* Trans. Mark Pontifex. ACW 22. New York: Newman Press, 1955.

———. *De natura and gratia.* CSEL 60: 231–99.

———. *Nature and Grace.* In *Answer to the Pelagians,* vol. 1. Trans. Roland Teske. WSA I/23. Hyde Park, N.Y.: New City Press, 1997.

———. *De nuptiis et concupiscentia.* CSEL 42: 209–52.

———. *De peccatorum meritis et remissione et de baptismo paruulorum.* CSEL 60: 1–151.

———. *De peccato originali.* CSEL 42: 167–206.

———. *The Grace of Christ and Original Sin.* In *Answer to the Pelagians,* vol. 1. Trans. Roland Teske. WSA I/23. Hyde Park, N.Y.: New City Press, 1997.

———. *De perfectione iustitiae hominis.* CSEL 42: 1–48.

———. *De praedestinatione sanctorum.* PL 44: 959–92.

———. *The Predestination of the Saints.* In *Answer to the Pelagians,* vol. 4. Trans. Roland Teske. WSA I/26. Hyde Park, N.Y.: New City Press, 1999.

———. *Retractationes.* CCL 57.

———. *The Retractations.* Trans. Mary Inez Bogan. FC 60. Washington, D.C.: The Catholic University of America Press, 1968.

———. *Sermones*. PL 38–39.

———. *Sermons,* vol. 1–11. Trans. Edmund Hill. WSA III/1–11. Hyde Park, N.Y.: New City Press, 1990–1997.

———. *Ad Simplicianum de diversis quaestionibus*. CCL 44.

———. *To Simplician--On Various Questions. Book I*. In *Augustine: Earlier Writings,* 376–406. Trans. John Burleigh. The Library of Christian Classics 6. Philadelphia: Westminster Press, 1953.

———. *De spiritu et littera liber unus*. CSEL 60: 153–229.

———. *The Spirit and the Letter.* In *Answer to the Pelagians,* vol. 1. Trans. Roland Teske. WSA I/23. Hyde Park, N.Y.: New City Press, 1997.

Ausonius. *Decimi Magni Ausonii Opera*. Ed. R. P. H. Green. Oxford: Oxford University Press, 1999.

———. *Ausonius,* 2 vols. Trans. Hugh Evelyn White. Cambridge, Mass.: Harvard University Press, 1919; repr. 1961.

Cassian, John. *De incarnatione Christi contra Nestorium haereticum*. CSEL 17: 235–391.

———. *Conlationes*. CSEL 13; SC 42, 54, 64.

———. *The Conferences*. Trans. Boniface Ramsey. ACW 57. New York: Paulist Press, 1997.

———. *De institutis coenobiorum*. CSEL 17: 3–231; SC 109.

———. *The Institutes*. Trans. Boniface Ramsey. ACW 58. New York: Newman Press, 2000.

Celestine I. *Epistola 4, ad episcopos provinciae Viennensis et Narbonensis* [*Cuperemus quidem*] PL 50: 429–36.

———. *Epistola 21, ad episcopos Galliarum* [*Apostolici verba*]. PL 50: 528–30.

Council of Carthage (418). *Concilium Carthaginense*. CCL 149: 67–78.

———. *The Canons of the Council of Carthage, A. D. 418*. In *Theological Anthropology,* 57–60. Trans. J. Patout Burns. Philadelphia: Fortress Press, 1981.

Council of Ephesus (431). *Concilium Ephesi. Conciliorum Oecumenicorum Decreta*. Ed. G. Alberigo et al. 3rd ed. Bologna: Instituto per le Scienze Religiose, 1973. [Critical edition reproduced and translated in] *Council of Ephesus,* in *Decrees of the Ecumenical Councils,* vol. 1, 37–74. Ed. Norman P. Tanner. London: Sheed & Ward, 1990.

Council of Orange II (529). *Concilium Arausicorum*. CCL 148A: 55–76.

———. *The Synod of Orange, A.D. 529*. In *Theological Anthropology,* 109–28. Trans. J. Patout Burns. Philadelphia: Fortress Press, 1981.

Cyprian. *De dominica oratione* CCL 3A: 87–113.

———. *Ad Quirinum (testimoniorum libri tres)*. CSEL 3/1: 33–184.

Dionysius Exiguus. *Collectio decretorum pontificum Romanorum*. PL 67: 229–346.

Epigramma Paulini. CSEL 16: 503–10.

Eucherius, Bishop of Lyon. *De laude eremi*. PL 50: 701–12.

Evodius, Bishop of Uzalis. *Epistula ad abbatem Valentinum*. PLS 2: 331–34.

———. *A Letter of Bishop Evodius to Abott Valentine*. In *Answer to the Pelagians*, vol. 4. Trans. Roland Teske. WSA I/26. Hyde Park, N.Y.: New City Press, 1999.

Faustus of Riez. *De gratia Dei et libero arbitrio libri duo*. CCL: 101–101B.

Flaminius, Joannes Antonius. *Vita S. Prosperi episcopi Rejensius*. In Surius, *Historiae seu vitae sanctorum*, vol. 3. Turin: Ex typographia Pontificia et Archiepiscopali eq. P. Marietti, 1875.

Gelasius I (Pope 492–96). *Appendix tertia: Concilia quaedam a Gelasio celebrata*. PL 59: 157–90.

Gennadius . *De viris inlustribus*. Ed. E. C. Richardson. TU 14/1: 57–97. Leipzig: Hinrichs, 1896.

———. *Lives of Illustrious Men*. In *Theodoret, Jerome, Gennadius, and Rufinus: Historical Writings*, 385–402. Trans. Ernest Cushing Richardson. Nicene and Post-Nicene Fathers II/3. New York: Christian Literature Publishing Co., 1892.

Hilary of Arles. *Sermo de vita sancti Honorati Arelatensis episcopi*. SC 235.

———. *Sermon on the Life of Honoratus*. In *The Western Fathers*, 248–80. Trans. F. R. Hoare. New York: Sheed & Ward, 1954.

Hilary of Poitiers. *Tractatus super Psalmos*. CSEL 61–61A.

Hilary (of Provence). *Epistula ad Augustinum (Ep. 226)*. [among Augustine's letters] CSEL 57: 468–81.

———. *Letter* 226. In *Letters* 211–270, 1*–29*, vol. 4, 95–102. Trans Roland Teske. WSA II/4. Hyde Park, N.Y.: New City Press, 2005.

Hincmar of Rheims. *De praedestinatione dissertatio posterior*. PL 125: 65–474.

Honorius, Emperor. *De constitutionibus imperatorum in causa Pelagianae haeresis*. PL 48: 379–97.

Hormisdas, Pope. *Epistula Papae Hormisdae ad Possessorem*. CCL 85A: 115–21.

Innocent. *Epistulae*. PL 20: 463–608.

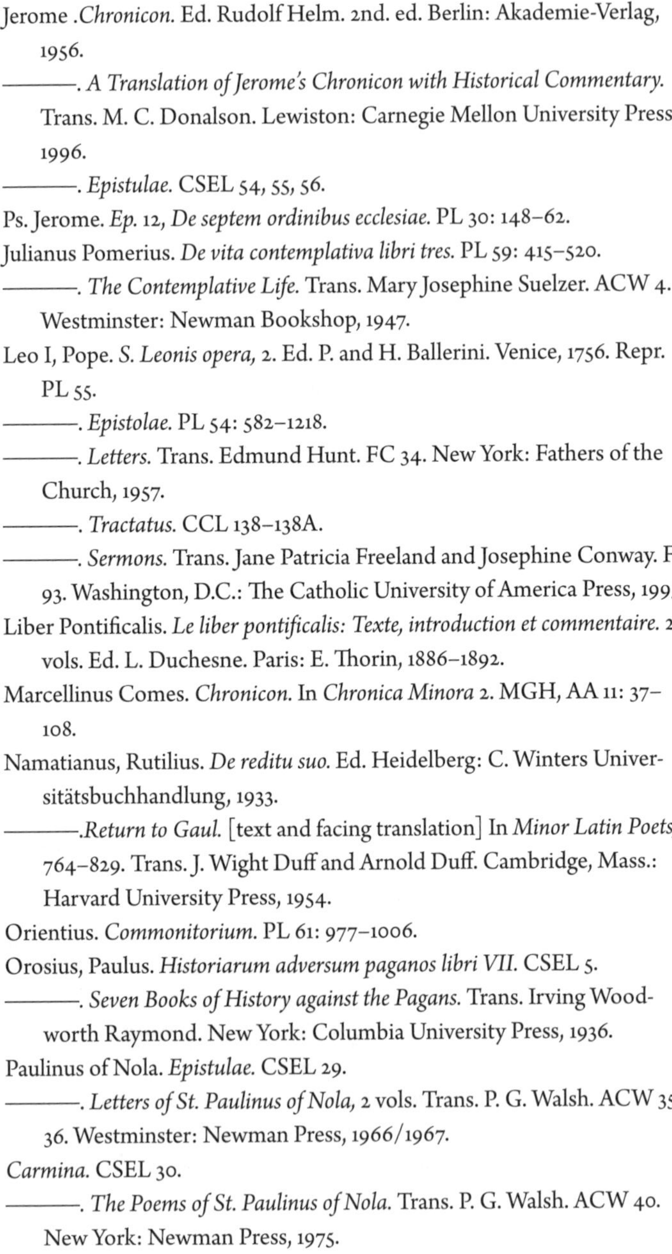

Jerome .*Chronicon.* Ed. Rudolf Helm. 2nd. ed. Berlin: Akademie-Verlag, 1956.

———. *A Translation of Jerome's Chronicon with Historical Commentary.* Trans. M. C. Donalson. Lewiston: Carnegie Mellon University Press, 1996.

———. *Epistulae.* CSEL 54, 55, 56.

Ps. Jerome. *Ep.* 12, *De septem ordinibus ecclesiae.* PL 30: 148–62.

Julianus Pomerius. *De vita contemplativa libri tres.* PL 59: 415–520.

———. *The Contemplative Life.* Trans. Mary Josephine Suelzer. ACW 4. Westminster: Newman Bookshop, 1947.

Leo I, Pope. *S. Leonis opera,* 2. Ed. P. and H. Ballerini. Venice, 1756. Repr. PL 55.

———. *Epistolae.* PL 54: 582–1218.

———. *Letters.* Trans. Edmund Hunt. FC 34. New York: Fathers of the Church, 1957.

———. *Tractatus.* CCL 138–138A.

———. *Sermons.* Trans. Jane Patricia Freeland and Josephine Conway. FC 93. Washington, D.C.: The Catholic University of America Press, 1995.

Liber Pontificalis. *Le liber pontificalis: Texte, introduction et commentaire.* 2 vols. Ed. L. Duchesne. Paris: E. Thorin, 1886–1892.

Marcellinus Comes. *Chronicon.* In *Chronica Minora* 2. MGH, AA 11: 37–108.

Namatianus, Rutilius. *De reditu suo.* Ed. Heidelberg: C. Winters Universitätsbuchhandlung, 1933.

———.*Return to Gaul.* [text and facing translation] In *Minor Latin Poets,* 764–829. Trans. J. Wight Duff and Arnold Duff. Cambridge, Mass.: Harvard University Press, 1954.

Orientius. *Commonitorium.* PL 61: 977–1006.

Orosius, Paulus. *Historiarum adversum paganos libri VII.* CSEL 5.

———. *Seven Books of History against the Pagans.* Trans. Irving Woodworth Raymond. New York: Columbia University Press, 1936.

Paulinus of Nola. *Epistulae.* CSEL 29.

———. *Letters of St. Paulinus of Nola,* 2 vols. Trans. P. G. Walsh. ACW 35–36. Westminster: Newman Press, 1966/1967.

Carmina. CSEL 30.

———. *The Poems of St. Paulinus of Nola.* Trans. P. G. Walsh. ACW 40. New York: Newman Press, 1975.

Paulinus of Pella. *Eucharisticus.* CSEL 16: 263–334.

———. *The Eucharisticus.* In *Ausonius,* vol. 2, 304–51. Trans. Hugh G. Evelyn White. Cambridge, Mass.: Harvard University Press, 1921; repr. 1985.

Pelagius. *Expositiones XIII epistularum Pauli.* PLS 1: 1110–1374.

———. *Pelagius' Expositions of Thirteen Epistles of St. Paul.* Vols. 1–3. Trans. A. Souter. Text and Studies 9, 1–3. Cambridge: Cambridge University Press, 1922, 1926, 1931.

Photius. *Myriobiblon sive Bibliotheca.* PG 103.

De praedestinatione et gratia. PL 45: 1665–78.

Salvian of Marseilles. *De gubernatione Dei.* CSEL 8: 1–200.

———. *The Governance of God.* In *The Writings of Salvian, the Presbyter,* 23–232. Trans. Jeremiah F. O'Sullivan. FC 3. New York: CIMA Publishing, 1947.

Shepherd of Hermas. *Shepherd of Hermas.*

———. Greek and Latin texts ed. and trans. J. B. Lightfoot. In *The Apostolic Fathers,* 297–483. London: Macmillian and Co.; repr. 1893.

Sixtus III, Pope. *Epistola* 6. PL 50: 607–10.

Sulpicius Severus. *Vita Martini.* SC 133: 248–316.

———.*The Life of St. Martin.* Trans. B. M. Peebles. In *Niceta of Remesiana, Sulpicius Severus, Prosper of Aquitaine,* 101–40. FC 7. New York: Fathers of the Church, 1949.

Valentine, Abbot of Hadrumetum. *Epistula* 216 [among Augustine's letters]. CSEL 57: 396–402.

Victorius of Aquitaine. *Cursus paschalis annorum* DXXXII. MGH, AA 9: 677–735.

Vincent of Lérins. *Commonitorium.* CCL 64: 147–95.

———. *Commonitories.* Trans. Rudolph E. Morris. In *Niceta of Remesiana, Sulpicius Severus, Prosper of Aquitaine,* 267–332. FC 7. New York: Fathers of the Church, 1949.

Zosimus, Pope. *Epistulae de causa Pelagii.* PL 45: 1719–23.

———. *Epistula Tractoria.* PL 20: 693–94 [fragments].

Literature

Abel, M. "Le '*Praedestinatus*' et le pélagianisme." *RTAM* 35 (1968): 4–25.

Amann, É. "*Praedestinatus.*" DTC 12, no. 2 (1935): 2775–80.

———. "Semi-Pélagiens." DTC 14, no. 2 (1939): 1796–1850.

———. Armitage, J. Mark. *A Twofold Solidarity: Leo the Great's Theology of Redemption.* Early Christian Studies 9. Strathfield, Australia: St Pauls, 2005.

Barclift, Philip L. "Predestination and Divine Foreknowledge in the Sermons of Pope Leo the Great." *CH* 62 (1993): 5–21.

———. "Shifting Tones of Pope Leo the Great's Christological Vocabulary." *CH* 66, no. 2 (1997): 221–22.

Baus, Karl. "Part Three: Inner Life of the Church between Nicae and Chalcedon." In *The Imperial Church from Constantine to the Early Middle Ages,* 264–69. Trans. Anselm Biggs. History of the Church 2. New York: Seabury Press, 1980.

Birch, Debra J. *Pilgrimage to Rome in the Middle Ages.* Woodbridge, U.K.: Boydell Press, 1998.

Bonner, Gerald. "Augustine, the Bible and the Pelagians." In *Augustine and the Bible,* 225–42. Bible through the Ages 2. South Bend: University of Notre Dame Press, 1999.

———. *Augustine and Modern Research on Pelagianism.* The Saint Augustine Lecture for 1970. Villanova: Villanova University Press, 1972. Repr.: "Augustine and Pelagianism in the Light of Modern Research," in *God's Decree and Man's Destiny: Studies on the Thought of Augustine of Hippo.* London: Variorum Reprints, 1987.

———. "Pelagianism Reconsidered." SP 27 (1993): 237–41.

———. *St Augustine of Hippo: Life and Controversies.* 2nd ed. Norfolk, U.K.: Canterbury Press, 1986.

Bonner, Stanley F. *Education in Ancient Rome: From the Elder Cato to the Younger Pliny.* Berkeley and Los Angeles: University of California Press, 1977.

Booth, Alan. D. "Date of Jerome's Birth." *Phoenix* 33 (1979): 346–52.

Braun, R. "Introduction." In *Opera Qvodvultdeo Carthaginiensi episcopo tributa.* CCL 60: v–cvi.

Brogan, Olwen. *Roman Gaul.* Cambridge, Mass.: Harvard University Press, 1953.

Brown, Peter. *Augustine of Hippo: A Biography.* 2nd ed. Berkeley and Los Angeles: University of California Press, 2000.

———. "The Patrons of Pelagius: The Roman Aristocracy between East and West." *JTS* 21 (1970): 56–72.

———. *The Rise of Western Christendom: Triumph and Diversity, A. D. 200–1000.* 2nd ed. Oxford: Blackwell, 2003.

Burns, J. Patout. "Augustine's Role in the Imperial Action against the Pelagius." *JTS* 30 (1979): 77–83.

———. *Cyprian the Bishop.* London: Routledge, 2002.

———. "The Economy of Salvation: Two Patristic Traditions." *TS* 37 (1976): 598–619.

———, ed. *Theological Anthropology.* Philadelphia: Fortress Press, 1981.

Callens, P. "Index Auctorum." In *Capitula sancti Augustini in urbem Romam transmissa.* CCL 68A: 387–89.

Cappuyns, M. "L'auteur du *De vocatione omnium gentium.*" *RB* 39 (1927): 198–226.

———. "L'origine des *Capitula* d'Orange 529." *RTAM* 6 (1934): 121–42.

———. "L'origine des capitula pseudo-Célestiniens contre le semipélagianisme." *RB* 41 (1929): 156–70.

———. "Le premier représentant de l'augustinisme médiéval, Prosper d'Aquitaine." *RTAM* 1 (1929): 309–37.

Capua, Francesco di. "Le due redazioni di una lettera di s. Leone." In *Scritti minori,* vol. 2, 177–83. Ed. A. Quacquarelli (Rome: Desclée, 1959).

———. "Leone Magno e Prospero di Aquitanio." In *Scritti minori,* vol. 2, 184–90. Ed. A. Quacquarelli (Rome: Desclée, 1959).

Casiday, Augustine. "Grace and the Humanity of Christ According to St Vincent of Lérins." *VC* 59 (2005): 298–314.

———. "Rehabilitating John Cassian: An Evaluation of Prosper of Aquitaine's Polemic against the 'Semipelagians.'" *Scottish Journal of Theology* 58, no. 3 (2005): 270–84.

———. *Tradition and Theology in the Writings of St. John Cassian.* Oxford Early Christian Series. Oxford: Oxford University Press, 2006.

Chadwick, Nora. *Poetry and Letters in Early Christian Gaul.* London: Bowes & Bowes, 1955.

Chadwick, Owen. "The Ascetic Ideal in the History of the Church." *Studies in Church History* 22 (1985): 1–23.

———. "Euladius of Arles." *JTS* 46 (1945): 200–205.

———. *John Cassian: A Study in Primitive Monasticism.* 2nd ed. Cambridge: Cambridge University Press, 1968.

Chéné, Jean. "Le semipélagianisme du midi de la Gaule d'après les lettres de Prosper d'Aquitaine et d'Hilaire à saint Augustin." *RechScRel* 43 (1955): 321–41.

———. "Les origines de la controverse semi-pélagienne." *Année théologique augustinienne* 13 (1953): 56–109.

Chisholm, John Edward. "The Authorship of the pseudo-Augustinian *Hypomnesticon* against the Pelagians and Celestians." SP 11 (1972): 307–10.

———. *The Pseudo-Augustinian Hypomnesticon against the Pelagians and Celestians,* vol. 1. Fribourg, Switzerland: Fribourg University Press, 1967.

Clark, Elizabeth A. *The Origenist Controversy: The Cultural Construction of an Early Christian Debate.* Princeton: Princeton University Press, 1992.

Clerck, Paul de. Lex orandi, lex credendi': The Original Sense and Historical Avatars of an Equivocal Adage." *Studia Liturgica* 24 (1994): 178–200.

Courcelle, Pierre. "Nouveaux aspects de la culture lérinienne." *Revue des etudes latines* 46 (1968): 379–409.

Couture, Léonce. "Saint Prosper d'Aquitaine." *Bulletin de littérature ecclésiastique* 2 (1900): 269–82.

———. "Saint Prosper d'Aquitaine II." *Bulletin de littérature ecclésiastique* 3 (1901): 33–49.

Daniélou, Jean, and Henri Marrou, eds. *The Christian Centuries,* vol. 1. Trans. Victor Cronin. New York: McGraw-Hill, 1964.

Daur, Klaus-D. "Einleitung." In *Arnobii Ivnioris: Commentarii in psalmos.* CCL 25: xi–xl.

Dekkers, Eligius. *Clavis patrum latinorum: Qua in corpus christianorum edendum optimas quasque scriptorum recensiones a Tertulliano ad Bedam.* 3rd ed. Turnhout: Brepols, 1995.

Dill, Samuel. *Roman Society in the Last Century of the Roman Empire.* 2nd ed. London: Macmillan and Co, 1925.

Djuth, Marianne. "The Hermeneutics of De libero arbitrio III: Are There Two Augustines?" SP 27 (1993): 281–89.

———. "Initium Fidei." *ATA,* 447–51.

Driver, Steven D. *John Cassian and the Reading of Egyptian Monastic Culture.* New York: Routledge, 2002.

Duchesne, L. *Christian Worship: Its Origin and Evolution.* Trans. M. L. McClure. 5th ed. New York: MacMillian, 1927.

———. *Origines du culte chrétienne.* 5th ed. Paris, 1925.

Duckworth, G. E. "Five Centuries of Latin Hexameter Poetry: Silver Age and Late Empire." *Transactions and Proceedings of the American Philological Association* 98 (1967): 77–150.

Durig, Walter. "Zur Interpretation des Axioms Legem credendi lex statuat supplicandi." In *Veritati Catholicae: Festschrift für Leo Scheffczyk zum 65. Geburtstag*, 226–36. Ed. Anton Ziegenaus et al. Aschaffenburg: Pattloch, 1985.

Elberti, Arturo. *Prospero d'Aquitania: Teologo e Discepolo.* Rome: Edizioni Dehoniane, 1999.

Ertl, N. "Diktatoren frühmittelalterlicher Papstbriefen." *Archiv für Urkundenforschung* 15 (1938): 56–132.

Fiedrowicz, M. *Psalmos vox totius Christi: Studien zu Augustins Enarrationes in Psalmos.* Freiburg [im Breisgau]: Herder, 1997.

Fixot, Michel. "Saint-Victor, à propos d'un livre recent." In *Marseille. Trames et paysages urbains de Gyptis au Roi René*, 235–54. *Actes du colloque de Marseille 1999.* Études Massaliètes 7. Aix-en-Provence, 2001.

Frank, K. Suso. "John Cassian on John Cassian." SP 33 (1997): 418–33.

Freeman, E. A. *Western Europe in the Fifth Century: An Aftermath.* London: Macmillan, 1904.

Frend, W. H. C. "The Two Worlds of Paulinus of Nola." In *Latin Literature of the Fourth Century*, 100–133. Ed. J. W. Binns. London: Routledge, 1974.

Gaidioz, J. "Prosper d'Aquitaine et le Tome à Flavien." *Revue des sciences religieuses* 23 (1949): 270–301.

Gehl, Paul F. "An Augustinian Catechism in Fourteenth-Century Tuscany: Prosper's *Epigrammata.*" *AS* 19 (1988): 93–110.

Glorie, F. "Prologemena." In '*Capitula Sancti Augustini' in urbem romam transmissa.* CCL 85A: 243–46.

Gori, Fr. "Prologomena." In *Arnobii Ivnioris opera omnia, pars III.* CCL 25B: v–xxii.

Gouilloud, A. *Saint Eucher, Lérins et l'église de Lyon au Ve siècle.* Lyon: Librairie Briday, 1881.

Grange, Antoine Rivet de la. *Histoire littéraire de la France*, vol. 2. Paris: Osmont, 1733.

Green. R. P. H. *The Poetry of Paulinus of Nola: A Study of His Latinity.* Brussels: Latomus, 1971.

Griffe, Élie. *La Gaule chrétienne à l'époque romaine.* 3 vols. Paris: Letouzey et Ané, 1964–1966.

Grossi, Vittorino. "Adversaries and Friends of Augustine." In *Patrology,* vol. 4, 461–503. Ed. Angelo Di Berardino. Trans. Placid Solari. Westminster, Md.: Christian Classics, 1986.

Grützmacher, F. "Cassianus, Johannes." RE 3 (1897): 746–49.

Haarhoff, Theodore. *Schools of Gaul: A Study of Pagan and Christian Education in the Last Century of the Western Empire.* London: Oxford University Press, 1920.

Hamman, A. G. "Introduction, notes et guide thématique." In *L'appel de tous les peuples/Prosper d'Aquitaine,* 8–18. Trans. [French] F. Frémont-Verggobi and H. Throo. Paris: Migne, 1993.

———. "Prosper von Aquitanien." *Theologische Realenzyklopädie* 27 (1997): 525–26.

———. "The Turnabout of the Fourth Century: A Political, Geographical, Social, Ecclesiastical, and Doctrinal Framework of the Century" and "Writers of Gaul." In *Patrology,* vol. 4, 1–32, 504–63. Ed. Angelo Di Berardino. Trans. Placid Solari. Westminster, Md.: Christian Classics, 1986.

———, ed. Patrologia Latina, Supplementum 3.

Hartel. G. "Praefatio." In *Sancti Pontii Meropii Pavlini Nolani carmina.* CSEL 30: v–xxxxii.

Harnack, Adolph. *History of Dogma,* vol. 5. Trans. Neil Buchanan. New York: Russell & Russell, 1958.

Hauck, A. "Prosper von Aquitanien." RE 16, no. 3 (1905): 123–27.

Helm, Rudolf. "Prosper Tiro." *Realencyclopädie der classischen Altertumswissenschaft* 23 (1957): 884–87.

Holder-Egger, Oswald. "Untersuchen über einige annalistische Quellen zur Geschichte des fünften und sechsten Jahrhunderts." *Neues Archiv der Gesellschaft für ältere deutsche Geschichtskunde zur Beförderung einer Gesammtausgabe der Quellenschriften deutscher Geschichten des Mittelalters,* vol. 1, 13–90. Hanover: Hahn'sche Buchhandlung, 1876.

Holmes, Scott T. *The Origin and Development of the Christian Church in Gaul during the First Six Centuries of the Christian Era.* London: Macmillan and Co., 1911.

Huegelmeyer, Charles T. "Introduction." In *Carmen de ingratis S. Prosperi Aquitani.*Washington, D.C.: The Catholic University of America Press, 1962.

Humphries, Mark. "Chronicle and Chronology: Prosper of Aquitaine, His

Methods and the Development of Early Medieval Chronography." *Early Medieval Europe* 5 (1996): 155–75.

Hwang, Alexander Y. "Augustine's Interpretations of 1 Tim. 2: 4." SP 43 (2006): 137–42.

———. "An Interview with Peter Brown: On Scholarship, Faith and Augustine." *Princeton Theological Review* 6 (1999): 20–27.

Inglebert, Hervé. *Les Romains chrétiens face à l'histoire de Rome.* Collection des Études Augustiniennes, série antique, 145. Paris: Institut d'études augustiniennes, 1996.

Jacobs, Andrew S. "Writing Demetrias: Ascetic Logic in Ancient Christianity." *CH* 69 (2000): 719–48.

Jacquin, M. "A quelle date apprait le terme 'semipélagien'?" *Revue des sciences philosophiques et theologiques* 1 (1907): 506–8.

———. "La question de la prédestination aux V et VI siècles." *Revue d'histoire ecclésiastique* 7 (1906): 268–300.

Jalland, Trevor. *The Life and Times of St. Leo the Great.* New York: Macmillan, 1941.

James, N. W. "Leo the Great and Prosper of Aquitaine: A Fifth Century Pope and His Advisor." *JTS* 44 (1993): 554–84.

Jones, A. M. H. *The Later Roman Empire 284–602: A Social, Economic and Administrative Survey,* vol. 1. Oxford: Oxford University Press, 1964.

Kaster, Robert. "Notes on 'Primary' and 'Secondary' Schools in Late Antiquity." *Transactions of the American Philological Association* 113 (1983): 323–46.

Kayser, H. *Die Schriften des sogenannten Arnobius iunior, dogmengeschichtlich und literarisch untersucht.* Gütersloh: C. Bertelsmann, 1912.

Kelly, J. N. D. *Jerome: His Life, Writings, and Controversies.* London: Duckworth, 1975.

Kennedy, V. L. *The Saints of the Canon of the Mass.* Studi di antichità cristiana 14. Rome: Pontificio istituto di archeologia cristiana, 1938.

Kéry, Lotte. *Canonical Collections of the Early Middle Ages (ca. 400–1140): A Bibliographical Guide to the Manuscripts and Literature.* History of Medieval Canon Law, 1.Washington, D.C.: The Catholic University of America Press, 1999.

Kidd, B. J. *A History of the Church to A.D. 461,* vol. 3. Oxford: Clarendon Press, 1922.

Klingshirn, William E., and Mark Vessey, eds. *The Limits of Ancient Chris-*

tianity: Essays on Late Antique Thought and Culture in Honor of R. A. Markus. Ann Arbor: University of Michigan Press, 1999.

Krabbe, M. Kathryn Clare. "Introduction." In *Epistula ad Demetriadem de vera humilitate: A Critical Text and Translation with Introduction and Commentary,* 1–136. PS 97. Washington, D.C.: The Catholic University of America Press, 1965.

Labbe, Philip. *De scriptoribus ecclesiasticis,* vol. 2. Paris, 1660.

Lamberigts, Mathijs. "Caelestius" and "Julian of Eclanum." *ATA,* 114–15, 478–79.

Lançon, Bertrand. *Rome dans l'Antiquité tardive.* Paris: Hechette, 1995.

———. *Rome in Late Antiquity: Everyday Life and Urban Change, AD 312–609.* Trans. Antonia Nevill. Edinburgh: Edinburgh University Press, 2000.

Lassandro, D. "Note sugli epigrammi de Prospero d'Aquitania." *Vetera Christianorum* 8 (1971): 211–22.

Letter, P. de. "Introduction." In *Prosper: Defense of St. Augustine,* 3–20. ACW 32. Westminster: Newman Press, 1963.

Leyser, Conrad. *Authority and Asceticism from Augustine to Gregory the Great.* Oxford: Clarendon Press, 2000.

———. "*Lectio divina, oratio pura:* Rhetoric and the Techniques of Asceticism in the Conferences of John Cassian." In *Modelli di santità, modelli di comportamento,* 79–105. Ed. G. Barone et al. Turin: Rosenberg and Sellier, 1994.

———. "Semi-Pelagianism." *ATA,* 761–66.

———. "'This Sainted Isle': Panegyric, Nostalgia, and the Invention of Lerinian Monasticism." In *The Limits of Ancient Christianity: Essays in Honor of R. A. Markus,* 188–206. Ed. William Klingshirn and Mark Vessey. Ann Arbor: University of Michigan Press, 1999.

Lienhard, Joseph T. *Paulinus of Nola and Early Western Monasticism.* Cologne: Hanstein, 1977.

Longpré, A. "Le De Providentia divina de Prosper d'Aquitaine et la question de son authenticité." *Revue des études anciennes* 80 (1978): 108–13.

Lorenz, Rudolf. "Der Augustinismus Prospers von Aquitanien." *Zeitschrift für Kirchengeschichte* 73 (1962): 217–52.

Loseby, S. T. "Marseille: A Late Antique Success Story?" *Journal of Roman Studies* 82 (1992): 165–85.

Lössl, J. *Julian von Aeclanum: Studien zu seinem Leben, seinem Werk, seiner Lehre und ihrer Überlieferung.* Leiden: Brill, 2001.

Macqueen, D. J. "John Cassian on Grace and Free Will." *RTAM* 44 (1977): 5–28.

Manitius, Max. "Über das Gedicht *de Providentia divina." Zeitschrift für die österreichischen Gymnasien* 39 (1888): 580–84.

———. "Beiträge zur Geschichte frühchristlicher Dichter im Mittelatter." *SB Akademie Wien* 117 (1889), Abh. 12, 20 f; 121 (1890), Abh. 7, 14.

———. *Geschichte der christlich-lateinischen Poesie bis zur Mitte des 8 Jahrhunderts.* Stuttgart: J. G. Cotta, 1891.

Marcovich, Miroslav. "The Text of St. Prosper's *De providentia Dei." Illinois Classical Studies* 8 (1983): 108–21.

———. "Preface." In *De providentia Dei: Text, Translation and Commentary,* ix–xii. Supplements to Vigiliae 10. New York: E. J. Brill, 1989.

Marán, Raúl Villegas. "En polémica con Julián de Eclanum. Por unan nueva lectura del *Syllabus de gratia* de Próspero de Aquitania." *Augustinianum* 43 (2003): 81–124.

Markus, R. A. "Chronicle and Theology: Prosper of Aquitaine." In *The Inheritance of Historiography 350–900,* 31–43. Ed. Christopher Holdsworth and T. P. Wiseman. Exeter: Exeter University Press, 1986.

———. *The End of Ancient Christianity.* Cambridge: Cambridge University Press, 1990.

———. "The Legacy of Pelagius: Orthodoxy, Heresy and Conciliation." In *The Making of Orthodoxy: Essays in Honor of Henry Chadwick,* 214–32. Ed. Rowan Williams. Cambridge: Cambridge University Press, 1989.

Marrou, H. I. *Histoire de l'éducation dans l'antiquité.* Paris: Éditions du Seuil, 1965.

———. *History of Education in Antiquity.* Trans. George Lamb. Madison: University of Wisconsin Press, 1982.

———. *Saint Augustin et l'augustinisme.* Paris: Éditions du Seuil, 1956.

———. *St. Augustine and His Influence through the Ages.* Trans. Patrick Hepburne-Scott. New York: Harper Torchbooks, 1957.

Marsili, Salvatore. *Giovanni Cassiano ed Evagrio Pontico: Dottrina sulla carità e contemplazione.* Studia Anselmiana philosophica theologica 5. Rome: Herder, 1936.

Mathisen, Ralph W. "Bishops, Barbarians, and the 'Dark Ages': The Fate of Late Roman Educational Institutions in Late Antique Gaul," in *Me-*

dieval Education, 3–17. Ed. Ronald B. Begley and Joseph W. Koterski. New York: Fordham University Press, 2005.

———. *Ecclesiastical Factionalism and Religious Controversy in Fifth-Century Gaul.* Washington, D.C.: The Catholic University of America Press, 1989.

———. "Emigrants, Exiles and Survivors: Aristocratic Options in Visigothic Aquitainia." *Phoenix* 38 (1984): 159–70.

———. "For Specialists Only: The Reception of Augustine and His Theology in Fifth-Century Gaul." In *Presbyter Factus Sum,* 29–41. Ed. Joseph T. Lienhard et al. Collectanea Augustiniana 2. New York: Peter Lang, 1993.

———. *Roman Aristocrats in Barbarian Gaul.* Austin: University of Texas Press, 1993.

Matthews, John F. *Western Aristocracies and Imperial Court A. D. 364–425.* Oxford: Oxford University Press, 1975.

McHugh, Michael P. "Introduction." In *The Carmen de providentia Dei Attributed to Prosper of Aquitaine: A Revised Text with an Introduction, Translation, and Notes,* 1–255. *PS* 98. Washington, D.C.: The Catholic University of America Press, 1964.

———."Prosper of Aquitaine." *ATA,* 685–86.

McLynn, N. B. "Paulinus the Impenitent: A Study of the Eucharisticos." *Journal of Early Christian Studies* 3 (1995): 461–86.

McShane, Philip. *La Romanitas et le pape Leon le Grand: L'apport culturel des institutions impériales à la formation de structures ecclésiastiques.* Montréal: Bellarmin, 1979.

Merdinger, J. E. *Rome and the African Church in the Time of Augustine.* New Haven and London: Yale University Press, 1997.

Mommsen, Theodore. "Introduction." In *Chronica minora* 1. MGH, AA 9: 341–84.

Montauzen, Germain de. "Saint-Eucher, évêque de Lyon et l'école de Lérins." *Bulletin historique du diocèse de Lyon* 2 (1923): 81–96.

Moricca, U. *Storia della letteratura latina cristiana,* vol. 3, no. 1. Turin: Società Editrice Internazionale, 1932.

Morin, G. "L'origine africaine d'Arnobe le Jeune." *Revue des sciences religieuses* 16 (1936): 177–84.

———. "Saint Prosper de Reggio." *RB* 12 (1895): 241–57.

Muhlberger, Steven. *The Fifth Century Chroniclers: Prosper, Hydatius, and the Gallic Chronicler of 452.* Leeds: F. Cairns, 1990.

Noris, H. *Historia Pelagiana.* Padua: Petri Mariae Frambotti, 1673.

Ogliari, Donato. *Gratia et Certamen: The Relationship between Grace and Free Will in the Discussion of Augustine with the So-Called Semipelagians.* Leuven: Leuven University Press, 2003.

Palanque, Jean-Rémy. "Les évêchés provençaux à l'époque romaine." *Provence historique* 1 (1951): 105–43.

Papencordt, Felix. *Geschichte der vandalischen Herrschaft in Afrika.* Berlin: Duncker and Humblot, 1837.

Pelland, Lionello. *S. Prosperi Aquitani: Doctrina de predestinatione et voluntate Dei salvifica.* Montreal: Studia Collegii Maximi Immaculatae Conceptionis, 1936.

Perler, Othmar. *Les voyages de saint Augustin.* Paris: Études Augustiniennes, 1969.

Pietri, Charles. *Roma Christiana: Recherches sur l'Église de Rome, son organisation, sa politique, son idéologie de Miltiade à Sixte (311–440)*, 2 vols. Rome: École français de Rome, 1976.

Plinval, Georges de. "Prosper d'Aquitaine interprète de saint Augustin." *Recherches Augustiniennes* 1 (1958): 339–55.

Pricoco, Salvatore. *L'isola dei santi: Il cenobio de Lerino e le origini del monachesimo gallico.* Rome: Edizioni dell'Ateneo and Bizzarri, 1978.

Prinz, Friedrich. *Mönchtum im Frankenreich: Kultur und Gesellschaft in Gallien, den Rheinlanden und Bayern am Beispiel de monastischen Entwicklung (4 bis 8 Jahrhundert).* Munich: R. Oldenbourg, 1965.

Ramsey, Boniface. "John Cassian: Student of Augustine." *CSQ* 28 (1993): 5–15.

Rees, B. R. *Pelagius: Reluctant Heretic.* Suffolk: Boydell Press, 1988.

Roberts, M. "Barbarians in Gaul: The Response of the Poets." In *Fifth-Century Gaul: A Crisis of Identity?* 97–106. Ed. John Drinkwater and Hugh Elton. Cambridge: Cambridge University Press, 1992.

Rondet, Henri. *Gratia Christi.* Paris: Beauchesne et Ses Fils, 1948.

———. *The Grace of Christ: A Brief History of the Theology of Grace.* Trans. Tad W. Guzie. Westminster, Md.: Newman Press, 1967.

Rousseau, Philip. *Ascetics, Authority, and the Church in the Age of Jerome and Cassian.* Oxford: Oxford University Press, 1978.

———. "Cassian: Monastery and the World." In *The Certainty of Doubt: Tributes to Peter Munz*, 68–89. Ed. Miles Fairburn and Bill Oliver. Wellington: Victoria University Press, 1996.

Sage, Athanase. "La volonté salvifique universelle de Dieu dans la pensée de saint Augustin." *Recherches augustiniennes* 3 (1965): 107–31.

Savignac, Jean de. "Une attribution nouvelle et une édition critique de l'*Hypomnesticon.*" *Scriptorium* 37 (1983): 134–40.

Schoeneman, K. *Bibliotheca historico-literaria patrum latinorum,* vol. 2. Leipzig, 1794.

Schaff, *History of the Christian Church.* Vol. 3: *Nicene and Post-Nicene Christianity, A. D. 311–600.* 5th ed. New York: Scribner's Sons, 1910.

Silva-Tarouca, Carlo. "Nuovi studi sulle lettere dei papi." *Gregorianum* 12 (1931): 547–98.

Silvan, Hagith. *Ausonius of Bordeaux: Genesis of a Gallic Aristocracy.* London: Routledge, 1993.

Standcliffe, Clare. *St. Martin and His Hagiographer.* Oxford: Clarendon Press, 1983.

Stewart, Columba. *Cassian the Monk.* New York: Oxford University Press, 1998.

TeSelle, Eugene. *Augustine the Theologian.* London: Burns and Oates, 1970.

———. "Pelagius, Pelagianism." *ATA,* 633–40.

Teske, Roland. "The Augustinianism of Prosper of Aquitaine Revisited." SP 43 (2003): 491–504

———. "General Introduction." In *Answer to the Pelagians,* vol. 4, 11–37. Trans. Roland Teske. WSA I/26. Hyde Park, N.Y.: New City Press, 1999.

C. Tibeletti. *Pagine monastiche provenzali: Il monachesimo nella Gallia del quinto secolo.* Rome: Borla, 1990.

———. "Valeriano di Cimiez e la teologia dei Maestri Provenzali." *Augustinianum* 22 (1982): 513–32.

Tillemont, L. S. Le Nain de. *Mémoires pour servir à l'histoire ecclésiastique des six premiers siècles,* 13, 16. Paris: Chez Charles Robustel, 1702, 1712.

Trout, Dennis E. *Paulinus of Nola: Life, Letters, Poems.* Berkeley and Los Angeles: University of California Press, 1999.

Twyman, B. L. "Aetius and the Aristocracy." *Historia* 19 (1970): 480–503.

Ullmann, Walter. "Leo I and the Theme of Papal Primacy." *JTS* 11 (1960): 25–51.

Valentin, L. *Saint Prosper d'Aquitaine: Étude sur la littérature latine ecclésiastique au cinquième siècle en Gaule.* Paris: Picard, 1900.

Van Slyke, Daniel G. "*Lex orandi lex credendi:* Liturgy as *Locus Theologicus* in the Fifth Century?" *Josephinum Journal of Theology* 11, no. 2 (2004): 130–51.

———. *Quodvultdeus of Carthage: The Apocalyptic Theology of a Roman African in Exile.* Early Christian Studies 5. Strathfield, Australia: St. Pauls, 2003.

Vessey, Mark. "Opus Imperfectum: Augustine and His Readers, 426–435 A.D." *VC* 52 (1998): 264–85.

———. "Peregrinus against the Heretics: Classicisim, Provinciality, and the Place of the Alien Writer in Late Roman Gaul." In *Studia Ephemeridis "Augustinianum"* 46, 530–565. Rome: Institutum Patristicum Augustinianum, 1994.

———. "Vincent of Lérins." *ATA,* 870.

Vogüé, Adalbert de. "Les débuts de la vie monastique à Lérins. Remarqus sur un ouvrage recent." *Revue d'Histoire Ecclésiastique* 88 (1993): 5–53.

———. *Les Règles des saint Pères,* SC 297–98.

———. "Les 'Règles des saint Pères' à Lérins," *Lérins* 287 (1980): 4–10.

———. "Understanding Cassian: A Survey of the Conferences." *CSQ* 19 (1984): 101–21.

Weaver, Rebecca Harden. *Divine Grace and Human Agency: A Study of the Semi-Pelagian Controversy.* Patristic Monograph Series, 15. Macon, Ga: Mercer UP, 1996.

———. "Hardrumetum." *ATA,* 411–12.

Wermelinger, Otto. *Rom und Pelagius: Die theologische Position der römischen Bishöfe im pelagianischen Streit in den Jahren 411–432.* Stuttgart: Anton Hiersemann, 1975.

Young, Joseph J. *Studies on the Style of the "De vocatione gentium." PS* 87. Washington, D.C.: The Catholic University of America Press, 1952.

Zumkeller, Adolar. "Die pseudoaugustinische Schrift 'De pradestinatione et gratia': Inhalt, Überlieferung, Verfasserfrage und Nachwirkung." *Augustinianum* 25 (1985): 539–63.

Index

Intrepid Lover of Perfect Grace: The Life and Thought of Prosper of Aquitaine was designed and typeset in Arno by Kachergis Book Design of Pittsboro, North Carolina. It was printed on 60-pound Natural Offset and bound by McNaughton & Gunn of Saline, Michigan.